THE STORY OF SUPERSTITION

THE STORY OF
SUPERSTITION

Philip F. Waterman

AMS PRESS

NEW YORK

Reprinted from the edition of 1929, New York
First AMS EDITION published 1970
Manufactured in the United States of America

Library of Congress Catalogue Card Number: 78-107770
SBN: 404-06849-9

AMS PRESS, INC.
NEW YORK, N. Y. 10003

This Book
is affectionately dedicated
TO MY WIFE

CONTENTS

CONTENTS

THE STORY
OF
SUPERSTITION

CHAPTER I

The Meaning of Luck

> *"Where it is a duty to worship the sun,*
> *it is pretty sure to be a crime to ex-*
> *amine the laws of heat."*
>
> JOHN VISCOUNT MORLEY.

1

I N the great open spaces of the Mojave Desert there lives a little animal called the "trade rat." The creature has earned that curious name. Its habit is to steal into your house or shed, to deposit there useless articles that it has purloined from some other shack, and to carry away something to be similarly bestowed elsewhere.

If the animal were a mere thief—if it stole objects which were of obvious use to itself—no special interest would attach to its habit. One could understand, even if one could not commend, so purely practical a procedure. But the inefficiency of the trade rat, its consummate waste of energy, its apparent inability to distinguish between conduct from which it derives some benefit and conduct that cannot possibly serve its ends—these considerations cover some of us with wonder and some with pity. Poor little trade rat! Think of what you might become and how happy you might be if you could be taught to conserve your energy and to be efficient like men and women!

But if it were possible for a thinking being, as superior to man as man is doubtless superior to the trade rat, to watch our conduct and to study our habits, the observer might be inclined to look upon us much as we look upon that humble inhabitant of the Mojave Desert. We, too, make any number of habitual and conventional gestures, which may have profound significance for us, but which to a distant observer, unfamiliar with our habits of thought, must appear both meaningless and useless. The ploughing of the soil and the sowing of seed, for example, would doubtless excite the admiration of the superhuman student, but he might question the practical utility of our harvest festivals. He might well view with approval the erection of a building and might regard the process as an efficient one, but he would not be able to understand the purely ceremonial laying of the corner-stone. That particular expenditure of effort would seem to him to be wasteful and senseless. He would find no difficulty in appreciating our dietetic habits and might become interested in our methods of preparing and consuming food, but grace before meat would give him pause, unless he could enter into our minds, as it were, and could know something of the motives which actuate us in pronouncing formulas of that character. He would watch us as we discharged our obligations of devotion in our various houses of worship. Unless, however, he had some method of obtaining information concerning the story of human institutions, sentiments, and conventions, how could he understand?

Not all of the ceremonial habits of men and women are of a solemn character like the laying of a corner-stone and the act of kneeling and praying towards Mecca. Our far-away student of human affairs might perhaps understand the facts of marriage, much as we strive to comprehend the mating of pigeons; but even though he might grasp the full meaning of that relation, how would he interpret the wedding-ceremony and especially the amazing popular customs that are everywhere associated with it? Why should guests throw rice at brides and bridegrooms? Is there any good reason why friends should tease young couples? Why is it that, in spite of the institution of marriage, a young man is generally permitted to kiss any maiden who happens to be standing beneath a sprig of mistletoe? Is there any connexion between that shrub and easy virtue? Would not items of that kind perplex the watcher?

Certainly the observer would note with amused tolerance the various funeral customs of the human race. Obviously dead bodies must be somehow disposed of. Our superhuman student might admire the ingenuity of men who take the precaution of burying corpses, thus avoiding the purely physical contamination that putrefaction would bring in its train. But he would raise his eyebrows with a most quizzical expression when there came before his notice the various ceremonial gestures with which the disposal of the dead is almost invariably accompanied. The savage wails at funerals in certain parts of the world and among certain peoples might be explained by him offhand (although the explanation would be but a fractional truth) on the basis of the idea that the survivors had been stricken with grief. But in view of so naïve a theory, would he not be confused when he came to observe the institution known as the "wake," which enjoys a vogue not only in Ireland but in many other sections of the globe?

If conventions appear on the surface to be unreasonable, what shall we say of that large segment of human behaviour which is frankly labelled "superstition"? If an average person wishes to say something good about himself or a friend, he knocks on wood. Why? Why should his remark have any evil effect, and how can the knocking on wood avert that unwelcome consummation? To say that there is no connexion between the wood and the flattering statement, and to affirm contemptuously that the timid creature is misguided who takes such precautions whenever he feels the urge to say something pleasant, does not remove the difficulty; for the question still remains: "Where do so many millions of people get such an idea? Where did the practice originate? What is its story?"

We may thus go through the whole field of human super-

stition. What is the source of the notion that the breaking
of a mirror will cause seven years of bad luck? Who designed
the various mystic signs and amulets that have been used in
all ages and are still popular in every land? Why is it so
widely believed that a mysterious power for good reposes in
such objects as the shoe of a horse or the foot of a rabbit?
On the other hand, what uncanny power for evil lurks in the
feathers of the peacock? If there is none, why do so many
people refuse to allow peacock feathers in their homes?

Nor does the problem stop at this point. What is the actual
history of those unseen beings who have filled human hearts
with terror for so many ages? Where did the idea arise that
Satan, the Prince of Darkness, has the leg and foot of a goat
and the horns of a bull? Who are the goblins, and where do
they come from? How do mortals know so many details of
the personal appearance, not only of devils and angels, but
also of ghosts, fairies, brownies, and gnomes? Who is the
famous bogy man, otherwise known as the bugaboo, who
now frightens children only, but who, not so long ago, was
the nightly dread of adults as well?

To find the answers to these questions it will be necessary
for us to cast off all preconceived notions and thus, unim-
peded by any bias whatsoever, to set out on a journey of
exploration. We shall pay a visit to the halcyon meadows of
fairyland, the woods that are haunted by goblins, the placid
fields of Elysium, and the dark pit of Tartarus. We may
confidently expect that, before our journey shall reach its
close, the supernatural world will have yielded its secret.

2

WHATEVER may be the fact in the case of the trade rat,
human beings are not intentionally inefficient. Laziness is
characteristic of the human animal, and while men and
women may be inspired to labour in order to achieve some
tangible, or at least desirable, result, they are rarely given

to the reckless and purposeless waste of either their efforts or their treasures. Nor do people deliberately create imaginary horrors, like ghosts and the bugaboo, in order to cringe in carking terror before fiends and furies who do not even exist.

The customs, ceremonies, institutions, sentiments, beliefs, and superstitions that, from one point of view, seem to be so wholly unrelated to anything practical, all have their histories, and were instituted in the first place because they were regarded not merely as useful, but as absolutely necessary in the serious economy of everyday life.

Consider, for example, the laying of a corner-stone. To-day that ceremony is usually regarded as having sentimental value only and as being distinctly less important as far as the permanence and strength of the structure is concerned than the proper drawing of plans and laying of bricks. If the architect is ignorant of the principles that underlie his art, or if the workmen are without skill, the building may collapse, whereas if the functionary who "lays the corner-stone" is stricken with stage-fright and fails utterly to lend dignity to the occasion, this will have no effect whatever upon the subsequent history of the edifice.

In times gone by, the opposite idea was in vogue. According to the priests and medicine-men who first instituted the solemn sacrifice of which the corner-stone ceremony is but an innocent relic, the magical performance of the foundation ritual, involving, as it did, the slaughter of a human victim as an offering to the gods, was far more important than mere workmanship. The spirits were the owners of the soil and were extremely jealous of the human beings who consumed its increase and who defaced the landscape with their dwelling-places. Those spirits were powerful creatures and if they were not continually appeased and kept in as good humour as possible, would destroy the human race and wipe out its puny treasures. The art of propitiating the gods, then, was the most important art in the whole world, for without it the other arts would be meaningless. Would it be practical to build a hut or to tend a flock or to plough a field if one neglected to offer to the supernatural beings their due, or if one was not careful to render the sacrifice in the approved ritual form? If the supernaturals did not receive what they demanded and in the manner in which they wished to receive it, the hut would burn, the sheep would die, the crops would wither, men and women would perish.

According to a Danish legend, there was once a curse upon the walls of Copenhagen. The people were industrious and cared for the important enclosure. But each time they built it, down it fell, and they were compelled to erect it once more, and then once more, and still once more. Finally the pious folks took a little girl, gave her some objects to play with, and, while she amused herself with the toys, walled her in as a sacrifice. Without the offering, all of the skill in the world would have availed nothing, but with the slaughter of the child the curse was lifted and the walls of the city were permitted to stand.

When the fort of Scutari was being built, a ghost is said to have appeared to the builders. The spirit demanded that a certain woman be buried alive in the foundation. Would it have been practical to proceed with the work and to pay no heed to the demand so solemnly delivered from the world beyond the veil? Needless to say, the sacrifice was duly rendered.

According to the Scriptures, the Lord Himself demanded this type of offering, so popular among all the gods in the early days. Thus, in the First Book of Kings there is a simple account of the devout manner in which Chiel built Jericho. "In Abiram, his first-born, laid he the foundation thereof, and in Segub, his youngest son, set he up the gates thereof, according to the word of the Lord, which He had spoken by means of Joshua the son of Nun."

It is most unfortunate, but it is also most true, that these cruel foundation sacrifices were not outgrown in the remote past. So profound is superstitious dread that it ever begets a remarkable conservatism, so that even when the principles on which a custom was founded cease to be accepted, the custom will none the less remain, for timid people will be afraid to abandon it. Thus the burying alive of human victims in order to remove, as it were, the curse from a building lasted into the present era. If the legends of the Germans are to be credited, two brothers lie entombed in the foundation of the Strassburg Cathedral. There is also a story of an archangel who called from heaven and commanded that the wife of the architect who had planned a particular edifice should be bricked up for the glory of the immortals. In such manner did men seek to satisfy the hunger of Heaven.

3

THE cruelty of human sacrifice naturally tended to sadden those tender-hearted people whose natures were full of the milk of human kindness. Those good souls did their best to mitigate the harshness of the religionists, and they finally succeeded in bringing about substitutions for men, women, and children in the offerings to the gods. In place of human victims the priests (as representatives of the gods) learned to content themselves with such substitutes as the first-fruits of both the flocks and the fields.

There is splendid reason to believe that this revolution in methods of holding commerce with the supernatural world was accompanied by the same sort of arguments that one still finds when more or less similar changes are timidly suggested in the concourse of believers. The conservatives appear to have advanced the view that the ways of Heaven are inscrutable, and that if the gory habit of murdering members of our own species is one that does not appeal to our mortal sensibilities, it is well to bow low in reverence and to proclaim: "Thy will, not mine, be done."

We may derive some hint of the nature of this argument from the following rabbinic legend: It seems that, when the Jews were told to make bricks without straw, they were unable to complete the quota that was assigned to them. Accordingly, so the story runs, Pharaoh commanded them to brick up children in the walls to fill the space that should normally have been occupied by more solid material. When Moses saw this cruel command being executed, he was filled with horror and he cried out to God in his righteous anguish. In answer to the piteous prayer of His prophet, God pointed out that the children who were being walled up were really ill-starred and, in order to prove this experimentally, He directed Moses to save one of the infants. The child so spared was named Micah.

Years passed and the day dawned for the Children of Israel to be delivered from the house of bondage. Moses was anxious to take with him the mortal remains of Joseph. On being informed that the body had been deposited in the Nile, he wrote on a piece of wood: "Arise, O Ox." (The ox was regarded as extremely beautiful, and this expression was intended as a subtle compliment to the great interpreter of dreams.) At once the casket containing the bones of Joseph rose to the surface, and they were carried with the Children of Israel into the promised land. The ill-fated Micah appropriated the magic splinter and secreted it in his garments.

Not long thereafter, when Moses was holding his long conference with the Almighty, the people became restless and demanded of Aaron that he manufacture for them an idol. The first high priest was extremely loath to do this. In fact, when he asked the people for their jewels, his intention was to cast them into the fire and to destroy them, thus teaching the moral that all idolatry is sin; but when he had cast the jewels into the flames, Micah threw in the charmed bit of wood on which the command had been inscribed: "Arise, O Ox." Thus, to the surprise of Aaron and to the joy of the sinful populace, when the oven was opened, there appeared not the melted mass of gold that the first high priest expected to find, but the golden calf which has become notorious in Jewish and Christian theology.

The implication of this legend as regards the heartless and relentless practice we are here reviewing is apparent. True (so runs the implied argument), it is cruel to entomb human beings in the walls of our buildings; but if the gods demand such sacrifices as the price of their divine favour, how can mortal man dare to oppose his puny feelings of humanity to the inscrutable will of Heaven and its hosts?

The transition from the practice of offering human beings to that of offering substitutes is reflected in a number of legends. Thus a ram was slaughtered in place of Isaac, and a doe in place of Iphigenia. In certain parts of Africa the shadow of a man is believed to be his soul. When a hut is about to be built, it is the habit of the people to steal up to some unsuspecting individual, to measure his shadow with a stick, and to cast the stick into the ground on which the hut is to be erected. No African will permit his shadow to be thus buried if he can possibly avoid it. For if his soul has thus been presented to the foundation gods, he cannot expect to live much longer. The burying of the shadow is a substitute for the earlier custom of entombing the man himself.

From such humble beginnings our modern ceremonies of the laying of the corner-stone have slowly developed. In the course of this development we have practically forgotten the ghastly origin of this impressive but innocuous ritual. The practice of holding some sort of solemn celebration in connexion with the building of a foundation has persisted long after the original reason for such an observance was definitely outgrown. So we invent new reasons. The ritual is "inspiring." The addresses are eloquent. We have deposited and sealed in the corner-stone, not a man, and not a woman, nor yet an animal, but some documents that may be of historic interest later, when the building has crumbled and the archæologists of the future unearth the stone in quest of information concerning our civilization.

4

PRIMITIVE men had plenty of reason to believe that over and above the world of sense there was a supernatural world, the inhabitants of which were cruel, and were bent upon the destruction of humanity unless they were appeased and humoured. Nothing appeared so self-evident as the fact that the human race dragged on its existence under the spell of a curse. The weeds grew readily enough, but crops had to be cultivated and tended. Health did not appear to spread from person to person, but sickness was contagious, probably because the presence of illness indicated the activity of the immortals in a particular locality at a particular time. Poor man was chilled in the winter and burned in the summer. At times there were unusual terrors, as, for example, when the sun, which generally shone all day long, was swallowed up by the dragon of eclipse. Enemies were everywhere. And to crown the hideous list of the various constituent items of mankind's environment, there were the mysterious, and therefore doubly terrible, facts of death.

In the face of these obstacles if any man did manage to live and attain some degree of comfort, this was because the powers of the supernatural world, for reasons of their own, had permitted him to do so. He was a lucky creature. But if another man fell by the wayside; if he could not find game; if the weeds choked his garden; if, indeed, he died, this was because he was signally out of favour in the sight of the gods. He was an unlucky creature.

The idea of luck among superstitious people has not changed much in the course of the ages. True, the modern child, or childlike grown-up who solemnly nails a horse-shoe over his door is less aware of the real nature of the charm than was the savage who first employed a similar device to protect his home from the malice of devils. The modern superstitious person usually performs a ritual without reference to its origin and without knowledge of its history. But he resembles the prehistoric performers of the same (or a similar) ritual in that he is confident that the ceremony will bring him luck; and his ill-defined idea of what that mysterious commodity is matches the notion that was prevalent among his ancestors when the human race was in its infancy.

To say that a horseshoe is "lucky" means that the object in question possesses a power to avert unpleasant circumstances and, perhaps, to attract pleasant ones. It is well known that this mystic potency has been ascribed in every age and in every clime to certain articles like the rabbit's foot and the four-leaf clover; while to others, as to the peacock feather, the opposite power has been imputed. In every such instance there is a definite reason why the particular something has been invested with this magnetic capacity either for good or for harm.

No doubt all of this seems reasonable enough, but the strange feature of the situation is that there has been so little disagreement among the most widely scattered races and among the most distantly separated peoples as to which objects are lucky and which are unlucky. The horseshoe is the repository of a beneficent influence in lands as remote from each other as Egypt, China, and America; while the howling of a dog or the breaking of a mirror will inspire terror almost anywhere. This wellnigh universal agreement is by no means accidental. Superstitions of this type all arose by a perfectly logical process out of a single conception that was common to primitive man. To appreciate and to understand that conception and to apprehend the process by which so many hopes, fears, conventions, rituals, arts, creeds, religions, persecutions, and even wars have developed out of it is to become privy to the underlying secret of the supernatural.

5

WHAT, then, is this idea, upon which the whole structure of the supernatural world rests? It is none other than the familiar theory that it is possible to bring to pass a desired result by simply imitating on a small scale that which one wishes to take place on a larger scale or more significant scale. Thus, if you want it to rain, you pour out a bit of water on the ground. This is the well-known "rain charm." If you harbour the desire to have your enemy die, you shoot an arrow in his general direction, and, even though he himself be miles away from the scene, he will succumb to the magic of this ritual. There are still some survivals of such a theory among ourselves. The small boy will "make a face" behind the bigger boy's back. This is the solemn ceremony of "killing with a look" by calling into play the dread magic of the evil eye. But this magic may be worked at a distance and the indignant lad will frequently relieve his feelings by distorting his face, even though the foe is not actually present in the flesh. Or he will shake his fist in the general direction of the absent bully. This is an empty enough ritual in these days, but in the ages gone by, it was regarded as a significant and consequential ceremony.

There are desires, however, that are not so definite as the wish for rain or for the death of an enemy. Suppose one is seeking luck, how shall he go about imitating on a small scale what he wishes to attain on a larger scale? Obviously the answer depends upon the specific meaning one attaches to the term "luck."

A person is generally conceded to be fortunate if circumstances so shape themselves that honour, power, wealth, health, contentment, and length of days become his portion. To these we may add the successful adaptation of oneself to the personalities of others, especially to those of the opposite sex, for no individual should be accounted truly "lucky" unless his love life is a happy one. Now, all of these desirable conditions and attributes are related to the general idea of life. Do people wish for honour and power? Then they do so because these enable them to live more intensely. Do people fear poverty and ill health? Then they do so because these tend to detract from the fullness of their lives. Besides, in the early days wealth was reckoned in terms of cattle and corn, both of which are alive and increase through the mystic union of the male and female creative forces. The millions of people who devote themselves to the age-old quest for luck, then, are really seeking life. What they want is, at bottom, more life and more abundant, here and hereafter.

The sad feature of this situation is that, in the world of real life, death, which must be the greatest evil since it is the negation of the supreme good, is the grim heritage of the entire race. Most people find it impossible to realize any of their ideals or to gratify any of their outstanding ambitions. And all people, even those who seem to be the "luckiest," are doomed to diappointment at last, for eventually every man is worsted in his lifelong struggle with death.

To the untutored mind of the savage the explanation of this unfortunate condition in which the human race finds itself is fairly plain. We are, it appears, mere pawns in the hands of supernatural forces, most of which are jealous of us and seek to impose upon us all sorts of unhappiness. These are the powers of darkness and destruction; they are the hosts of Death. But the fact that human beings do survive for a while at least is proof that not all of the supernaturals are enemies of men; some are the powers of light; they are the hosts of Life. The problem of the savage, then, is that of so using the mysterious force of imitative magic that the armies of Life will put to rout those of Death.

If one travels today among any typical group of savage (which is another way of saying "primitive") people, the method of doing this will be apparent. To imitate on a small scale the cosmic power of creation, which is life, the pre-scientific individual imitates the relation of love, from which animation appears to be generated. There are, according to the primitive view, two forces of creation, one male, and the other female. Either of these may be enlisted for the purposes of man in the never-ending war against Destruction and Death. Thus there are some people who honestly believe that if a woman will uncover herself before a hailstorm, the fury of the elements will at once subside because of the inability of the fiend who is present in the atmospheric disturbance to remain in the presence of the generator.

But there comes a time in the development of every people when such crudity is frowned upon for the reason that such practices do not harmonize with the growing modesty of the society. Then, as we should expect, substitutions take place, for folks do not readily abandon the search for luck. Instead of adoring the actual creators of the human body, and of employing them as paraphernalia of devotion in the relations of men with the spirits, certain conventional signs, emblems, plants, and animals are used for this purpose. These become endowed with the virtues of those generators they were intended to represent; sometimes they become gods; sometimes they become shields against demons and are carried into battle or are worn as amulets, particularly at such times as men have reason to believe that they are walking in the valley of the shadow and require special protection.

One of the earliest and most universal emblems of the female creator is the mystic sign of the horseshoe. The fa-

mous head-dress of the Egyptian goddess Isis was a horseshoe, and there are numerous divinities in different parts of
the world who are represented with similar devices upon
their heads. In Rajputana, India, there are temples constructed on the plan of a horseshoe for the reason that the
symbol of life is one of the sacred emblems of the deities
therein worshipped.

The Head-dress of Isis

Originally the nailing of a horseshoe above the door was
an act of piety. Its purpose was that of protecting the people who dwelt in the house against devils and against sorcery. To the extent that it was regarded as an effective
shield against such supernatural terrors it brought luck in
its train. The forces of Death could not prevail against it.
For the horseshoe was the generator; it was the repository
of the mysterious power of life.

6

THE idea that there is a supernatural world inhabited by
two warring factions, one creative and the other destructive,
is the foundation upon which most modern conventions, social habits, beliefs, and even arts rest. Painting and sculpture originated in the efforts of primitive people to devise
representations of Life, in order that they might attain luck.
Dancing originated as pious ritual, a sacred representation
of the power of creation. Upon this corner-stone rests most
of the beauty of human life. Ugliness and intolerance, alas,
rest upon it too. If we but knew—

The supernatural world was called into being by timid people in order to serve as an explanation of the sad plight in which the human race found itself. The spirits who lived in that world were for the most part demons and fiends whose incessant activity was responsible for all the ills that flesh is heir to. But there were among the immortals some angels of light who were interested in the promotion of life and in the increase of living things. In the struggle between the two spiritual armies men and women were intensely interested, for everything they had and prized was at stake. In order to encourage the powers of life and to frighten away the devils of death various devices and rituals were employed. Those who were most skilled in the proper ues of those weapons in the spiritual war became the priests and the medicine-men. They were the first doctors, who taught their people about the supernatural and about the methods of inducing the good spirits to do the will of their petitioners. The methods of bringing about this delightful consummation centred about the mystery of love. For love is Life, the arch-enemy of Death.

Still, this is not the entire story. In the very earliest days men knew little of love, and did not understand the relation it bore to life. There are still savages who are as ignorant in this matter as so many tiny children. It was not until the forward and more scientific among the early races began to formulate rules on the basis of experience and observation that this relation between life and love was at length discovered. This was the first great heresy in the history of human belief. But it did not remain a heresy for long. Soon it was recognized as a wellnigh self-evident truth, which promptly became the basis of man's effort to attain luck.

And basically the rule holds today as it did yesterday that the purpose underlying all attempts at commerce with the supernatural, whether that commerce take the base form of superstition or the nobler form of religion, is that of improving one's luck. Does this easily demonstrable truth tend to degrade the spiritual institutions of man? Or does it rather tend to elevate the basic impulse of life, which is love?

CHAPTER II

The First Great Heresy

*"Nothing is so firmly believed as what
we least know."*

MICHEL DE MONTAIGNE

*"But Faith, fanatic Faith, once wedded
fast
To some dear falsehood, hugs it to the
last."*

THOMAS MOORE

1

IN the central part of Australia there lives a tribe of
rude and uncultivated people known as the Arunta.
These people have not been brought into close contact with
the theories and principles of modern science, and the experience of the ages has taught them but little concerning
the nature of the world they inhabit. They are a credulous
people and retain the ideas that their forefathers believed
in the dim ages of long ago. They live in the twentieth century, but they are not of it.

People like the Arunta serve at least one excellent purpose from the point of view of those who seek the truth
about the history of the human mind. For they represent the
past; they are living specimens of primitive man.

The Arunta do not know that there is any relation whatever between life and love. Like the lower animals they
have their love life, but are utterly without appreciation
of its significance. As questions arise in the minds of un-
taught children, so they arise in the minds of those primitive
people. "Where do we come from?" "What is the answer
to the mystery of creation?" And the answer of their holy
men, whose sacred function it is to conserve the traditional
mythology, is illustrative of the dim ideas our fathers once

entertained about the true inwardness of the world they lived in.

Generation, in central Australia, is a result of the activity of discarnate spirits anxious to be born. The human mother is but the passive channel through which a soul passes from the shadowy to the material world. Spirits who desire bodies take up their residence in a particuar sacred stone and wait for maidens to pass by. Young women who do not desire children give that rock a wide berth, but occasionally it happens that a girl finds it necessary to pass the enchanted spot. At such times the maid pretends to be old and hence unfit to become a mother. She stoops over and uses a walking-stick in order to deceive the spirits and make them believe that she is feeble.

2

THIS single illustration will suffice to demonstrate the singularly childlike innocence of the first human beings who inhabited our planet. But, as happens sooner or later in every race and among the adherents of every creed, there arose certain gifted people who were characterized by what we should call "scientific curiosity." These people were sceptical and were unwilling to accept the traditions and teachings of their medicine-men without pausing to check them up with their own independent observations. To such individuals the connexion between love and life first became apparent.

The teaching of this fact was doubtless the first instance of the sin of heresy. On the one hand there were the accepted spiritual theories of the tribe and the ritual practices based on them. On the other hand there was the new doctrine, supported of course by ample evidence, but threatening to undermine the very foundations of that revelation which it was the function of the authorized priesthood to guard and to expound.

It is likely that the first heretics suffered the kind of martyrdom that had fallen to the lot of sceptical investigators in all ages. After all, the problem that they raised was a practical one, for their teachings clashed not only with the theories of the people, but with the vested interests of the primitive clergy. These holy men had attained their professional standing in good faith by assiduous study of such lore as was available to them. Thus among the ancient Druids the course of preparation for the priesthood required some twenty years. Could the priests be expected to abandon the fruits of all that honest labour without a struggle?

That such martyrdom was indeed the fate of the early sceptics a number of myths and legends attest. Prometheus was chained to a rock, and a vulture was appointed to devour his vitals as he writhed in pain; and what was his crime? He had brought fire to mankind, and the gods were jealous. Even in the Scripture we are informed of the jealousy of God, which was aroused because men had eaten of the tree of knowledge. "And the Lord God said: 'Behold, the man is become as one of us, to know good and evil; and now, lest he put forth his hand and take also of the tree of life, and eat, and live for ever—' Therefore the Lord God sent him forth from the garden of Eden, to till the ground from whence he was taken."   Even as late as the beginning of the sixteenth century we have the legend of Faust arising out of a similar situation. For that folk-tale exemplifies, as one authority puts it, "the priest's shudder at the fumes of the laboratory."

3

BUT however sinful it may have been accounted to believe that love and life are connected with each other in a relation of cause and effect, the fact, once stated, was so patent that it was bound to be generally accepted. The old doctrine probably died hard, but its eventual doom was certain. This was nothing short of a spiritual revolution.

Still the popularizing of the basic fact of biology did not undermine religion. On the contrary, it gave religion a new lease of life. The customs and ceremonies of earlier times were for the most part retained, but since the original reasons for them had become obsolete, new meanings were read into them. The ancient foundation was demolished, but a new one was substituted, and the structure remained.

The first manifestation of religious feeling is always concerned with human love life. It is still true that the great crises in the development of the affectionate side of human nature are coincident with the great crises in man's religious development. That is why among practically every people the age of puberty is the age of initiation or confirmation. The awakening in the soul of a child of the mysterious impulses tends to arouse within him a sense of the mystery of all things, and for the first time he feels a profound urge to enter into emotional contact with the supernatural.

It is for this reason that primitive religion, even before the first dim perception of biological truth, expressed itself in the form of sacred dances and excesses. Therefore when it became known that these excesses were bound up in sober fact with the creation of life itself, the greatest of blessings, the orgies themselves became more significant than ever before. The supernatural world began to be peopled with beings whose prime concern was love. Even the demons of darkness were filled with the unholy desire to marry the daughters of men, and the gods in the sky were envious of the happiness of lovers.

To this day we retain in many of our wedding-customs the ancient precautions that were taken to guard against the malice of lovesick devils and even to propitiate the love-lorn divinities.

CHAPTER III

The Demon Lover

*"It is the customary fate of new truths
to begin as heresies and to end as superstitions."*

THOMAS HENRY HUXLEY

1

IT WAS once widely believed that every snake (like
every toad) bore in its head a precious jewel. To call
that belief into question was in itself sinful—deserving,
perhaps, of such punishment as the right-thinking might see
fit to inflict upon the erring.

According to an old Sanskrit story, there lived, once upon
a time, a beautiful damsel who coveted this zoological
jewellery and who killed a cobra in order to extract the
valuable stone from its head. In pursuance of the doctrine
of blood revenge then prevalent, it became the sacred duty
of the snake tribe to avenge that murder—just as it was the
unquestioned duty of Hamlet to avenge the murder of his
father. In the interest of justice, the King of the serpents
called into play that magic with which snakes have always
been familiar, and took the form of a young man, smart and
dashing. In this guise he proceeded to woo the unsuspecting
maiden.

His suit prospered and in due course a date was set for
the wedding. The impressive ceremony was duly pronounced
and the young couple retired to the bridal chamber. The
bride looked lovingly at her husband, who tenderly smiled
in reply, but when he opened his mouth, she observed, horrible to relate, that his tongue was forked and that it
trembled. Alas for the maid, her bridegroom did not have
the tongue of a man, but that of a snake.

Bright and early the next morning the father of the bride and his friends stood before the door to tender their greetings to the happy pair. But the sun rose to the meridian and proceeded to its resting-place in the west, and neither bride nor bridegroom nor sound issued forth from that fatal chamber. An attempt was made to awaken the couple with music, but it was in vain. At length the door was broken down and the unhappy parent entered the room. There he saw the terrible vengeance of the snake. On the couch lay the inert body of his beautiful daughter. The bridegroom was nowhere to be seen. Presently, however, a black cobra emerged from the bed and left the house through an aperture in the wall.

2

TURNING from this old Sanskrit tale to the ancient Hebrew Book of Tobit, which is preserved in the collection known as the Apocrypha, we discover a slightly different version of the venerable demon-lover superstition.

Tobias and the Angel Raphael were travelling together, and one evening they encamped on the bank of the Tigris River. A giant fish leaped out of the stream and attempted to devour the young man. At first Tobias was frightened, but the angel said to him: "Take the fish." So he seized the creature and brought it to land.

As it turned out, this incident was a fortunate one. As Raphael explained to his companion, if a jealous demon tormented a bridegroom and his bride, the pair had but to burn the heart and liver of that fish in the chamber, and the evil spirit would flee, never to return again. Needless to add, the youth retained the organs that possessed such marvellous power. Soon, indeed, he had an opportunity to test their efficacy.

It seems that in the town to which they were going, there lived a beautiful girl named Sara. Marriages, as is well known, are arranged in heaven, and it had long been common gossip among the angels that Tobias and Sara were destined for each other.

But one serious difficulty stood in the way of the union. A demon was enamoured of the fair Sara. For her part, she utterly refused to have any commerce with him, and he in turn was determined that no human being should have the maiden as a wife. Seven times she had been betrothed and married, but each of her ill-fated bridegrooms had been slain by the jealous spirit on the bridal night.

Tobias was the eighth bridegroom. But this time shameful defeat lay in wait for the Devil. When the couple retired to their room, Tobias prayerfully burned the heart and liver of the fish, and the demon fled into Egypt, where the angel bound him.

3

SOMETIMES the demon lover is a mysterious creature like the snake, sometimes he is one of the fallen angels, who occupy positions of greater or less honour in hell, but occasionally he is the ghost of a man, who once lived and moved as a member of human society.

Such a being is Nathuram, who terrorizes the natives of a certain section of India. He is the ghost of a notorious libertine who was put to death for corrupting the morals of ladies. Although dead, he retains an indecent interest in human affairs, and no family is safe from his depredations. To pacify him it is necessary for the women to sing certain immoral songs and to go through obscene motions for his ghostly amusement. But he is especially jealous when a marriage takes place. On an occasion like that people must be careful. Accordingly his image is placed in the bridal chamber after a wedding, in recognition of his rights.

But even if the demons are not in love with the bride,

they are jealous of human happiness in general. It is always necessary to be specially cautious when speaking words of praise, and particularly if the praise is directed towards oneself or one's friends. When boasting, it is considered a good thing to knock on wood to drown our voices so that the imps will not hear. The practice goes back to the time when our fathers lived in wooden huts.

Now, a wedding is primarily an occasion of joy. Therefore care must be taken to deceive the spirits and to make them believe that it is really one of sorrow. Among some primitive people the practice is common of breaking crockery at the time of marriage. There are two or three reasons for this, but one of them is contained in the dread of the supernatural. The demons must be made to feel that the wedding is not really a pleasant affair, but one which involves the destruction of property and hence is a season of distress.

In addition to all this, there were some spiritual horrors of a less personal nature that arose to plague a bride and groom. The relation of love had in it the divine element and involved the dangers that always inhered in that which was holy. As no one might look upon the face of God and live, so those people played with death who approached the mystery of life. As many of the traditional rites connected with marriage were originally intended to protect the bridegroom against the malice of the demon, others were devised to shield the pair from the killing power of the very holiness that was inseparably connected with love.

At nuptial ceremonies people frequently feel the urge to cry. This may be due to the more or less unconscious realization of the seriousness and solemnity of the occasion and of the momentous family reorganization that the significant pronouncements imply. The bride's parents are losing a daughter; the groom's parents, a son. While these considerations are sufficient to explain the phenomenon of nuptial sadness, it may be that a dim racial memory also plays a part in eliciting tears from the eyes of the company. One frequently hears the bride comfort her mother with the words: "Remember, this is my wedding, not my funeral." In the dark ages of long ago, people were far from sure that the happiness of the marriage would not culminate in the tragedy of a burial.

4

THE superstition of the demon lover lasted into modern times and formed one of the bulwarks of the witchcraft proceedings that clogged the court calendars of Europe for so many centuries. If one might trust the records of numerous trials, one would believe that thousands of men and women were guilty of being actually wedded to devils. If there were doubters in the dark ages of credulity who denied the possibility of such unions, the sceptics either kept their opinions to themselves or took their lives in their hands. To hold an irreligious opinion of that character was to live in constant terror of the Holy Inquisition and its punishments.

During the Middle Ages there were male and female demons who were available respectively as husbands and wives of human beings. The males were called "incubi" and the females "succubi" or "succubæ." It happened that there were more incubi than succubi, and hence many more women were burned at the stake for contracting demon marriages than men. Still, there were some male culprits. For example, there was a priest who evaded justice for forty years, during which time he was married to a demoness, but at last he was discovered, tried, convicted, and burned alive.

But for every man who was concremated for this sin, hundreds of women paid the supreme penalty. There were certain rules by which the inquisitors were guided in their task of unmasking such females. Thus, it was well known that devils usually sought out girls whose hair was luxuriant and attractive. The wise men of Europe were agreed that Saint Paul had this fact in mind when he admonished women to cover their hair "because of angels."

5

ALTHOUGH it was generally agreed that marriage between a human being and one of the immortals was not only a possibility, but a daily occurrence, there was a dispute among the learned as to whether or not such unions were sinful. The majority felt, of course, that such carnal commerce with the inhabitants of the supernatural world was both horrible and abominable. But the mystics, taking their cue from the Jewish cabbala, saw in the "facts" concerning the incubi and succubi a genuine opportunity of achieving the goal of all mysticism—namely, union with the transcendent world.

The cabbalists believed that there were spiritual maidens called "sylphs" who were willing to become the brides of philosophers—provided, of course, the latter had attained sufficient mystical insight and cabbalistic proficiency to merit so exalted a union. The sylph, unmarried, was not, strictly speaking, one of the immortals. Instead, she had a long span of natural life, but at the end of a number of centuries she was destined to perish utterly, for she enjoyed no place in the divine scheme of immortality beyond the grave. But if she married a righteous and worthy philosopher, her span of natural life may have been decreased, yet she became, like her husband, ultimately immortal. On the other hand, if she chose a spouse who did not merit eternal bliss, then both husband and wife became mortal. They passed away completely and the wicked philosopher was spared the eternal torments of hell.

6

AMONG civilized people today the belief in the existence of demon lovers has passed away. No longer do the fanatics stand around the roaring fires and hurl epithets and imprecations upon the writhing wives of the incubi. Philosophers no longer hunch themselves over ponderous volumes of cabbalistic lore in the hope that through such study they may fit themselves to become husbands of ethereal sylphs. But the customs that originated when such ideas were in flower are still with us, and to this day we go through motions that were designed in the first place to protect husbands against the ungovernable jealousy of ghostly rivals.

Why do brides wear veils at wedding-ceremonies? Why is a "best man" necessary? What of the bride's maids and ushers who make up the bridal party? Were they originally merely friends whom the young couple delighted to honour, or did they have a serious and significant mission to discharge? Who started such a curious practice as that of throwing rice at weddings? Why do the bride and bridegroom find it necessary to sneak away? Why is a wedding considered a peculiarly appropriate occasion for playing practical jokes on the principal celebrants?

Not all of the answers to these questions are simple. The customs connected with weddings have different roots. For instance, there was more than one reason for the appointment of a "bridal party" even in the earliest days. Accordingly in this place it will be possible to offer but a portion of the whole truth by way of answers to our questions. But the full solution of this riddle of the wedding-ceremony and its attendant customs will appear in bold relief as we probe deeper and deeper into the secret of the supernatural.

7

THE bridal veil was originally a disguise. If there was a demon lover who desired the girl for himself, he would be more than likely to work harm to the human rival whose suit had been successful. It was necessary to deceive the devil, to throw him off the track, to confuse him so that he should not know which pair was really being married. Hence the actual bride was disguised and her fiancé did not visit her on the day before the ceremony. This upset the calculations of the evil spirit.

Even if the demon did manage to discover who the wife-to-be really was, in spite of the veil and the bewildering presence of the bridesmaids, he would still be confronted with the difficulty of identifying the husband. How should he set about determining which was the groom and which the best man? How much greater must his confusion have been when a number of groomsmen were at hand!

Now, it is well known that the spirits are disturbed whenever they think that human beings are happy. That is one of the reasons why there are still many good people who associate morality and holiness with drabness and ugliness. The gods will not like it if people seem to be enjoying themselves. Make this life as miserable as possible, and maybe the deities will relent and give you some compensation in the next world. It is a practically universal habit to speak of a beloved child as a "little beggar." This is merely a custom today, but it is a hold-over from the time when it was essential to impress the gods with the idea that the little fellow was afflicted already and that it was not necessary to harass him further.

The danger that is attendant upon happiness is particularly present in the union of two lovers. Therefore the

bride and groom are teased; their belongings are misap-
propriated; they are made the target of friendly abuse—all
to make the immortals believe that they are miserable and
that it would be a waste of energy to add to their unhappiness by imposing supernatural punishments. Among some
savages the bride is beaten by her family, and among others
the property of the couple is deliberately destroyed or
stolen.

The methods of dealing with the jealous supernaturals at
the time of a wedding are of two kinds. In the first place,
we have the devices that were originally intended to deceive
the spirits by introducing doubt as to just which pair was
being married. In the second place, there were offerings of
rice. The rice was thrown into the air as a sop to the
injured feelings of the spirits.

This important grain was also useful as a charm to keep
the soul of the groom in his earthly body. It was notorious
among primitive people that the souls of bridegrooms were
likely to run away rather than stay and face the dangers
of marriage. The souls of men and women frequently left
their bodies, even during lifetime, for temporary sojourns
elsewhere. When savages saw their reflections in water or
in glass, they felt that those images were the spirits of the
living disporting themselves in reflecting surfaces. That is
why it is bad luck to break a mirror. You might injure your
soul if it is in the looking-glass at that time. Orthodox Jews
still cover all the mirrors in their houses at the time of a
death, so that the spirit of the departed will go to heaven,
instead of going, by force of habit, into the mirror.

The unfortunate habit of the human soul to take untimely
leave of its clay abode was (and is) an ever present source
of worry among primitive people. The peril has always
been most keenly appreciated by those folks who shared the
theory that the animating principle was the breath. Our

word "spirit" is derived from the Latin *"spiritus,"* which
means "breath" or "breeze" or "spirit." Similarly the Hebrew word *"ruach"* has each of those meanings. At one time
the three were regarded as identical. Thus, to satisfy ourselves with but a single illustration, in the story of the dry
bones as told in the Book of Ezekiel, one recalls that, after
the bones had come together and had been covered with
sinews and skin, the bodies thus formed were still exani-
mate. But they were quickened when the four winds blew
upon them the "breath of life."

This conception is at the bottom of the custom of pronouncing a magic formula whenever someone sneezes. Sometimes the sneeze is a good omen, indicating the entrance
into the body rather than the departure therefrom of a
spiritual reality. In certain parts of Africa the phenomenon
is a source of happiness because it shows that an ancestral
spirit has "possessed" the individual. Xenophon looked
upon the sneeze as a favourable sign, and Aristotle alluded
to the popular judgment that this mysterious emission of
air was somehow divine. In the miracle worked by the
prophet Elisha, when the dead child of the Shunammite
woman was restored to life, the boy sneezed seven times
and then opened his eyes. The soul had re-entered his body,
and this re-entrance had caused the sevenfold manifestation of the nasal mystery.

Usually, however, the sneeze is an unfavourable sign.
As a precaution against the possibility that the soul will
take its departure in the course of the involuntary demonstration, superstitious people still repeat such magic charms
as the German *"Gesundheit* (Good health)" or the more
pious English ejaculation "God bless you."

Clearly, then, it was a simple matter for the soul of the
groom to escape all difficulties by departing at the time of
a wedding. The rice induced it to remain.

8

EVER since men began to people the world with spirits, those ethereal beings were thought of as somehow interested in the love life of human beings. It mattered not whether the spirits were gods or demons (and in the earliest times it was scarcely possible to distinguish between the two); they were supposed to concern themselves in season and out of season with the mystery of love.

Out of that primitive conception there have slowly evolved the more exalted ideas of modern religionists, poets, artists, and dreamers. We have seen that some of our modern wedding-customs are the fruitage of the old demon-lover theory. To what extent such notions have been the seeds from which many of our finest institutions have flowered we shall have ample opportunity to observe.

CHAPTER IV

The Divine Lover

*"An honest God is the noblest work
of man."*

ROBERT GREEN INGERSOLL

1

HOSPITALITY has long been recognized as a virtue. The idea that a host stands in a singular relation to his guest and owes him special duties has come down from the remotest and mistiest past. But it is significant that those duties have not expanded and become more numerous with the development of the race; on the contrary they have become fewer and less rigorous with the passing of the ages. Among civilized people the virtue of hospitality is a polite grace—nothing more. Among savages, quite the other way, the claims of a guest have behind them the mysterious sanctions of religion, and the terrors of primitive superstition.

Long ago, before there were domestic animals to herd or crops to cultivate, human beings derived their subsistence from hunting and fishing. The earth was covered with virgin forests, in which men and beasts alike wandered in search of prey. Under such conditions it was a frequent occurrence for a man to find himself at nightfall far from his own humble and rude dwelling-place. In that event, he looked round for the dwelling of some other hunter, for he was confident that shelter would not be denied him. As a matter of fact, the host had probably been entertained on many occasions in just that way, and fully expected to seek and obtain hospitality on occasions yet to come. Therefore the virtue of protecting a guest became something more than a refined grace. It was essential to the progress of the race, and there grew up around it a host of superstitious ideas that made of hospitality a sort of unwritten law, which men were afraid ever to violate.

So far this is all easy enough to understand, but there is one feature of primitive entertainment that must shock the sensibilities of a modern. Among the duties that early people everywhere felt that they owed to their guests was the loan of their wives. Far from being a vice, this was a most sacred obligation. It had behind it the commands of the whole spirit world. It was one duty that no pious and dutiful individual would dare to call into question.

2

THE main reason for this is to be found in the belief that gods were in the habit of taking human form in order to associate in intimate fashion with women. Even the Bible tells us that the sons of the gods used to descend to earth and to court maidens. The offspring of such divine unions were giants. Now, it must be remembered that the woman who was courted by a stranger had no means of knowing whether her suitor was a disguised divinity or merely a mortal male in quest of female companionship. If the girl was under the impression that her lover was a god, it was necessary for her to wait and see whether or not her baby proved to be a giant, for only in that event could she know that she had been purified and uplifted by the embrace of deity.

To illustrate the uncertainty that always prevailed as to whether a stranger was a man or a god, one may study the case of Abraham. Three angels went to pay him a visit and to tender him the welcome assurance that his aged wife was destined to have a child. Abraham had no means of knowing that the visitors were supernatural beings in disguise, and had he been unwilling to entertain all guests who presented themselves at the entrance of his tent, he would have run the risk of refusing hospitality to the angels of heaven.

The angels went from Abraham's tent to the dwelling-place of Lot, where in the evening the house was besieged by the wicked inhabitants of the city. Lot went out to the people and begged them to desist and to leave his guests in peace. He went so far as to offer his own daughters to the populace; for he was ready to sacrifice their cherished honour for the safety of the strangers who had placed themselves under his care. If he was willing to turn his daughters over to the lustful hordes, it is surely reasonable to infer that he would have been as content to abide by the primitive idea of his duty as a host, and to give his children to those guests for whose security he was so piously and so properly solicitous.

But not merely did angels and lesser divinities sojourn incognito among men in order to court their daughters. Even the highest gods and their official representatives often paid this compliment to the human race. Zeus, the ruler of Olympus, frequently paid loverlike visits to girls. It is well known, for instance, that he courted Leda in the shape of a graceful swan, and Europa in the form of a bull.

The same great ruler of Olympus was attracted by the charms of Io, the beautiful priestess of the Temple of Hera. The god was not above seducing this servant of his wife, but when he was charged with this misdeed, he vigorously denied his guilt. Hell hath no fury like a goddess scorned, and to protect himself, Zeus turned Io into a white heifer and gave her to Hera. Later he assisted his beloved to escape, but the divine wife sent a gad-fly to torment her human rival and to drive her from land to land. At last Zeus screwed up enough courage to change her back into her own form. By this time she had reached Egypt, where she became the mother of Epaphos, the reputed ancestor of a number of peoples, the child of the maiden and the god.

The sacred literature of various religions is full of similar tales. Since the gods were so ready to enter into such intrigues, is it any wonder that primitive men, anxious to form unions with the supernatural world, were so eager to lend their womenfolk to strangers? In the words of La Croix, "This traveller, this beggar, this depraved and ugly being . . . who knew but he might be Brahma, Osiris, Jupiter, or some god in disguise, who had descended among mortals to . . . put them to the test? And would not the woman in such a case be purified by the embrace of a divinity . . . ?"

3

DEAD indeed was the soul of a maiden who did not cherish the ambition of becoming, like Io, the mother of a divine babe. But since the fates rarely allotted such exalted destiny to mere women of flesh and blood, the next best possibility was to seek a liaison with a priest, or holy man. He was a human being to be sure, but he was an official representative of divinity.

The great Bible of the Hindus tells the following story. Once upon a time a great Rajah died and left behind him two widows, but no sons. It was horrible to contemplate that so great a dynasty should thus perish from the earth. To avert this misfortune a sage undertook to visit each widow in turn and to raise up seed for the departed. Though renowned for his goodness, the wise man was repulsive in personal appearance. One of the widows therefore closed her eyes when she saw him, and her son was born blind. The other turned pale with disgust, and her child was born white. The blind boy could not become the ruler because of his handicap, so Pandu, the white child, became the Rajah.

Pandu was popular and grew to be a famous leader. All would have gone well with him had not a curious stroke of ill fortune befallen him. One day when he was out hunting, he chanced to see two deer disporting themselves together. He shot an arrow at the pair, but it turned out that the creatures were in reality not deer, but brahmins in disguise. One of these powerful persons threw off the mask and inflicted upon the Rajah the terrible curse that he should meet his death in the arms of his wife.

In the face of this irresistible imprecation Pandu determined to remain aloof from his wife. But this left open the very difficulty the dynasty had faced prior to his own birth. In his predicament he consulted an ascetic, who advised him to resort to the identical eugenic device that had been responsible for his own entrance into the world. He therefore commanded his spouse to visit a brahmin, but the good woman was even more fortunate than her mother-in-law and found as her lover, not a mere holy man, but a god. This stratagem saved the life of the ruling line, but not of Pandu himself. For in a moment of weakness he met his death after the manner of the curse.

If we would appreciate the true inwardness of stories like that (and one might multiply them), it is necessary to enter into the minds of the people who first conceived them. Just as the person of an ambassador today is somehow identified in law with the Government from which he is accredited, so the holy men of antiquity and of prehistory were looked upon as almost identical with the divinities whose representatives they were.

Thus the queens of ancient Egypt were regarded as the brides of the god Ammon. True, the deity himself did not deign to approach his earthly wife, but the Pharaoh was the honoured envoy of that powerful divinity, so that the god appeared to the queen in the likeness of the king.

This feeling was prevalent among practically all people in a certain stage of culture. It explains why so many ancient monarchs looked upon themselves not only as quasi-divine because of their official positions, but as actually divine because of literal descent from the great spirits of the supernatural world. The Incas of ancient Peru were the descendants of the Sun. The inscription on the famous Moabite Stone begins with the words: "I am Mesha, the son of [the god] Chemosh."

The gods are farther off today. But how much farther? Are there any relics of the old conception that holy men or men of power are privileged to represent Heaven and to indulge in amours on behalf of God? The "holy man" theory has not passed away completely. It is the foundation of the notion of the "divine right" of kings. There was a time when the ruler did not reign by the mere sanction of the supernatural. He was the official ambassador of the court of deity. Sometimes he was God Himself.

And a cursory reading of the lives of European kings will demonstrate the tendency of those august persons to take the liberties that Zeus used to take in the days when he was monarch of the sky.

4

A LOVE-LORN god has always been more dangerous than a love-lorn devil. The power of the demon was limited, and he was easily hoodwinked. We have observed that, in one case at least, he could not abide the smell of the burning heart and liver of a fish. If the bride wore a veil, and if the bridesmaids and groomsmen did their work with efficiency and dispatch, he would become confused and would not know on whom to inflict his diabolical revenge. It was merely necessary to tease the young couple in order to persuade him that the happy occasion was really one of sadness and that the plight of the joyous pair was bad enough without his magic interposition. And, finally, if all of these expedients failed, it was possible to buy him off with a few handfuls of rice.

But the gods, though not less lustful than the demons, were less childish and less easy to hoodwink. Since there were (and are today in certain places) gods who were attracted by the charms of girls and who were jealous of their human lovers, it was necessary to make real concessions to the divine ardour and to stand aside with humility while the divine passion was gratified.

To understand the history of this sort of thing and of the modern conceptions and practices that are outgrowths of it we may examine a singular convention that obtained in Europe under the feudal system. It was the rule that when a serf was married, he was compelled to pay a sum of money to his lord for the privilege of enjoying his wife's company on the first night of the nuptial union. This custom did not spring into existence full-grown; but the remuneration was exacted in payment for a right that the lord at one time had exacted for himself. But where did the ruler get the notion that he had this privilege? Where did the right come from in the first place? Unfortunately the history of this particular licence is a bit obscure and we shall not be able to marshal enough facts to furnish a complete demonstration of our conclusion. Still, we do know that the ruler, in the earliest days, was a human god. We also know something about the numerous divine kings (like the genial but notorious Roman Saturn) whose cults once dotted the globe. Apparently they enjoyed the favour of all women whom they deigned to admire. In the light of what follows we may be justified in concluding that the prerogative of the feudal lord was derived in the first place from a prehistoric "divine right."

In ancient Rome the god Priapus looked with a jealous eye on human maidens. He was not merely a powerful god, but he had in his charge the mysterious force of creation, so that, if he became displeased with humanity, he might always forbid the crops to grow, the flocks and herds to prosper, and the human race to increase, multiply, and enjoy the mystic blessings of life.

Among the prerogatives of Priapus was a privilege similar to the "right of the first night" claimed by the old feudal lords of Europe. It was a part of the Roman marriage ceremony for the young couple to repair to his temple and there for the bride to sit upon his image. This idol, a nude figure, was particularly obscene—that is to say, the formation of the body was such as to render it evident that the deity it stood for was the god of reproduction. For a girl to sit upon the idol was in effect to confer a favour upon it—to sacrifice to it her maidenly purity. Until she had duly rendered this offering to the deity, her husband was not eligible to be the beneficiary of her wifely attentions.

To this day the Hindu god Siva, whose images resemble those of the Roman Priapus, exacts the same offering from brides. Siva is a most important divinity, being the third person of the Hindu Trinity. A marriage among his worshippers would surely be accursed if the bride refused to grant to this highly sexed god the right that is so generally recognized as belonging to him.

One of the most interesting gods in the whole supernatural world is Legba, who is worshipped in that part of western Africa that is known as the Slave Coast. His function is similar to that of Priapus and Siva, and his images are, if anything, more obscene (from our point of view) than those of the other two. He habitually squats down and admiringly examines his own horribly disproportioned body. As a rule this divinity is male, but occasionally female. Like other people, Africans sometimes dream when they sleep, and now and then they dream of love. Not being students of modern psychology, the inhabitants of the Slave Coast must seek some answer in accord with their feeble lights to the question of the cause and "meaning" of those dreams.

They believe that Legba visits human beings while they
sleep and that his (or her) caresses cause the sleeper to
dream.

5

NOT content with this sporadic and promiscuous philander-
ing at night, Legba has his wives, who commit unspeakable
excesses when his mysterious festivals are celebrated. When
the ceremonies begin, the priests administer to the worshippers a consecrated drink, which fills the devotees with lust.
The people then adjourn with Legba's wives and go to the
bush for the further celebration of the mysteries. But it
must be understood that the inhabitants of the Slave Coast
are otherwise not impure. It is a recognized religious duty
among them to offer this sacrifice to Legba, but when the
religious festivals are not going on, they would be mortally
afraid to be unchaste.

In both Africa and India there are temples that have attached to them certain maidens who are called wives of the
god. Some of these brides of divinity are selected at birth,
and dedicated at a tender age to the service of their divine
husbands. The particular service that is required of them
is the raising of funds for the temple through the plying of
an immoral trade, the various intricacies of which they are
sedulously taught. They are the famous "dancing women,"
and, as we shall see, they are by no means the only women
who, in the slow evolution of spirituality, have sold their
charms for the support and glory of the gods and goddesses.

Sometimes, however, the brides of a god were not supposed to offer themselves to the general public. The Temple
of Bel in Babylon had a high chamber that was furnished
with a bed and a table. There the beauty who had been
honoured by being chosen as Bel's wife for the night met
the god—in the person of one of his priests. According to

Herodotus, there was a similar temple at Thebes. It was not
accounted a disgrace for a woman to be thus selected. It
was the proudest of distinctions.

This sort of worship was not confined to any one locality.
In a certain village of ancient Peru there was a stone which
had the shape of a man and which was venerated as a god.
This divinity demanded a wife, and a bride was selected
for him. After the elaborate wedding-ceremony the bride
lived a virtuous life, and her only duty was to offer sacrifices to her husband on behalf of the people. The virgin
bride was highly honoured, for she shared in the divinity of
her stony spouse.

6

THE root of the divine-lover theory is the idea that the
god is interested in individual human beings, and particularly in their love life. Holy as he is, he is not above
lusting after his own creatures, whom he sometimes deliberately seduces and sometimes unites with himself in the
holy bonds of sacred wedlock. In its crudest stages the
theory recites that the god demands a sacrifice like that
which was offered by every Roman bride to the passionate
Priapus. Then comes the stage where the idol no longer
receives this attention, but the favour of the deity's chosen
bride is accepted by him in the likeness of his priest. Next
comes the practice of devoting one's first act of love to
the benefit of the temple. We shall call this practice the
"Dance of the Gods."

But as the sensibilities and moral feelings of mankind
develop, these crass habits are sooner or later outgrown.
From such humble beginnings some of the highest exemplifications of spirituality have come into being. Thus
it happens that in some of the nobler religions the sacrifice
of virginity takes the more idealistic form of a vow of
perpetual chastity.

Even in ancient times people believed that a virgin was closer to the gods than other people. Side by side with the Dance of the Gods and the theory on which it rested, there was the idea that love had in it an element displeasing to the spirits, and that one who had never experienced the delights of affection was more godly than one who had. Ancient Roman law would not countenance the execution of a virgin. Such procedure might have brought down on the entire State the wrath of supernatural powers. If capital punishment of a chaste maiden was called for, it was the legally recognized duty of the executioner to deprive the girl of her purity before depriving her of her life.

Because virginity was so highly esteemed, it was natural that many goddesses should have been thought of as possessing that attribute, even some who had given birth to many young ones. Minerva had children, but she was called the "Virgin." Diana was known both as the "Virgin" and the "Mother." Hera, the jealous wife of Zeus, was not at all times exactly a virgin, but she took an annual bath at a mysterious fountain, and these ablutions had the magic property of restoring to her the pristine purity of her divine maidenhood.

Throughout the ancient world there were women who were literally "inspired" by the gods, and through whom important revelations were vouchsafed. The Pythian priestesses and the sibyls were such inspired women, magically "possessed" by the immortals—and they were of necessity virgins. The ancient Germans also had their prophetesses, who were virgins. These were specially chosen by signs of supernatural favour, or (what amounted to the same thing) they were elected by accredited holy persons, as were the famous vestal virgins of Rome.

Vesta was the goddess of the hearth. Sacred to her was a special fire that was kindled in a ritual manner at the beginning of every new year. When the year reached its close, the fire was carefully and reverently extinguished, and a new one made in the required manner. At other times, however, the sacred flame was not to be put out, and it was the prime duty of the vestals to tend it and to see that it continued to burn.

The superstition of the "holy fire" is one of hoary antiquity. It is the embodiment of the mystic power of light, the enemy of darkness. Light and life have always gone together as have darkness and death. Ghosts and devils walk at night in preference to the day-time. Is it altogether strange that the female guardians of Vesta's fire were required to be of unsullied virginity? If they permitted the fire to go out, the particular girl who was guilty received a whipping for the glory of the goddess. But if any vestal lost her honour, she was buried alive.

The requirements that a vestal had to meet were fairly rigorous. To be appointed in the first place she had to be between the ages of six and ten, both her parents had to be living, and she had to be free from any bodily or mental defects. When selected, she went through a ceremony of initiation. Her hair was cut off, and she wore a special veil thereafter. The exact origin of the institution is not known, but that it had much to do with the idea of the divine lover is shown by the fact that the pontifex, in beginning the ceremony of initiation, addressed the girl as *"Amata,"* or "Beloved."

One of the most astonishing facts about the supernatural world is the similarity of the sentiments, institutions, symbols, superstitions, conventions, and religious practices that are designed in different parts of the world as channels of communication and influence between it and the world of men. Long before there were any white men in the Western hemisphere, the Peruvian Indians had developed an institution closely resembling that of the vestals. The Inca, or ruler of Peru, was a semi-divine individual, who was a lineal descendant of the Sun. That the sun is important to the welfare of men is recognized today by the scientific fraternity, who affirm that from its rays all of earth's energy is ultimately derived. Primitive folks went further and looked upon Sol as a personal god, who would send his rays to fructify the fields if he so desired, but would withhold them if, for any reason, his mood was hostile to humanity. Therefore much of the content of early religions was designed to induce the Sun to send his fertilizing light. One of the favourite means of doing this was to light ritual fires for purposes of imitative magic.

To obtain light and heat from the Sun the Peruvians kindled a sacred fire by friction. Their sacred flame was tended by selected maidens, who were called "Virgins of the Sun." If the fire happened to go out, this was a sure sign that Sol was angry and had to be placated. To this end a feast was held. The Virgins of the Sun prepared special cakes and goblets of fermented liquor, which were served to the Inca and his nobles. The festival closed with dancing.

The Virgins of the Sun lived in special convents and were there watched over and taught by elderly women who had been cloistered for the better part of their lives. The convents themselves were closed to the whole world, except the Virgins, the Inca, and his queen. If one of the sacred maidens lost her virtue, she was, like the vestal under similar circumstances, buried alive, and the entire village from which she had come was destroyed.

But the curious feature of this institution lay in the fact that the "Virgins of the Sun" were also known as the "Brides of the Inca." The reason for this was that the descendant of Sol had certain privileges where they were concerned. Whenever he so desired, he selected the most beautiful in the convents and moved his favourites to his own palatial halls. He had many palaces, and possibly he placed some brides in one and some in another. If at any

time he tired of a particular girl, he sent her away; then
she returned to her original home, where for the remainder
of her life she was venerated by the entire populace. For
she was more than merely human. She was partly divine.
She was a Bride of the Inca.

7

THE idea that heavenly beings are interested in the affections of human beings is present in some of the highest
religions of modern times. But the forms in which that idea
has expressed itself among moderns are far nobler and more
spiritual than in the ages gone by.

The ceremony of Consecration of a Virgin, which is to be
found in the Roman pontifical, partakes of the nature of
a divine wedding. When the veil is bestowed, the following words are spoken by the celebrant of the occasion:
"Receive the sacred veil, that thou mayest be known to
have despised the world, and to be truly, humbly, and with
all thy heart subject to Christ as His bride; and may He
defend thee from all evil, and bring thee to life eternal."

8

A SPLENDID illustration of the relation between love and
the supernatural world may be found in the career of Saint
Gertrude, a Benedictine nun of the thirteenth century.
Her life-history has been duly and authoritatively recorded
in a book published in Paris in 1898 and entitled: *Révéla-
tions de Sainte Gertrude*. From that volume William James
quotes the following:

"Suffering from a headache, she sought, for the glory of God,
to relieve herself by holding certain odoriferous substances in her
mouth, when the Lord appeared to lean over towards her lovingly,
and to comfort Himself in these odours. After having gently
breathed them in, He arose and said with a gratified air to the

saints, as if contented with what he had done: 'See the new present which my betrothed has given Me!'

"One day at chapel she heard supernaturally sung the words *'Sanctus, Sanctus, Sanctus.'* The Son of God, leaning towards her like a sweet lover and giving to her soul the softest kiss, said to her at the second *'Sanctus'*: 'In this *Sanctus* addressed to My person, receive with this kiss all the sanctity of My divinity and My humanity.' "

CHAPTER V

The Dance of the Gods and the Secret of the Mistletoe

> *"Our virtues are most frequently but vices disguised."*
>
> FRANCIS, DUC DE LA ROCHE-
> FOUCAULD

1

THE mistletoe is a parasite of the oak—the holy oak —which has been an object of human devotion from time immemorial. On the sixth day of the month the ancient Druids, clad in white robes and carrying a golden sickle, used to go out to cut the mysterious parasite from its sturdy and rugged host. Then they sacrificed two white bulls and offered prayer. For this was a solemn occasion.

The ceremony was a most practical one. The holy plant had many powers. It was called the "all-healer"; it was an antidote against poison; and, most important of all, if animals drank a potion made from it, they became magically fruitful. Thus did the Druids connect the mistletoe with love.

But this mysterious shrub was not an unmixed blessing to mankind, for, according to Norse mythology, it was responsible for a world-wide calamity. It caused the death of the god Balder.

Balder was a popular divinity. He was equally beloved of gods and of men. His countenance literally shone, for rays of holy light that issued from his handsome face illuminated the space around him. He was the darling of the universe.

But Balder was afflicted with bad dreams, which indicated that his divine life was in peril. Accordingly his mother became alarmed at the portents and she exacted of practically everything in nature the promise not to harm her son. Wood, stone, metal, and earth all agreed to spare the life of the beloved divinity. But the mother neglected to exact this promise of the mistletoe, since she did not imagine that so little a shrub could be powerful for harm.

The gods of the Norsemen were inclined to be playful, and they invented a pleasing game of throwing things at Balder, whom the covenant with the elements had rendered virtually invulnerable. This gave an opportunity to the Devil to destroy the favourite of gods and men. It seems that there was in the pantheon a blind god, who, because of his handicap, was not able to take part in the sport. So the Devil made a dart of mistletoe and gave it to the sightless deity with the offer to guide his hand while he threw it at Balder. The dart did its work, and the good god fell to the ground.

After the funeral, which was a most elaborate affair, the goddess Hel, who was in charge of the dead, was entreated to permit Balder to return to the land of the living. She finally agreed to grant this exceptional permission, provided that all the world would weep and thus convince her of the god's universal popularity. So all the world wept for Balder. Men, women, animals, trees, metals, and stones all shed tears. But one wicked giantess, who was probably the Evil One in disguise, refused to cry—so it was all in vain.

The story of Balder is a typical primitive explanation of the origin of winter. Balder of the shining face, the beloved of everybody and everything except the Devil, was the sun, honoured and revered everywhere. Opposed to the luminary was the spirit of darkness, who caused the blessed light to descend to the realm of the dead. But the Wicked One could not accomplish this without the aid of that mystic power which is at once the destroyer and the generator. Love sometimes causes much evil, and therefore it is not surprising that the mistletoe, which was an antidote against poison and which rendered cattle fruitful, had also called into being the winter, the season of cold and darkness, the period of the year when, especially in the North, nature appeared to be dead.

2

A PLANT that possessed such a combination of mysterious powers as those of generation and destruction naturally attracted to itself much reverence. It was sacred to the lovely Venus, who was worshipped under different names in many lands and in many climes. And in some of the temples of that goddess it had a particular significance which has bearing on its curious modern association with kissing.

The Babylonian Venus was known as Mylitta. According to the law in that land, it was the duty of every woman, once in her life, to go to the temple of the goddess and there to submit to the caress of the first stranger who tossed her a coin, pronouncing as he did so the formula: "I invoke the goddess Mylitta."

It made no difference whether the girl was rich or poor, beautiful or ugly, modest or bold, of noble or humble parentage—the law of the land made it incumbent upon her to discharge her obligation to the local Venus. Some of the maidens who combined modesty with wealth and station rode to the temple in covered chariots and took their seats under the watchful eyes of many personal attendants. Others made the journey alone and unattended. But all alike wore the symbolic crown of fig-leaves on their brows, bound themselves with the symbolic cords, and assumed their places under the symbolic mistletoe.

Venus herself is no longer the Queen of Love. Her cult, as far as the Western World is concerned, is a matter of interest to historians alone. But customs that arise in the course of man's struggle to serve the ends of the supernatural and thus to bring blessings upon himself tend to survive long after the ideas on which they were originally founded have passed away. The loverlike prerogative connected with the suspended plant is less significant now than it was of yore. But it is from such beginnings that the custom of kissing the girl beneath the shrub has come down to the youths of modern times.

3

IT is not known what part of the silver collected in that manner went to enrich the priests who were in charge of the temple. But we do know that even in modern times there are similar temples, where the entire gains of the traffic go to the support of the priesthood. For example, in certain parts of India there are (if these practices have been abolished, the abolition must have been extremely recent) certain sanctuaries which feature "dancing-girls," who are the recognized brides of the idol there worshipped. The girls are selected early in life and go through an elaborate and solemn ceremony of marriage to the god. They are then carefully trained in the arts of arousing and gratifying the animal lusts of men and they sell their charms and abilities to provide revenue for the temple. If male children are vouchsafed to them, the boys are educated for the priesthood; if they have female children, they are trained to take up the duties of their mothers.

It is possible that the first temple dedicated to this kind of worship was that of Mylitta at Babylon. But so popular and so successful did the institution wax, and to such an extent did the temple expand and flourish, that the cult was copied throughout the then known world. Or perhaps it would be better to say that the spiritual development of human beings everywhere follows certain more or less specific lines, and the worship of Venus is but one phase in the normal evolution of the supernatural. However that may be, the fact remains that cults of that character were widespread. In every country the goddess appeared under a different name, and her worship flowered with new and distinctive ceremonies. Thus we hear of Mylitta, Anaitis, Astarte, Urania, and many others—but all of them were manifestations of the personality of Venus.

Anaitis was the Venus of Armenia. To her a vast temple was reared and she enjoyed a wide sacred enclosure that was set aside for her worship. The girls passed a certain time in that enclosure, where they extended their hospitality to all strangers who requested it and paid for it. After the prescribed period of service had passed, the girls emerged from their seclusion, but they left for the use of the priests all of the money they had collected. The life they had led did not render them unfit for matrimony. On the contrary, the girls were regarded as uplifted by their experience, and those were the most honoured and most sought after as wives who had been (by actual count) the most popular with the strangers who had visited the temple.

The island of Cyprus was recognized as the particular home of Venus. According to the myth, Venus was born of the foam of the sea. The gods had allotted Cyprus to her; but when she appeared on that island after having risen from the waves, the maidens of the place looked down on her and derided her. So enraged did the goddess become that she commanded the girls to sacrifice their purity to her, by associating freely with any strangers who asked for their companionship. Perforce the girls obeyed, but they did so with such shameful reluctance that Venus, in her anger, turned them into stones. After that they repented, and agreed to obey the goddess thenceforth cheerfully and willingly. Thereupon they regained their natural shapes, and from that time until quite late (there is record of the custom during the days of Justinian) they used to walk beside the sea, to greet the sailors and other folk who dis-

embarked on the island. They sold themselves for the glory
of their divine mistress.

This type of observance became especially popular with
seafaring men. Possibly for that reason it was extremely
frequent all around the shores of the Mediterranean. There
were such temples in Greece, Italy, and Africa. They were
situated on high hills, in full view of the seamen who rode
the waves. Perhaps they had something to do with the rise
of the mermaid legends, for they were veritable sirens, like
the famous Lorelei, who tempted sailors and lured them
from their courses.

4

THE success of the cult of Venus was due in large measure
to the fact that it was pleasing to men. It not merely afforded gratification of carnal lusts, but filled people with
the self-righteous judgment that in seeking pleasure they
were really performing acts of piety, reverence, and devotion. In other words, it offered the joyous assurance that in
doing precisely what one wanted to do, one was not urged
on by selfish impulses, but was guided merely by the righteous will to obey the behests of Heaven.

But this was not the only reason for the cult's prosperity.
No religion has ever thrived that did not express the highest sensibilities of the people whose spiritual hunger it
sought to appease. Doubtless there were some people who
visited the Temple of Mylitta solely because there they
found opportunity and licence to commit sin. But the
priests of Venus, however grasping they may have been and
however willing they were to appropriate the price of
womanhood's shame, were, according to their lights, spiritually minded people. The writings which they have bequeathed to posterity show clearly that their souls tran-
scended mere sordidness and avarice. To the minds of Venus'

worshippers, the goddess did not degrade maidenhood, but
elevated and exalted it.

5

THE ceremonies of ancient religions were at bottom
magic devices intended to make "two ears of corn or two
blades of grass to grow upon a spot of ground where only
one grew before," to increase the size of flocks and herds,
and to multiply human beings. The laws of population, and
the principles that underlie scientific husbandry, were, of
course, totally unknown. Instead the wisest of the people
held to the theory that the only effective method of inducing "Mother Earth" to yield more and more living things
was to make magic use of the power of creation as this
manifested itself in their own bodies. Generation was then,
as it is now, among decent people, both mysterious and
holy.

The Upright Symbol of Sex

The Roman god Bacchus, in common with many other
ancient divinities and the Hindu god Siva in our own day,
had as his most sacred symbol an upright representation of
his own power of creation. In the month of March, when,
after the long sleep of winter, it was essential to induce
nature to be reborn, the Romans celebrated the feast of
the Liberalia (for Liber was one of the names of Bacchus).
The physical symbol of the god was reverently placed in a
chariot, where it was garlanded with blossoms and was
conveyed through fields and cities by rejoicing throngs.

The intention was not culpably obscene. It was simply assumed that such a happy parade of an idol that so patently represented creation would result in the profuse generative activity of Mother Nature.

But the ceremonies of Bacchus did not end with this parade. The finest citizens of the land, together with the most sedate and demure of women, laid aside their usual decorum during Liber's feast and gave themselves over without restraint to the sort of conduct required by the deity who held fertility in his charge. The women either removed their clothing or covered themselves with wild and strange apparel, and ran out into the open country. In their hair they placed ivy or the vine, both of symbolic significance, and the most pious wore head-dresses of live serpents for the glory of their god. They screamed and they danced, and they worked themselves up to such a state of ecstatic excitement that they were known, as one authority says, "not only to feed upon raw flesh, but even to tear living animals with their teeth and eat them warm and palpitating."

Bacchus was the Roman counterpart of the Greek Dionysos. The festivals of Dionysos in Greece were of course similar to those of Liber in Rome. Wine was freely drunk, dancing and shrieking featured the occasions, and all the worshippers worked themselves into a frenzy. After such celebration the people were confident that they had experienced sensible union with their god. For had they not actually felt a new spirit enter into them? Had they not been conscious of sensations that were foreign to them except when under the spell of such mystic ceremonies? Was this not proof that they were "inspired"? Was this not a clear demonstration that the god himself had actually and palpably "possessed" them?

The Liberalia in Rome was followed by the festival of Venus. The details of that celebration need not concern us.

It will be sufficient for us to consider that, in the more solemn and less orgiastic portion of the ritual, the women proceeded to the Quirinal, where stood the erect emblem of generation. They took this symbol and reverently formed a procession to carry it with respectful attendance to Venus' temple. There they tendered it to the goddess and sought unrestrained joy.

6

IN ancient Egypt the goddess Isis was the Venus who was worshipped with similar rites and for similar reasons. Osiris and Isis, the great deities of Egypt, were essentially per-sonifications of the mysteries of reproduction,—Osiris being male, and Isis female. As in almost though not quite all of the early theories, the sun was male (and therefore a manifestation of Osiris), and the earth was female (and therefore a manifestation of Isis). The principal function of Egyptian religion was that of inducing Osiris and Isis to show affection towards each other and to bring forth in consequence a blessed abundance of crops, herds, and hu-man beings.

For the proper celebration of the feasts of those divini-ties certain specific symbolic paraphernalia were required. Since one of the most important of the symbols of Osiris was a bull, and Isis was usually represented by the cow, the images of the sacred cattle were borne respectively by the priests of the god and the goddess. In the procession the nursing cow of Isis was followed by the young girls who were consecrated to the service of Heaven. They carried a basket of holy cakes, which were round, with a hole in the centre, and were intended to represent the function of motherhood. After the maidens came an hon-oured priestess who carried a golden vessel, in which was the most sacred emblem of them all, the upright sign of creation.

The historian Herodotus has given us an account of one of the feasts of Isis. The people of a particular town rushed to the water, where they hastily jumped into boats without standing on the order of their jumping, and apparently without selecting their partners. As they sailed in the boats, some played musical instruments, and the rest sang. When they approached another city, they moved to the bank, where the visiting girls shouted insults at the women on shore. The offended hostesses then proceeded to dance (doubtless a ritual dance), while the female visitors lifted their garments and made indecent displays of their persons.

7

THE importance of this type of ritual for our study lies in the fact that out of it grew the art of dancing. Up till a few years ago (comparatively speaking), there was no such thing as an art divorced from the supernatural world. Painting was always pious painting; drama was sacred drama; even the alphabet was an outgrowth of mystic symbolism; and dancing was an effort to influence the supernaturals by the force of imitative magic.

To this day there are relics of the old orgiastic dance festivals at harvest time among the European peasantry. These are the demonstrations of gladness in which all men indulge at that season. In former times the joy of carnival time knew no bounds. The people drank freely of intoxicating liquor because they felt somehow that this weakened moral resistance and increased lust, and they wanted the gods to lose their divine powers of resistance and to give way to fruitful lusts on those occasions. They worked themselves up to a pitch of excitement in the hope that the gods would do likewise. And they indulged their passions without restraint—also as an example to the gods and goddesses of fertility.

It is no accident that Bacchus, the god of procreation, was also the god of wine. The use of liquor was originally an act of devotion, as, in a measure, it still is. Particularly at the festival in the spring of the year was it considered virtuous to drink to excess. The drinking of wine is still considered meritorious among Orthodox Jews at the Passover, which falls about the time of Easter, but which was also the season of the Liberalia, the festival of Venus, and the Teutonic and Anglo-Saxon spring festival of the goddess Eastre (or, as it is sometimes spelled, Eostre).

8

THE Dance of the Gods usually implied a ceremonial friendship between men and women. But this was not always so. The Greek festival of the Thesmophoria, for example, which was observed in the autumn in honour of Demeter and her daughter, was a feast for women alone.

Demeter was the goddess of the earth. She had a lovely daughter, Persephone, whose father was none other than the love-lorn ruler of the immortals, the mighty Zeus. One day Persephone was out in the field playing aimlessly and plucking wild flowers. While engaged in this innocent pastime, she espied a pretty narcissus and proceeded to grasp it. But unfortunately the flower was connected with a magic trap. No sooner had the child's hand closed over the narcissus than the earth opened itself and swallowed her. Zeus himself had entered into a dark conspiracy with Hades to seize his own little daughter and to imprison her under the ground. No one saw the crime except the Sun and the Moon.

The divine mother was heart-broken. She took a torch in her hand, and for nine days she wandered about looking for her lost little girl. On the tenth day, however, the luminaries informed her of what they had seen.

This was not a direct help to the bereaved parent. She must find a means of compelling Hades to give back her child. It was a problem similar to that which confronted the gods of the North when Balder the Good was treacherously slain. While she pondered over this difficulty, she continued to wander disconsolately, till at last, disguised as an old woman, she sat down to rest beside a well. The well became known as the Fountain of Maidenhood, and was situated in Eleusis.

The daughters of the King went to draw water and they met the disguised goddess. Naturally, they did not recognize her. But they were kindly girls and good listeners, so Demeter beguiled them with a false story. She pretended that she had been captured by pirates, from whose cruel prison she had escaped, and she begged them to find employment for her as a nurse-maid. They took her to their own royal residence, where she was placed in charge of the baby of the family. She used her divine arts in the care of the child and was caught in the act of baptizing it with fire. Then the outraged Queen knew that she had to deal with no mortal person, and the goddess threw off her disguise and announced that she was no less than Demeter, mistress of the soil. She then directed that a temple be erected to her and gave detailed instructions concerning the nature of the worship she would deem acceptable.

Meantime the divine grief had not abated and Demeter did not bother to be fruitful. Therefore there were no crops; the flocks and herds perished for want of grass; the people were famishing; and, most important of all, the gods were neglected because their worshippers had nothing to offer on the altars. Alarmed at this unfortunate state of affairs, the gods pleaded with Demeter, but she refused to take any steps till Persephone was restored to her.

After much persuasion Hades consented to permit Persephone to return to her mother, but he slyly gave her a seed of the mystic pomegranate, a fruit that has played a prominent role in the drama of the supernatural, and this magically bound her to the earth. The upshot of the matter was that, while the child was permitted to spend a part of each year above ground, she had to go back to the underworld for a season. This is the Greek version of the origin of winter.

Demeter was satisfied with this arrangement, compromise though it was. She returned to her rightful abode among the gods, but not until she had revealed to the people certain mysterious truths and certain occult rituals, which became known as the mysteries of Eleusis.

Whatever may have been the real origin of those mysteries and of similar mystery cults in various lands, the fact remains that they played a prominent part in the spiritual development of mankind. To this day they are regarded as important divine revelations in that school of opinion known as theosophy. They formed the beginnings of that sort of activity which is embodied in our secret societies. The mysteries were, in fact, the first secret orders.

9

THE mysteries of Eleusis took place immediately before the sowing of the seed in the fall. They were extremely elaborate. New candidates were initiated and rituals were pronounced and acted. There was sacred dancing and ceremonial handling of holy emblems. Most significant were the dramatic representations of the myth of Demeter and her daughter. After a candidate had passed through the various degrees of membership, each involving a revelation of some new verity, he was shown an ear of corn, which the worshippers recognized as the supreme truth in the whole series of ceremonies.

Originally Demeter and Persephone were one and the same. But when they became separate beings, the mother was the soil, and the daughter the produce of the soil, or the corn. The grain appears above ground for a part of the year, but goes perforce to the underworld, the realm of the dead, for the remainder. Balder in the chilly Northland, and Persephone in sunny Hellas, explained this natural phenomenon.

But the myths were more than mere explanations. They and the rituals that were presumably based upon them were of supremely practical significance. The weeping for Balder helped to render Mother Earth fruitful. Possibly it acted as a charm to bring the rain in its season. The mysteries of Eleusis repeated in dramatic and artistic form the sacred story of the resurrected goddess. Such representations assisted the cycle of the seasons to keep in proper order and to culminate in the fruitful activity of the soil. Such myths and such rituals were very common in antiquity. The deities who thus descended to the underworld and were brought back are legion. This is the mystery of mysteries.

At the Thesmophoria, or annual festivals of Demeter and Persephone, it was the custom to sacrifice swine. When the girl was to be shown descending into the earth, the incident was portrayed by throwing the pig into a sacred cavern. Thus the animal that is so hated by observant Jews and Mohammedans, as it was abhorred by the ancient Egyptians and others in the early days, was fairly divine at Eleusis. Was not the swine identified with Demeter's daughter? Could the creature hope for a more signal honour?

Whatever may have been the significance of the pig (and we shall not conclude our journey through the supernatural world until we have discovered it), the other emblems of Persephone's feast were frankly concerned with life and love. The upright sign of sex was paraded, and so were a mystic cake shaped like a serpent, and also a fir-cone. These were all intended to suggest the idea of fertility. Women alone took part in the ceremony, but it was a pious duty of the celebrants to indulge in indecent jokes at each other's expense.

The women also celebrated in honour of Demeter and Persephone the feast of the Halloa. On that occasion, in addition to the holy jokes, always of an indecent nature, the symbols of both sexes were handled for magical purposes. At the close of the festivities a banquet was held, at which sacred cakes were served. The cakes were shaped like the organs of the human body. It is interesting to note that the effectiveness of cakes of that sort was widely assumed. As far back as 1500 b. c., buns were used in the ceremonies of Astarte.

10

It is difficult for moderns to understand the seeming indecency of primitive and classical spirituality. But, after all, if one can enter, so to speak, the minds of the earlier peoples and can view the world through their naïve and untrained eyes, the matter will be fairly simple. The surrender of one's honour for the glory of a god or a goddess was a form of sacrifice. In fear and trembling, people laid at the feet of the immortals that which they prized most highly. Upon what could righteous people place a greater value than their honour? Even this they were willing to offer to the powers above.

Nor were women alone in rendering that sacrifice. If the maidens offered their purity to Venus, so did the lads to Adonis. Adonis was one of the gods who died every year and who was reborn in the spring, as his devotees rejoiced. To him men sacrificed their purity.

In addition to the goddesses like Venus, and gods like Adonis, there were deities who were of two sexes. Legba in Africa today is sometimes male and sometimes female. Brahma seated upon the lotus is at once both a god and a goddess. Venus was now and then represented with a beard.

The Dance of the Gods reached its most frenzied peak

when the object of adoration was at one and the same time
a type of Adonis and of Venus. For such a divinity combined in a single spiritual person the whole mystery of creation. And creation was love, and life, and prosperity.

CHAPTER VI

The Obscene Saint

> *"A man who is unable to count above five, who walks naked* coram populo, *adorning his person only with feathers and tawdry ornaments, would ordinarily be called insane; but if he has a black skin and lives on the banks of the Congo, he is considered an average specimen of normal humanity."*
>
> SIGMUND FREUD

1

AMONG the curious features of the Dance of the Gods one may have remarked the use of buns in the ceremonies of certain important divinities of bygone days. Bread is the staff of life and it was employed in the service of the gods because the principal object of the rites was that of procuring the blessing of bread. If the cakes were baked in obscene shapes, this was due to the profound conviction that likeness of that sort would effectually stimulate the production of more life, more happiness, more luck.

Like holy bread, eggs played a prominent part in the divine dance. Though not recognized as the staff of life, the egg is apparently the source from which it mysteriously springs. Hence it was used on those important occasions when the powers of creation were being invoked.

The spring festival of the Jews is called the Passover. It is connected by the Jewish tradition with the story of the departure from Egypt, but a study of its ritual and symbols will reveal the fact that it is far older than that event. It bears all the ear-marks of the typical spring festival, and when the Scripture says that Moses asked Pharaoh to let his people go into the wilderness to perform their devotions, it was doubtless that feast that he had in mind.

The main feature of the Passover celebration is a meal called the "Seder." The table is graced with symbols that are supposed to represent incidents in the tale of the Exodus. There is pure horse-radish, supposedly to illustrate vividly the bitterness of the house of bondage; there is salted water to depict the Red Sea; there are unleavened cakes to take the place of the bread that was baked in the sun and did not have time to be leavened; there is a burnt bone to represent the paschal lamb; and a burnt egg to symbolize (?)—no one knows. It is also the custom to serve hard-boiled eggs to the guests, though the significance of these edibles is not made clear in the tradition.

The symbols of the annual Seder Supper will serve as a splendid illustration of the tendency of pious people to pour old wine into new bottles. The old customs and signs are retained long after the original belief that called them into being has passed away. But the habits and rites are not merely retained as such. New interpretations are assigned to them; the old foundations are removed and new ones are provided for them to rest upon. But simply as a matter of history it is well to recognize that the customs of the Passover, to mention but one of the many spring festivals of various groups, did not originate in the manner in which folk-lore says that they originated.

The eggs and cakes that figured so prominently in the different spring devotions and rituals of the earth were generally connected with the worship of that female divinity who, in whatever place she was worshipped and under whatever name, bore the title of Queen of Heaven. That honour was held among the ancient Saxons and Teutons by the well-known goddess Eastre.

It is no secret in these days that the various months of the year, like the various days of the week, were at one time sacred to special divinities. Thus Monday is the Moon's day; Tuesday is Tiw's day; Wednesday is Woden's day; Thursday is Thor's day; Friday is Frigga's day; Saturday is Saturn's day; and Sunday is the Sun's day. The months of the year were also assigned to special deities to whom they were sacred. Even among such rigid monotheists as the Jews, for example, there is still a religious month called Tammuz (which was the proper name of the god Adonis) and there is a month Sivan, named after that amazingly lustful god who is worshipped to this day in India under the name Siva.

Sacred to Eastre was the month of April. At that time a festival was celebrated in her honour. Highly coloured eggs were used in the rites, as were holy buns.

Sacred cakes in ancient times were frequently baked in suggestive shapes. The Romans made their ritual buns in the form of organs of either sex. In Sparta the cakes were sometimes made in the form of the female breast, and such cakes were worn by bridesmaids at weddings. But at times conventional symbols were used. It is interesting in this connexion to note that the ancient Egyptians, years before the advent of Christianity, used to impress on their spring buns the sign of the cross.

2

THE customs that we have been investigating were by no means wiped out at one fell swoop. The worship of sex is still frankly the religion of a large part of mankind, and, while it has given way in the highly civilized nations to more advanced and even sublime expressions of spiritual feeling, still, the change from early crudity to the noble conceptions of modern times was not an abrupt one. A highly spiritualized creed may be propagated among primitive folks who have not reached the necessary stage of culture to appreciate it, but if it is, the rude people will combine the new teaching with the old. They may even interpret the higher faith in terms of the lower.

That this is true in lands that are known to be far removed from the centres of western thought will not surprise many people. No one will be amazed to find that in modern India the days set apart for the worship of Siva and those set apart for the adoration of Sakti, his wife, are spent in what amounts to a form of carnal indulgence. It may not appear unduly strange that at certain festivals of Siva the priest takes the place of the god and unites in loving union with those women whom Siva has not blessed with offspring through the instrumentality of their own husbands. Nor will one be thoroughly astonished to read of feasts of Sakti in which the goddess is represented by a beautiful maiden, who accepts the caresses of male worshippers after the service of dancing and hymns has been properly completed.

But it will be astonishing to most people to learn that in certain sections of France it used to be the custom of the peasantry to celebrate as holy a day as Palm Sunday in a suggestive manner. Cakes made in the old familiar shape were attached to palm-leaves and were then blessed and preserved by the women during the remainder of the year. Doubtless they served as charms. They were typical repositories of luck.

In like manner, no one will be shocked to learn that at the Roman Bacchanalia in the spring, part of the worship consisted in the pouring of wine by the women over the symbol of the god's generative power. But it is shocking to learn that as late as the year 1585 in the town of Embrun, in France, the identical symbol belonging to Saint Foutin was revered in precisely the same manner.

Saint Foutin was said to have been the first Bishop of Lyons. Somehow he became connected in the minds of the people with the idea of creation. Possibly they identified him with certain priapic divinities whom they had been accustomed to worship in the days before Christianity. At any rate, his rites were suggestive. A jar was placed beneath his emblem, to catch the wine with which it was regularly anointed. This wine was left to sour, and then it was known as "holy vinegar." The women drank it in order to be blessed with children.

At Isernia, in Italy, a similar worship flourished. It was not suppressed till the year 1780. The saints who were worshipped there were Saints Cosmas and Damian. They were given to the curing of diseases at the festival that was celebrated in their honour, on the seventeenth of September.

The method of cure was as follows: The suppliants purchased at the Isernia Fair certain wax representations of the parts of their bodies that were afflicted. The wax objects were then taken to the church, where they were presented to the saints along with an offering. The devotee then approached the priest, before whom he uncovered the ailing or the affected part, and the clergyman poured upon it some "oil of Saint Cosmas."

In theory it was possible for a man suffering from arthritis or angina pectoris to present himself at Isernia for cure. But, as a matter of fact, most of the seekers for relief were women, and practically all of the wax images offered for saintly attention represented the generative parts. Many of the prayers were for children, but there were also invocations for the cure of diseases of creative organs.

In addition to the saints mentioned, one might mention others of a similar character in Europe. The roll includes Saint Giles in Brittany, Saint René in Anjou, Saint Guerlichon of Bourges, and others.

3

SUPERSTITION always dies hard. The evolution of the supernatural from the depths of savage conceptions to the heights of modern religion has been a slow process. Spiritual progress is still slow.

In the words of an old Arabic proverb, "Men resemble the times they live in more than they resemble their fathers."

CHAPTER VII

The Magic Wand

> *"The districts where an account of a*
> *modern miracle is received with least*
> *derision are precisely those which are*
> *most torpid and most isolated. The*
> *classes whose habits of thought are*
> *least shocked by such an account are*
> *those which are least educated and*
> *least influenced by the broad current of*
> *civilization."*
>
> W. E. H. LECKY

1

PART of the standard equipment of every magician is a wand. At one time the staff was supposed to possess a significant power. But today even the man who admits that his profession is merely that of entertainer finds it necessary to use it. The performer who frankly advertises that his seeming magic is at bottom nothing more than clever trickery and illusion carries a wand, if only for the atmosphere it creates.

In the past, when the science of the occult and the black art were widely pursued and still more widely feared, the rod was employed for purposes more directly practical. Fairies are known to carry long, tapering wands, usually with stars at the tips. Kings, those semi-divine hold-overs from the dark days of superstition, wield sceptres. Why? What is the true story of the wand and of its royal counterpart, the sceptre?

The glittering star at the end of a typical fairy's wand was originally intended to represent the sun, from which powerful rays were proceeding. In the same way, in the

well-known Eastern symbol known as the "star and crescent" the real meaning of the device is the union of the sun
and the moon. The two are locked together in loving embrace in order that, as a result of their caress, nature will
be fruitful.

Sceptres vary slightly in different countries and among
different peoples. As a rule, the staff of royalty is not a
plain stick, but is tipped with some device or other that, to
the eye of a student, is usually symbolic of love. The French
kings, for example, used to have two sceptres. On one was a
fleur-de-lis, and on the other was a hand raised as if about
to confer a blessing. The flower is emblematic of motherhood. As for the hand, it is still used in Mediterranean countries as a charm against the evil eye. The very fact that the
hand is universally used as an instrument of blessing shows
that it bears a relation to the supernatural. It is an organ by
which magic is frequently worked. At Copenhagen one finds
a bronze relief of Zeus Sabazios. The god holds in his right
hand a pine-cone; in his left is a sceptre the tip of which is
in the shape of a hand.

There is reason to believe that staffs as symbols of royal
authority were used as early as the old stone age. Nevertheless, for a long time no hard and fast distinction was
made between the rod of the king and that of the magician.
The Greek and Latin words for "sceptre" were used also to
denote other staffs, which fact in itself shows that no difference was originally recognized between the varieties of potent wands. Among the plains Indians of North America
carved wands were used as sceptres. Common individuals
were not permitted to carry them. Their use was restricted
to chiefs and to medicine-men (who were, of course, official
magicians). It is clear, then, that originally, at least, the
royal sceptre and the magic wand were one and the same.

The magic wand is one of the oldest instruments known
to the human race. Perhaps it is actually the oldest, and

hence the most venerable, invention designed for the purpose of bending the forces of nature to the will of man. Among the ancient wands of which we have record are those of Moses and Aaron in Scripture. According to some interpretations, these two were really one and the same, and we shall refer to the staff in the singular for that reason.

It is clear from the biblical accounts that the rod of Aaron was nothing new, for the magicians of Pharaoh also had magic wands which were potent, if not as potent as those of the brothers. Thus when Moses was asked for a sign, he cast his staff on the ground, and it became a serpent. The royal magicians then followed his example, and with the same astonishing result,—but the serpent of Moses ate up the serpents of the others. Moses stretched out his staff over the waters, and frogs came up to plague the Egyptians. But "the magicians did so with their secret arts, and brought up the frogs over the land of Egypt." On the other hand, Aaron struck the dust with his wand and thus produced the plague of vermin. The magicians found that they were unable to perform that particular miracle; in other words, that while their rods were powerful, Aaron's was more so.

On a later occasion the rod of Aaron budded and brought forth fruit in the Tabernacle in order to demonstrate the right of the tribe of Levi to serve as a priestly caste. For this reason according to the Old Testament it was placed "before the Testimony," while according to the New Testament it was kept inside the Ark itself. Clearly it bore some relation to the holy Ark.

Since the Bible assigns such magic potency to Aaron's wand, it is not strange that the ancient Jews surrounded it with a whole wealth of legend. According to the rabbinic accounts, the rod had a most remarkable history. It was created on the sixth day, and when Adam was expelled from the garden, it was turned over to him to be passed on to his descendants. Each of the patriarchs possessed it in turn and they doubtless used it for the performance of wonders. At last it came into the possession of Joseph, who carried it with him to Egypt when he was sold by his jealous brothers. When that seer and interpreter of dreams passed away, the Egyptian nobility proceeded to steal his belongings, and among other things they appropriated the rod. In the division of the spoils the wand passed over into the keeping of Jethro, the priest of Midian, who planted it in his garden.

Once planted, it was not long before the magic virtue of the staff became apparent. People found that they were likely to be injured if they so much as touched it, and even the strongest men found it impossible to dislodge it from the ground. Because of this, Jethro made the promise that he would give his daughter Zipporah in marriage to the man who should be able to uproot the powerful and mysterious shoot. After Moses had killed the Egyptian and was living as a fugitive in Midian, he reached the house of Jethro. He saw the rod and was able to read the ineffable name that was engraved upon it. This name has always been full of magical possibilities. Lilith used it to obtain wings and to fly out of the garden when she became disgusted with Adam. Moses used it to enable him to pull the staff from the ground. That is how he happened to become the husband of Zipporah.

The early Christian Fathers also surrounded this rod with legends of their own. Thus it was said that the wand was taken in the first place from the tree of knowledge. It was in the possession of the patriarchs and was handed on by them to subsequent generations, but an angel took it and buried it. Jethro unearthed it and passed it on to Moses and Aaron, who in turn gave it to Joshua, and so on till it was again buried, this time in Jerusalem. At the time of the birth of Jesus it was once more exhumed. It was carried by Joseph to Egypt and there turned over to James, the brother of the Saviour. Just as, according to the Jewish legend, the

Egyptian nobles had stolen it from the estate of Joseph, so according to the Christian story Judas Iscariot stole it from James. When the time came for the Crucifixion, it was found that there was no wood for the beam of the cross, so Judas furnished the rod, which was used for this purpose.

Moreover, the legends of the Mohammedans exalt the rod of Aaron. It seems that when Moses stood before Pharaoh and cast his staff on the floor, the fact that the wand transformed itself into a serpent was the smallest feature of the miracle. According to the Mohammedan story, the snake was as large as an exceedingly tall camel. This enormous reptile seized the throne and raised it into the air. Then putting it down again, the serpent said: "If it pleased Allah, I could swallow up not only the throne, with thee and all that are here present, but even thy palace and all that it contains, without anyone's perceiving the slightest change in me."

2

It is clear that the rod of Aaron combined the properties of two living things. It blossomed and grew like a tree, and it changed itself into a serpent. It so happens (and the coincidence is at least interesting) that many of the gods of antiquity carried rods of one kind or another, and the myths connected with those symbols show that they also were combinations of the tree and the serpent. It is also true that both the tree and the snake were venerated as gods by primitive men. A study of tree-worship and serpent-worship and of the combination of the two will demonstrate how the idea grew that there was magic potency in certain staffs. From such a study one will be able to understand why the wand is a necessary part of the magician's paraphernalia and why the sceptre is an essential feature of the equipment of a king.

3

Not so many many years ago the earth was wellnigh covered with trees. In those days the people believed that the forests were populated with nymphs and fauns, fairies and witches, elves, brownies, and gnomes. The fairy-tales that have come down to us from remote antiquity describe the forests. One had but to travel a short distance from one's village to come upon a virtually unexplored wood. There one would be likely to meet not only the fox and the wolf and the hare, but also the dryad and the magician.

It was dangerous indeed to venture alone into a wood. In addition to the natural perils that the traveller had to face, there were the supernatural terrors, constant hints of which were thrown out by the awful whistling of the wind, and the moaning and groaning, as the leaves and branches were stirred.

The sounds with which the forest was filled were obviously caused by something. What could be responsible for them? Clearly the spirits of darkness who lurked in the dread shadows. Even if some sceptic had proved that the noises were caused largely by the wind, this would not have served to allay the fears of timid people. For were not the winds and the spirits essentially identical? Did not all ancient races use the same word to describe wind and spirit? Does not our very word "spirit" come from the Latin *"spiritus,"* which means "wind"? Would not a modern individual begin to tremble if he found himself alone in a wood as darkness closed in upon him? True, such fear would be justified because the lost man would be in genuine peril, but would not his dread resemble the creepy feeling with which one reads a ghost story at midnight? Can one blame a primitive and untutored person if when he traversed the vast forests of yore he was

Like one that on a lonesome road
Doth walk in fear and dread
And, having once turned round, walks on
And turns no more his head
Because he knows a frightful fiend
Doth close behind him tread?

But if the voices of the forest were terrible, they were also useful. The demons of darkness walked in their shade, but the trees themselves were sacred to the gods. Hence, if one could but understand it, the voice of the wood was the voice of deity. Thus, the oak forest at Dodona was an oracle of Zeus, and the initiated priesthood of the forest could tell what the leaves were saying. They were talking in the language, as it were, of the King of the gods. They were revealing the future and were expounding the divine will.

The holy oak, the king of the forest, was everywhere sacred to Jupiter, the King of the gods. It was sacred to Yahweh, the great God of the Hebrews. The Hebrew word for oak is *"elon,"* which may originally have signified "the tree of El" or God. There is reason to believe that the oak was at one time not merely sacred to the King of the gods, but that Jupiter himself was, in the first instance, an oak-tree and nothing more. The giant of the wood was frequently blasted by lightning, a mysterious phenomenon frightful to contemplate, and showing, according to primitive logic at least, that the majestic tree and the terrible thunder were somehow related to each other. As Jupiter grew and developed, however, he became manlike and was elevated farther and farther above his trembling worshippers. In the course of time other trees became sacred to him also, as the pine, the palm, and the ash.

While the holy oak was most frequently the object of human reverence, other trees, shrubs, and blossoms were sacred to various divinities. To mention but a few, the periwinkle was sacred to Cupid, the laurel to Apollo, the poplar to Hercules, and the alder to Pan. Some trees were sacred to female divinities. Thus the myrtle, like the rose and poppy and mistletoe, was sacred to Venus, the pomegranate to Persephone, and the olive and mulberry to Minerva.

4

AT Mamre, in Palestine, there still stands what is left of the famous "oak of Abraham." If we may credit the story connected with it, the patriarch stood in its shade when he received the angels who came to tell him that his wife would bear a son. It was also in that sacred spot that he carried on the negotiations for the purchase of a burial cave for Sarah. At the time of the crusades many Christians made pilgrimages to the oak, and devout celebrations took place under its consecrated leaves. What was the nature of the first religious observance that was ever held under the shadow of that holy oak? We can only surmise.

We know, of course, the nature of the worship that was offered to Mylitta in the sacred grove of cedars at Babylon. We are familiar with the lament of Israel's prophets that lewd exercises were conducted in Palestine "under every green tree." We know furthermore that the tree used to be regarded everywhere, and most properly, as a symbol of life. Graceful plants like the myrtle were female, but most trees, like the towering oak, were signs of the male sex. To this day one may find streamers and coloured rags attached to trees in Africa. The natives put them there in the hope that nature will be rendered fruitful by the grateful spirit of the erect plant.

Finally, we know that the first temple of the gods was the grove. This is an axiom of the science of comparative religions. Even when, in somewhat later times, the priests directed that circles of stones be set up to enclose a devoted spot (there are remnants of those circles in every part of the globe), these were always placed within or near sacred groves. Even Pliny made the statement: "The trees are the temples of the gods."

5

THE garden of Eden contained two magic trees, which Adam and his wife were forbidden to molest. One was the tree of knowledge of good and evil, and the other was the tree of life. The latter is universally known, for many races have venerated the arboreal symbol of generation. For example, the Scandinavians revered the ash as their "tree of life." If an ash happened to fall, the omen was a dreadful one, and the timid observers turned pale with terror. If any impious mortal dared to cut one down, the penalty was death.

The primeval couple succumbed to temptation and ate of the tree of knowledge. As a result they discovered that they were naked and that nakedness was wrong. Hence they made for themselves aprons of fig-leaves.

The fig, like the vine, was sacred to Bacchus, and for two reasons. In the first place its fruit and leaves have a suggestive shape, and in the second place it is full of seeds and hence apparently connected with the function of creation. The fig was carried in state at the holy processions of Bacchus, and the famous statues of the obscene god Priapus were regularly made of fig-wood. We have not forgotten that in the Temple of Mylitta the maidens who waited for an opportunity of sacrificing their purity wore upon their brows wreaths of leaves from that mystic tree. To this day the fig-leaf is used by sculptors as a conventional emblem.

The tree of life in the Mohammedan religion is the Tooba. It is to be found in the seventh heaven, where it graces the space at the right of the Eternal. The Prophet himself saw this plant in the seventh heaven. Gabriel was standing beside it.

The mystic tree of Buddhism is the Bo. It has been identified with the fig. The Bo tree plays a most significant part in the mythology that has grown up about the person of Buddha.

Siddhartha Gautama, called the Buddha, was a scion of a noble and wealthy family. While still a young man, he married, and for a while he enjoyed luxury, position, and power.

But Gautama, possibly because he chanced to see a corpse, became filled with a sense of the futility of worldly pleasure and the emptiness of reality. If all life must be conquered eventually by death, isn't the world a cheat? Isn't it a delusion and a snare?

In the still watches of the night the young prince ran away. He was determined to renounce the world and to discard his material possessions. He even exchanged clothes with a beggar so that nothing remained to him but the bedraggled vestments of poverty. Clad in such garments, he went forth in quest of wisdom; and the particular wisdom he sought was an answer to the riddle of reality—a perception of the nature and value of life and death.

For years the holy lad studied in the company of hermits, but the secret was withheld. Like Omar Khayyám, who also sought knowledge of ultimate truth, he "evermore came out by the same door as in he went." But at length he passed through a miraculous experience of spiritual rebirth. In this way there was revealed to him what patient study and ceaseless inquiry had been powerless to unfold.

He was lying under the Bo tree when the revelation took place. For a day and a night he remained there, and then he ventured forth to share his knowledge with mankind. The wisdom that he had found was Buddhism—the inspiration of the fig.

6

To describe tree-worship in detail would fill many volumes. As forests once covered the earth, so did the worship of the woods. Groves have their supernatural as well as their natural histories. As the winds danced among the leaves, so did the happy divinities of the woodland. Among the trees the gods danced, and their worshippers with them.

But one can hardly dismiss the subject without describing the adoration of the holy palm, for of that devotion vestiges are extant to this day.

In tropical and semi-tropical lands the palm was generally sacred to the Sun. Now that luminary was a god whose divine function it was to kiss his bride, who was known everywhere as "Mother Earth." As a result of this celestial affection the earth became instinct with life; the fruits were brought forth in due season, and humanity was blessed.

Because of the association of the palm with the Sun, the graceful tree was frequently employed in devout exercises of different kinds, especially those affectionate rites of the Dance of the Gods, harvest festivals, and wedding-ceremonies. The upright trunk was regarded as suggestive of the male; the curved and tapering branches, so like the mythical sylphs in form, were thought of as female. A favourite theme with the sculptors of Assyria was that of a god holding a pail and giving pollen to the palms. The Hebrews of Palestine felt the inspiration of the palm and used it for ritual purposes. The reverence for that particular tree naturally passed over into Christianity. The early Christians used to make a religious symbol by placing a beam across the palm, and hanging to the transverse bar of the cross thus formed the mystic signs "alpha" and "omega," thus:

Among modern religionists the palm is still used in connexion with certain rites, which, though they bear indications of a humble origin, are interpreted in higher and more spiritual terms. For example, on the Feast of Tabernacles, in the fall of the year, the Jews use for their worship an instrument that is called a *"lulab."* This is made of a palm shoot, three twigs of myrtle, and two willow branches. The myrtle and the willow are attached to the base of the *lulab*, and the shoot is then bound in such a manner that it becomes a long and graceful wand. With the *lulab* a Palestinian citron (resembling in appearance a large lemon) is always used. The palm and the citron are paraded through the temple, and each worshipper shakes the object towards the north, south, east, and west, then upwards and downwards.

This waving of the palm is considered a most important ritual among Orthodox Jews. In some countries special provisions are made to enable the poor and the sick to perform this rite. The congregation keeps one *lulab* or more on hand for the use of the poor, and one is taken to the homes of the sick, so that they too may fulfil the commandment. An observant Orthodox Jew will not eat breakfast during the Feast of Tabernacles until he has discharged the sacred obligation of waving the *lulab*.

While ceremonies of that sort in the higher religions are interpreted in terms of poetry and spirituality, there can be no question as to their origin. The custom of parading round the altar with a mystic representation of generation is a very old one. The waving of these symbols in every direction was to protect the people from the insidious wiles of the demons of death and to insure the rebirth of all nature at the end of the winter that was about to set in.

Poetry, ancient and modern, abounds in figures of speech that may be traced back to the old idea that the prosperity of men and women was dependent upon the union of Father

Sun and Mother Earth. The rays of the sun still "kiss" the earth. No grander illustration may be found of the tendency to use loverlike symbolism (the old, wellnigh forgotten language of tree-worship) to express truly exalted ideas than that afforded by the Psalmist when he said: "The righteous shall spring up like the palm-tree: like a cedar in Lebanon shall he grow high. Planted in the house of the Lord, in the courts of our God shall they spring up. They shall still flourish in high old age; they shall be vigorous and covered with foliage; to declare that the Lord is upright: He is my rock, there is no fault in Him."

7

WE must resist the temptation to wander too far from the straight line of our inquiry into the nature and history of the magic wand. By this time the reader may have been led to suspect that the wand is a "golden bough" or sacred branch—in short, a relic of a long forgotten adoration of trees. If this is so, the reader has divined just half of the truth.

The rod of Aaron budded, and, according to legend, it was planted in the ground—but it was not entirely vegetable for all that. When cast upon the ground in the presence of Pharaoh, it became a snake—a most gigantic reptile, if we may credit the Mohammedan story. Morover, it shared the ability to transform itself into a serpent with the wands of the King's professional magicians.

The rod of the Exodus, then, was a representation of both the tree and the serpent. In this respect it resembled the caduceus of the Greek god Mercury. That symbol, which was used for self-protection by the messenger of the gods, was a rod round which two snakes were coiled. The emblem has not been discarded even to this day, for it is the sign of the medical profession.

But why should the caduceus become the emblem of

medicine? What is the connexion between healing and the
serpent? Why are there two snakes instead of one? What,
if any, is the significance of the fact that they are coiled
about a wand?

The Caduceus

The healing serpent did not limit its ministrations to the
gods of Olympus. In Holy Writ there is a description of a
charm that must have borne a striking resemblance to the
potent talisman of Mercury. Nor is the emblem unknown
in Buddhism.

An Early Buddhist Emblem

The biblical story of the caduceus is as follows: The
Children of Israel (as was their wont) murmured against
Moses and gave vent to their anger because they had been

lured away from the comparative security of bondage. To punish the people for this petulance, the Lord sent serpents to plague them. The reptiles bit the rebels, and many of them died.

The timid folk repented forthwith. Thereupon God had mercy upon them. He instructed Moses to erect a bronze serpent upon a pole, and He promised that if any sufferer from snake-bite would but look at the image, he would be cured at once.

Now, it happens that the Hebrew word that is used to denote this brazen serpent is "Nechushtan." According to the tradition current among the rabbis of the Talmud, this word is "dual" in form; that is to say it is neither singular nor plural, but refers to a double object or a pair of objects. Thus it is at least probable that the snake which worked miracles of healing among the Hebrews of ancient times was a caduceus—a pair of sacred serpents coiled about a pole.

However that may be, it is important to recognize the significance of the pair of serpents as opposed to that of the solitary reptile. The two snakes coiled about a pole were supposed to be locked in affectionate embrace.

8

THE snake in olden times was a universal object of reverence and awe. In Dodona the Greeks maintained a sanctuary of Zeus, where the whispering of the oak-leaves and the cooing of Venus' doves constituted a code by which the gods revealed hidden truths to the devoted virgins. But besides the holy oaks and the doves the grove contained its divine snakes, which played a prominent role in this eternal drama of revelation. On a certain occasion the virgins were required to strip themselves of all clothing and in this state of nature to present food to the serpent. If he accepted the offering, that indicated that the year would be a prosperous one; if he refused it, the omen was sinister—like the falling of an oak.

This practice was comparatively harmless, for whether the divine reptile took the food or rejected it, life must have gone on just the same, albeit the atmosphere may have been overcast with gloom because of a sense of impending disaster. Still the depression of such occasions was compensated for by the joy present at other times, when the serpent ate what the nude maidens offered him.

But snake revelations were not always vague and of an indefinite nature. They did not always concern themselves with such hazy predictions as the forecast that a year was destined to be prosperous or disastrous. Near the city of Rome, for example, there was a cave where sacred serpents were maintained. To that cavern the virgins went to render offerings to his snaky majesty. If he accepted the food, that was an indication that the particular girl who had given it to him was pure and would have many children; if the snake refused the food the girl either was not pure or was destined to give birth to few children. The maids whom the snake rejected were not desirable as brides, so one can understand the tragedies that were enacted at that holy cavern, and one can appreciate the importance of the revelations that were vouchsafed there.

9

SERPENTS were not only prophets, healers, and channels of communication with the supernatural fountain of truth; they were also lovers. Snakes were claimed as the ancestors of some of the world's most famous men.

According to the traditions that passed current in antiquity, Lucian, the Syrian Greek, was the child of a snake, and so was the Emperor Augustus. Scipio Africanus did not go so far as to insist that he was literally the son of a reptile, but he claimed the honour of having been nursed by one. Philip of Macedon was convinced that he was not really the father of Alexander the Great, but that the child's father was a serpent that had been observed on the couch of Olympia.

One of the earliest of the Christian sects was that of the Gnostics. Among these believers were some who were known as Ophites, who worshipped sacred serpents, which they kept in consecrated baskets. The Eucharistic service in that sect consisted of the coaxing of the snakes out of the baskets by means of bread, after which the reptiles were kissed and hymns were sung. The Ophites not only worshipped serpents, but looked upon the snake as a representation of the Saviour Himself! For had not the serpent given wisdom to the world when he induced the ancestors of humanity to eat of the tree of knowledge?

As late as the third century the great Persian Christian Manes, founder of a heretical sect, taught that the Saviour was an incarnation of a serpent which had passed over the bed of the infant Mary when she was a child of a year and a half old. Manes did not create this fantastic idea out of nothing. He simply applied to the teachings of Christianity the old superstitions with which he was familiar. Those superstitions had their beginnings in the dark days of prehistory, but they were evidently still flourishing in the third century of our era.

10

THE history of the supernatural is full of accounts of the power of sacred animals. But there is no animal whose worship was more widespread than was that of the snake. Even in ancient Ireland, where there were no snakes, those creatures were worshipped. Their fame spread and they were known in the Emerald Isle by reputation. No better illustration might be offered of the esteem in which the reptile was once held by devout people than that afforded by the census of religions which was taken in Kashmir in the sixteenth century. Siva at that time had forty-five temples, Vishnu had sixty-four, Brahma had three—but the Snake, most popular of all, had seven hundred institutions of worship dedicated to him.

To this day the serpent is an object of human reverence. Not only is he the chief god of Africa, but the dragon (a magnified snake, similar to that in the Mohammedan legend of the plea of Moses before Pharaoh) is revered in modern China.

The African cult of the snake is as elaborate as any religion can possibly be. Houses are erected for reptiles. Sometimes the house is a mere hut where a serpent is maintained and is tended by a woman. But some of the temples are ornate affairs, with many priests in attendance, and each temple is the home of a single snake. To the serpents both prayers and sacrifices are offered; and it is said that human beings are sometimes sacrificed to the sacred snakes. In time of trouble, and particularly at times of drought and failure of nature to bring forth her fruits, the natives repair to the temples of the reptiles, and invoke those creeping Gods.

11

WHY has the snake been an object of such widespread reverence? Why has he of all animals been regarded as the healer, the prophet, and the creator?

There are two reasons. In the first place it is the habit of snakes to shed their skins at certain periods of the year. Primitive men, not familiar with biology, but anxious to explain those natural occurrences with which they were familiar, concluded that the sloughing off of the skin was a device of the snake to renew its life. The serpent was immortal; instead of dying it merely dropped its skin and continued to live. Hence it was not only mysterious, but it was a special repository of immortality.

More important still was the shape of the animal and its ability to raise its head and thus stand erect. To the ancients this was suggestive of the creation of life. Hence the snake became the god of creation, the dispenser of life and its fullness, the supreme giver of luck, and the enemy of sickness, as sickness is the adversary of life. In time the serpent came to be associated with other qualities that were also related to the general idea of life. The creature became the symbol of wisdom, and of cunning.

The mythology of every people contains one or more tales of serpents or of the Serpent. In the earliest of myths he was a god. He fell from popular favour, as many other gods have so fallen throughout the ages, and he eventually became a devil. The fall of the snake is one of the intimate secrets that we shall try to uncover in our investigation of the inside story of hell.

12

PRIMITIVE people have their own laws of thought. It is an axiom among savages that an object is somehow connected with anything it happens to resemble. As like causes like, so like may be used to influence like, either for good or for evil. If the followers of Pythagoras refused to eat beans, this was because they detected in such food a resemblance to certain parts of the male body. The prohibition still present among some rude peoples against the eating of snakes and eels arose out of a similar observation.

In New Guinea the temples of the Snake are decorated with figures of nude human beings, whose postures are obscene and whose bodies are so proportioned as to suggest abnormal development of the power of creation. According to the mythology of that land, there once lived a woman who was beloved of a god. One day she was out bathing, and the deity approached her in the form of an eel. Therefore to this day the people of that part of the world do not eat eels.

We have doubtless indicated enough to render plain why it was true that in the great mystery religions of antiquity the serpent played so large a part. In the ark of Osiris that was paraded at his festivals, there was always an egg, an upright symbol of sex, and a serpent. In the festivals of Greece and Rome the women who wished to show exemplary piety carried live snakes in their hands or wore them entwined in their hair.

13

NOT only was the serpent a god to whom sacrifices were offered and in whose honour rituals were recited, but he was also the sacred symbol both of heaven and of the nations of earth. The famous Pythian Apollo represents the god leaning against a stump round which is coiled a snake. Minerva usually wore a wreath of serpents. In general it was rather common for gods to be sculptured in company with serpents.

In like manner human beings associated themselves with such mascots. The English word "dragoon" is derived from the Latin *"Draconarii."* These were the picked troops of Rome, and their banner was not a woven flag, but a real snake upon a pole. As late as the time of Marcus Aurelius it was the custom of Rome legions to march forth to battle under the standard of the serpent or dragon—not a mere representation, but a genuine snake. A standard bearing a dragon was carried in the crusades by Richard Cœur de Lion. In the days of Henry III the motto of England's King was: "The dragon knows not how to spare."

The snake was associated with human beings for the same reason that prompted its association with gods. Mercury was the messenger of divinities, and, as such, it was essential that he be protected against the evil eyes of those against whom the contents of messages were at times directed. In like manner armies feared the evil eye and similar sinister magic. The powers of destruction could best be overcome by the use of a symbol of life. The reptile was such a mystic symbol.

Nor would it be correct to state that the use of the snake as an emblem of life has died out among civilized people. While we have done our best to banish this sort of crude symbolism from our consciousness, we still retain it in the realm of the unconscious mind, as the Freudians have discovered. It is surely not strange that an idea that dominated humanity for so many ages and in so many lands still has survivals in our unconscious memories. Freud tells us that to dream of snakes indicates a certain type of suppressed desire. Back in the pre-scientific ages this fact was dimly perceived by the sages. The Talmud says that it is a good omen to dream of a snake. . . .

14

THE magic wand has come down to us from the days when tree-worship and serpent-worship were combined in the universal adoration of the mystic force of generation. The rod is more than a branch and it is more than a snake; it is a combination of both. It is an embodiment of the greatest of miracles—the miracle of birth. It is the symbol of life, and and hence it works wonders.

Even today the snake charmers of the Orient are skilled in the art of causing a serpent to stiffen up and to become like a staff. This is the magic wand.

CHAPTER VIII

The Magic Fountain and the Bridal Bouquet

"Flowers are Love's truest language."
PARK BENJAMIN

1

FOR ages it has been customary to use flowers at weddings and funerals. To be sure, flowers are employed at other times also, chiefly on loverlike occasions. Thus, if a swain has quarrelled with his beloved, he is likely to send a floral gift as a peace-offering. But the use of blossoms at the time of marriage and at the visit of the Grim Reaper is peculiarly conventional.

The common explanation of such floral conventions has to do with the loveliness and fragrance of flowers. Flora will help to brighten a room in which they are placed. They will cheer the sick, comfort the mourner, and add to the joy of the wedding-ceremony. But does this explanation account for all the facts? Does it offer a key, for example, to the singular superstition of the bridal bouquet? The bride casts that nosegay to her unmarried girl friends, and it is widely believed that the maid who catches it will be the next to marry. Where did such a notion arise? Why should flowers possess so important a virtue as that of obtaining a husband for a maiden?

2

FLOWERS among primitive peoples are symbolic of female sex energy. Especially was the lotus regarded by the ancients as the sign of the mother, the female creator.

The lotus was to the female sex what the upright emblem of Priapus was to the male. The Hindus still represent

Brahma as seated upon a lotus, and when he is pictured in that manner, he is called Kamal-a-yoni—that is to say, "the great god who is at the same time both male and female." It is almost needless to add that the lotus and flowers like it (the lily, for example) were sacred to Venus and were widely used in the religious art and rituals of bygone ages.

In the circular stamens of the lotus one can detect the sign of the two crossed triangles. This is an old mystic symbol, still used by the theosophists. It is revered as the holy emblem of the Jewish religion and is called "the Shield of David." Under one name or another it has been honoured from time immemorial.

The Shield of David

3

In the ages gone by, people were convinced that all illness could be traced to one of two causes: either the sick man was "possessed" by an evil spirit, or else he was the victim of some dire enchantment. In either case his unfortunate situation was traced to the malign activities of the powers of destruction. The methods of cure, therefore, consisted of a number of devices that were designed to enlist the mysterious power of generation and to employ it either to drive away the spirit or to serve as an antidote to the spiritual poison of witchcraft.

The sending of flowers to the bedside of a sick man originally had nothing to do with the loveliness of the gift. The thought that the fragrance of the blossoms and the beauty of their colour would serve to cheer the sufferer may have entered the minds of primitive people, but no such æsthetic consideration was the compelling motive behind the custom. Flowers were curative agents, because they were embodiments of the power of sex. This is also the reason why the bridal bouquet possesses so happy and so mysterious a virtue. The maiden who catches the nosegay as it is thrown from the hand of the bride receives unto herself this powerful symbol, which embodies the mystery of life.

4

IF it was desirable to employ sex symbols at the bedside of a sick person, it was essential to make use of them in the actual presence of death. If life is always to be desired, both here and hereafter, it is clearly the duty of the survivors to fortify those who have been called away by presenting to them the weapons of life. Among such weapons are flowers, especially the lotus and lily.

But there is an additional reason why the powers of generation are in such universal use at the time of death: not only must the dead be protected when the Grim Reaper is at hand, but the living are also in danger. The peril of the living arises not merely from the obvious fact that the destroyers are present, but also from the presence of the ghost.

In the world of superstition, flowers are the protectors of humanity. They save maidens from spinsterhood, brides from barrenness and marital unhappiness, sick people from the further power of their tormentors, discarnate souls from utter destruction, and living people from the depredations of ghosts.

Besides all this the flower speaks the language of love. It is the conventional peace-offering after lovers' quarrels. It is unquestionably effective as a herald of peace at such times. For flowers are repositories of life.

5

AMONG the goddesses who grace the Chinese pantheon one will discover an interesting being whose title is Puzza, which corresponds to the Hindu title Buddha. Her story is as follows: Once there were three nymphs who descended from the celestial regions to bathe. While they were in the water, a lotus flower appeared on the garment of one of them. It is dangerous (from the view-point of myth-makers) to eat a lotus, for it works enchantment—yet there is ever something about it that is tempting.

The nymph upon whose clothing the flower appeared succumbed to the temptation, and by eating the magic plant she became a mother. After her son was born, she went back to her abode in heaven. Her child grew up and became a great leader. He was a sage, a law-maker, and a warrior. His mother naturally became an object of reverence. The lotus made her not only a mother, but also Puzza.

In this case the magic flower appeared and worked its wonder while the nymph was bathing. This is not accidental. For, as the flower is female and an embodiment of motherhood, so is water. One cannot understand the supernatural force of flowers without also knowing something of the mystery that was once ascribed to the liquid element.

Aphrodite, the personification of female love, arose, as we have learned, from the sea. Other great leaders, divine or semi-divine, have arisen from the water to embark upon glorious careers and to fulfil noble destinies. Sargon when a child was placed in a box on the Euphrates. He was rescued by a royal party, and when he grew to manhood, he became the mighty ruler of Assyria. Moses was similarly placed in a basket on the River Nile and was rescued by the daughter of Pharaoh.

If it is not given to the general run of the pious to arise

from the water like Aphrodite and Sargon and Moses, the common people might at least be protected against evil by the magic charm of that liquid. The use of water for purposes of protection, both in the childhood of a believer and at the hour of death, is fairly common among many different peoples. For example, in Bengal there is a tribe whose traditions combine the baptism idea with the romantic "Apple of Love" theory. A mango branch is cast into a well, which becomes holy at its touch. The child is then carried to the well, and the water is drawn and poured to the accompaniment of appropriate prayer.

6

THE reason why water has been so generally regarded as a special sign of the female creator is that the liquid was identified with certain body-fluids. It is not necessary to go back to prehistory to prove this. Pliny says that to touch one's door-posts with body-fluids will drive the witches away from one's home. The Manichæans and Albigenses, two heretical sects, used those liquids as charms against sickness.

If a person desired to enter the faith of Mithra, the ancient sun-god, it was necessary that he be literally "washed in the blood." The neophyte was placed in a hole in the ground, and the hole was covered with leaky boards. A bull or goat or ram was then slaughtered in the ritual manner on those boards, and its blood was allowed to leak down upon the person beneath. The bull, the goat, and the ram are all peculiarly potent creatures, masters of herds, and as such they were all sacred to those deities whose special concern was generation.

In the woods of Bohemia there lies a little town known as Ronsberg. In that town is a fountain that is reputed to have miraculous powers. According to an inscription found there,

Baal Shem, the founder of a great Jewish sect of mystics, visited the spring in the winter of 1744 and bathed in its icy waters three hundred times. "He found the waters heal all ills, relieve all evil, and restore fecundity to sterile women."

This wondrous fount of holy water was forgotten for many years. In January 1928 it was rediscovered. Thousands of mystics have journeyed to Ronsberg since that time in order to reap the remarkable benefits that the fountain is said to bestow. The water is bottled by hopeful pilgrims, who carry it to their native villages, where it doubtless blesses the friends of the righteous with health, fortune, prosperity, and fruitfulness.

It is well known that what is now the State of Florida was discovered by Ponce de León, who set sail in quest of the Fountain of Youth. For an explorer to seek a magic spring of that type in this day and age would be a most unusual procedure, but at one time the superstition of the Fountain of Youth was widespread. From what has gone before it is easy to understand why the idea of rejuvenation was associated with that of a magic spring.

But this is not all. Water, properly consecrated, has worked many miracles other than the mere curing of illness, the warding off of demons, and the restoration of youth.

In the life of Saint Hilarion by Saint Jerome, we find the following story: There was once a Christian named Italicus, who used to engage in chariot races with the pagan Duumvir of Gaza. The Duumvir was something of a magician, and by casting spells he managed, for a time, to win all the races. Italicus told his story to Saint Hilarion and bespoke his intervention. The saint objected to the idea of taking any part in the race at all, but at last consented to work a miracle. He gave to Italicus a bowl of holy water, which he himself had consecrated.

The appointed day for the race dawned. Crowds came
from afar, and the circus grounds were gradually filled
with the throng. The signal was given, and the contenders
started.

Italicus promptly sprinkled some of the holy water on his
horses, who raced ahead at unheard-of speed, while at the
same time the steeds of the Duumvir appeared to be rooted
to the spot. The crowd filled the air with their cries. Some
demanded the death of the man who had cast so powerful a
spell. Others acclaimed him and judged that the miracle was
proof of the power of his God. The result of the episode was
that many pagans, having witnessed the spectacle, abandoned their errors and embraced the faith of Saint Hilarion.

7

WATER has ever been regarded as one of the most effective
enemies of the demons of death. It is notorious among superstitious people that no demon or ghost or supernatural destroyer of any kind can cross water. This is one reason why
holy water is used at funerals among many different peoples. Some people merely pour out water at the time of a
death.

One recalls a significant incident in the well-known "Legend of Sleepy Hollow." Ichabod Crane found that he was
being followed by a headless ghost on horseback. He hur-
ried as fast as he could, for he knew that, since the headless
horseman suffered from the limitations that are common to
all ghosts, he could not cross a stream. Only when he had
put water between himself and the supernatural being could
he feel confident that he was safe at last.

The strange fact that devils, ghosts, and the like are nowhere able to cross water is understood among students of
the psychology of dreams. People frequently dream that
they are being pursued by demons or similar horrors. It is
generally the belief of the dreamer that if he can but reach

a stream and wade into it, he will be safe. Apparently we have retained in our minds much of the primitive notion of the war of Life against Death. We have banished it from the sphere of consciousness, and it has taken up its abode in the dim realm of the unconscious.

CHAPTER IX

The Apple of Love

> "Earth's crammed with Heaven,
> And every common bush afire with
> God;
> And only he who sees takes off his
> shoes;
> The rest sit round it ana pluck black-
> berries."

ELIZABETH BARRETT BROWNING

1

THE wearing of fruit blossoms by a bride is reminiscent of the old "Apple of Love" that was so well known to myth-makers everywhere. This mystic fruit was not of necessity the particular object that we call the apple. But its shape was the same. Thus in India the love-apple is the mango; in China it is the peach; and our own brides usually wear orange-blossoms.

There is general agreement on the point that the tree in the centre of the garden of Eden was an apple-tree. The Scripture nowhere specifies the species of tree that was forbidden. At the same time, the universal idea that the dangerous fruit was the apple must have had its origin somewhere. Nor is it difficult to determine where.

According to the popular religion of ancient Greece, there lived, once upon a time, a hero named Heracles. This individual, who was the son of Zeus, was a towering bully, who was as unscrupulous as he was powerful. When offering sacrifices to him the worshippers used to utter curses, for the hero enjoyed the atmosphere of vulgarity. Still, he was not really a "bad" character, for he had a big heart, and it was he who liberated Prometheus from the condign punishment that the gods had visited upon him for the crime of giving mortals the blessing of fire.

Heracles was an enemy of the serpent, and on at least two occasions he killed powerful reptiles. When he was but a babe, Hera sent two snakes into his bed and he strangled them with his tiny bare hands. Later in life he set forth to obtain the golden apples of the Hesperides, which Zeus had given to his wife for a wedding-gift. The tree on which those golden apples grew was guarded by a dragon with a hundred heads, but Heracles killed the monster and obtained the fruit.

In the early days of Christianity the people were familiar with the Greek representation of Heracles at the tree, round the trunk of which the dragon was coiled. The picture served not only as a representation of the labour of the pagan hero, but also as a symbol of the fall of man as portrayed in Genesis. It is possible that from this substitution of a biblical for a pagan interpretation of that popular illustration of an ancient tale the idea arose that Eve tempted Adam with an apple.

2

But the question still remains: Why did Zeus give to Hera a golden apple-tree? Why not a pear-tree or a cherry-tree? The answer is that the apple is a symbol of love, sacred to Venus. Romantic young couples used to offer love-apples to their divine patroness. On the walls of Pompeii a young man and a maiden are to be seen offering such fruit to Venus.

Possibly the first love-apple that Venus ever received was the golden one awarded to her by Paris. It happened in this manner: The earth was becoming overcrowded with human beings, and so Zeus, in order to cut down the population, decided to stir up a war in order to wipe out the surplus. To that end he saw to it that there was born the lovely Helen, whose beauty was so marvellous that tall

cities were "snared" by it. Then the King of the gods offered a golden apple to be awarded to the fairest of the
goddesses. Hera, Athene, and Aphrodite (Venus) applied
for the prize. Naturally, they were unable to agree among
themselves as to which one was worthy, so Zeus arranged
that the matter should be laid before Paris, who would
render his decision and award the apple.

That goddesses should resort to the bribery of a judge was
apparently taken for granted. Athene offered victory in war
should Paris decide in her favour. Hera offered the judge a
throne. Venus offered him Helen.

He awarded the apple to the goddess of love. Thereupon
he was enabled to take Helen away from her husband, and
the great Trojan war for her recovery began.

3

ACCORDING to Hindu legend, the first man tempted the first
woman with the fruit of the mango-tree. The fact that this
fruit is shaped like the apple contributed to its position as
the Hindu love-emblem.

In the pre-scientific ages the notion passed current among
the learned that the apple was able to excite human beings
and to awaken love within them. "Strengthen me with
flagons of wine," says the Song of Songs, "refresh me with
apples, for sick of love am I." Later in the same scriptural
song the bard cries out: "Oh that thy breasts might be like
clusters of the vine, and the smell of thy nose like apples."
And later still: "I raised thee up under the apple-tree: there
thy mother brought thee forth."

Before the days of biological classifications people did
not make accurate distinctions between different species of
animals and plants. Flies were thought of as birds, because
they had wings. In like manner the apple, the citron, the
pomegranate, and fruits of similar shape were commonly
grouped together. This much is certain—they were all sacred

to Venus; they were all thought of as symbolic of the female sex; and they all had magic properties for good and (as in the first temptation) for evil. They were all apples of love.

The girl who fell in love with Bacchus and died for love of him was changed into a pomegranate-tree. In the Temple of Solomon, the pomegranate was a prominent item of decoration. The pomegranate is full of seeds and for that reason is suggestive of motherhood. It was through the magic inherent in a single seed of that fruit that Persephone was forced to remain under the ground for a period of each year.

According to the cabbalists of the Middle Ages, the apple was one of the attributes of God—nothing less. It was a mystic attribute of beauty. One of the great text-books of Jewish mysticism says: "Beauty diffuses itself into the world as an apple."

The citron is still used by Orthodox Jews at the Feast of Tabernacles, though the original significance of the fruit is no longer recognized. Can one wonder any longer what was the primeval meaning of the orange-blossom that our brides wear, which they regard as so essential an item of their costumes?

It is probable that the Empress Anne of Austria did not know the original significance of the pomegranate and did not appreciate its connexion with the idea of love. But she selected it as her special device, and beneath it she had the legend inscribed: "My worth is not in my crown."

CHAPTER X

The Door of Life and the Threshold Superstition

> *"Stronger by weakness, wiser men become*
> *As they draw near to their eternal home:*
> *Leaving the old, both worlds at once they view*
> *That stand upon the threshold of the new."*
>
> EDMUND WALLER

1

IF an Orthodox Jew is taken seriously ill, his friends may repair to the synagogue and go through the ceremony of changing the sick man's religious name. The theory is that when the angel of death is sent to summon a human soul, the Hebrew patronymic is specified as a means of identification. Now, if the prænomen has been changed in the interim between the dispatching of the grim messenger and his arrival at the residence of the doomed, it will be difficult for him to identify the man whose soul he has been instructed to carry away.

This is but one of many methods that frightened human beings have devised for the purpose of hoodwinking the immortals. And why not? If a man has reason to feel that Destiny has some evil in store for him, it is but natural for him to try, either to change the will of the Fates, or, if that is impossible, to deceive them and render them impotent to afflict him.

Among primitive people a man's name is mysteriously bound up with his soul. To alter the sacred title that has been bestowed upon a person at birth is an act of serious import. Such an alteration has far-reaching consequences. A savage by another name is not the same man—a change has been effected in his very soul.

Among moderns the popular expression "He has become another man" and others like it are merely figures of speech, but among more primitive peoples the conception is prevalent that it is possible for a person to make radical alterations in his own soul and thus to become literally a different individual. One of the most popular methods of averting the evil decrees of Destiny is that of effecting such a spiritual change by being born again. Such rebirth is not merely spiritual, but physical as well. A religious pantomime is enacted in which the sufferer takes the part of an infant that is being ushered into the world.

A popular method of curing diseases in the early days was that of passing the patient through a hole in a tree or a rock. In England it used to be the custom among the lower classes to cure rickets by slitting the trunk of an ash-tree and then passing the ailing child (head foremost) through the slit. The wound in the tree was carefully bound up, and if it healed, the child was cured.

In India, where the cow is a sacred animal, the natives have been known to manufacture artificial cows for purposes of being born again. Rich rajahs manufacture these cows out of gold or silver and after the ritual divide the metal among the priests who officiated at the ceremony. Poorer men use caves as vehicles of rebirth. In the north of India there is such a cave. It has two openings. Pilgrims journey to that place from afar. The ceremony of going in at one entrance and emerging from the other is called "passing through the cow."

2

BUT the idea of rebirth is present in acts that do not involve such elaborate ceremonial. In former times all doorways were sacred, for the reason that the one who passed through them was undergoing a sort of birth. One still hears of the custom of carrying one's bride over the threshold. And it is usually unlucky to step upon a threshold instead of across it.

To stumble on a threshold is a most unlucky sign. Pythagoras advises people to turn back if in their egress from a house they accidentally kick the threshold. Sometimes it is considered "bad luck" to sneeze in the doorway, and it frequently is thought inadvisable to sit upon the door-sill.

In western Africa, in time of an epidemic, the natives smear blood upon their gateways. This is reminiscent of a number of gateway customs. For example, in ancient Egypt swine were sometimes sacrificed upon the threshold. These offerings were intended for Osiris. In ancient Babylon lambs were offered in the same sacred place and the blood was sprinkled upon the door-posts.

The sanctity of the doorway is attested by a great number of customs and superstitions. There are special ways of crossing a threshold in order to do so auspiciously—for example, one should step over it with the right foot in place of the left, the reason being that, in the lore of superstition, the right side of the human body is frequently supposed to be more potent than the left. Some primitive peoples will actually grovel before the doorway and touch their foreheads to the threshold.

Orthodox Jews place upon the door-posts a small object known as the "Mezuzah." This contains a biblical passage and is supposed to be a fulfilment of the command: "Write them upon the door-posts of thy house and upon thy gates." As a matter of fact, the similarity of the mezuzah institution to like institutions of other peoples proves that originally it was a door-post amulet, if not a door-post god. The pious Orthodox Israelite will kiss the mezuzah upon entering or leaving.

It is not uncommon for some special rite to be performed when opening a door for the first time in the morning. Thus the Arab will piously pronounce: "Bismillah."

The reason why the doorway is sacred is that it was originally one of the symbols of the female creator. As such it was worthy of respect.

3

JUST as human beings are accustomed to enter a house via the door, so the denizens of the spiritual world use this opening for ingress and egress. It is then most important to guard this aperture against the entrance of demons, ghosts, and other minions of the powers of darkness. When a death occurs, the wicked immortals are particularly active and it is necessary to take special pains to guard against them. Among the precautions that human beings take on such occasions is that of placing a wreath or crape or something of that sort upon the door.

Even in normal times, when the presence of death is not manifest, it still is wise to guard the doorway against spiritual enemies. This is especially true of gates that lead to palaces or great buildings. In ancient Babylon and Assyria before such gates winged bulls and lions with human heads stood sentinel. In Egypt sphinxes guarded the approach to tombs, temples, and the like.

It is probable that out of such conceptions has arisen the idea of decorating palatial doorways by flanking them with crouching lions or other animals. In addition to such animals there are other devices that serve a similar purpose. For example, the woman's face once popular as a decoration on a door-knocker is a development of the Medusa head which was intended originally to ward off the evil eye.

4

IN the light of the facts we have been considering, it is

easy to understand why doorways have been venerated and why people have been at such pains to guard them against the evil spirits. But one should not leave this subject without mentioning the fact that, in addition to the reverence which was paid to doors which were actual and necessary apertures in buildings, special archways have been erected simply and solely to aid man in his dealings with the supernatural world. For example, in China and Japan special archways are frequently placed before the doors of temples. In Korea these archways are placed also in front of government buildings. The triumphal arch of the Romans served in the first place a magical purpose. The soldier who returned from a victorious campaign was beset by a number of hostile spiritual influences. One of the methods of coping with such eerie dangers was that of walking through the arch and thus gaining for himself the strength that could come alone from such symbolic rebirth.

A favourite device before a Mohammedan tomb is the high archway. This is definitely appropriate. It is the door of life.

5

ONE need not wonder that ancient people thought of life as a mystery. It remains to this day the supreme mystery. What is the nature of life, and what its source? Learned professors of proto-zoology have advanced theories. The question however, remains unsolved.

> Into this universe, and *Why* not knowing,
> Nor *Whence*, like water willy-nilly flowing:
> And out of it, as Wind along the Waste,
> I know not *Whither*, willy-nilly blowing.

The ancients endeavoured to solve the problem on the theory that life is the product of two kinds of supernatural energy working through each other. One was the female energy, and the other the male. Divine motherhood, in the arms of divine fatherhood, produced life.

But the idea went further. Divine motherhood, again with the aid of divine fatherhood, might increase life's fullness, protect it, and save it beyond the grave. To this end do the Mohammedans erect the doorway of life at the entrance to the tomb.

CHAPTER XI

The Fear of Ghosts

"Sunset and evening star,
And one clear call for me!
And may there be no moaning of the
bar,
When I put out to sea.
But such a tide as moving seems
asleep,
Too full for sound and foam,
When that which drew from out the
the boundless deep,
Turns again home."

ALFRED TENNYSON

1

THE howling of a dog is said to be a sign of impending death. If a bird flies into one's house, one may expect misfortune. According to some, this brings with it "bad luck," while according to others, the particular ill of which the entrance of the bird is a sign is that of death. If one watches a funeral procession through a window, one is likely to suffer in consequence, and the dire calamity that must result from counting the vehicles in a cortège is well known in the concourse of the superstitious.

The connexion of the dog with the idea of death is not difficult to understand. In the first place, all members of the canine family are beasts of prey and are willing to feed upon carrion. In the second place, mythology ties up the dog with the abode of the departed. According to the ancient Greek idea, the realm of Hades was guarded by the three-headed Cerberus.

The peril that lurks in the practice of watching a funeral cortège (and, by that same token, in counting its vehicles) lies in the fact that the ghost of the departed is likely to entice one's soul away. Nothing is more widely believed among primitive peoples than the notion that the animating principle is given to the unfortunate habit of departing from the body from time to time. Death, according to the savage idea, is simply the permanent, as opposed to the temporary, departure of the soul.

Among the less intellectual classes of France, Germany, and Switzerland one discovers the practice of taking a tile off of the roof at the time of a death. Sometimes this is done before the sick man has actually expired, the reason being that his soul may thus depart more easily and the pains incident to a lingering passing may be avoided. In China people go so far as to make a hole in the roof for this purpose. Among other peoples the practice obtains of simply opening a window at the time of a visitation. Where conventions of that type are present, it is often the habit to leave the aperture open for but a brief interval, in order that the spirit, having departed, will not be tempted to return and haunt the survivors.

The theory that the ghost may thus fly away from its discarded body has given rise to the use of the bird as a symbol of the soul. Sometimes it is believed that the spirit hovers for a time over the grave, in this winged form. One may readily understand, then, why it is that the flight of a bird into a house is an ill omen. Possibly at one time this incident was more than a mere portent. It is likely that, in the days when the supersition first arose, the intruding creature was thought of as actually tempting (or even carrying) the soul away from the body and thus causing the death instead of merely indicating that it was about to occur.

2

WHY should the ghost always act as an agent of mischief? Why are folks unable to enjoy the companionship of the departed, just as they did when the spirits were incarnate? Why is it that the very thought that a ghost may be present in a room will almost invariably elicit the emotion of terror? Let your cultivated sceptic sit alone at midnight, and let him read a story of haunting in the privacy of his study, and, with all his presumptive knowledge of the origin and history of the belief in ghosts, he will be afraid.

In the view of primitive men, the lot of the dead was unpleasant as compared with that of the survivors, who continued to strut upon earth. The departed continued to exist, but in a shadowy place like Sheol, where existence was not particularly joyous. The invidious distinction between the lot of the living and that of the dead gave rise to jealousy. Even a mother, after she died, might degenerate into a vindictive spirit and might deliberately injure the darling of her former days.

If this was true of a parent, it was doubly so of one who was murdered or whose death was untimely. This is one of the reasons why savages are usually convinced that murder is a crime. They have not risen to spiritual heights from which they might appreciate the majesty of the Ten Commandments, and the idea that their neighbour is entitled to have his right to life respected is foreign to them. But that the act of killing may be followed by a supernatural visitation is something they do understand—and fear.

A savage usually regards it as spiritually dangerous to fell a tree. To kill an animal is fraught with eerie peril. When it becomes necessary to do either of those things, the savage will frequently perform some elaborate rite to propitiate the spirit he has rendered discarnate. If such danger is present when an animal or a tree has been deprived of life, how much greater is the peril when a man has been slain! The outraged ghost might haunt the whole village and engage in acts of destruction. The murderer is therefore committing a crime against the security of his fellows.

Since ghosts are so disposed temperamentally that they are harmful to the living, a number of methods have been devised to lay them. We still carry out corpses feet first, so that the spirits cannot see their way back. We are careful not to offend anyone who has "passed on." *De mortuis nil nisi bonum.* As if it were more important to spare the feelings of the dead than of the living! True, the dead are gone and cannot defend themselves—but there is the point exactly. Primitive men felt that the dead could defend themselves. The reticence of early men, out of which ours has sprung, did not arise out of gallantry, but out of fear.

3

THE precautions that human beings take to avoid being haunted are many. Some are distinctly curious. For example, in some places there is a custom known as "telling the bees." Some interested individual goes to the hives, knocks in order to attract the attention of the insects, and tenders to them the whispered information that their owner has passed away. To this intelligence may be added the name of the new owner. Some people go further and put crape upon the hive. This sort of thing prevents the ghost from enticing the bees away.

Nor are bees the only animate property that the spirit is likely to carry off. In some sections of France crape is placed upon the pigsties and is even tied upon the cat. Sometimes the trees must be "told" and they too must be dressed with the sign of mourning.

One of the most widespread practices with regard to death is the custom of wailing, from which our modern funeral dirges and eulogies have obviously developed. Not only do savages cry and howl both in the presence of the corpse and at stated occasions for a definite period, but they sometimes mutilate their bodies, tear out their hair, and rend their garments—all in a ritual manner. The emotion of grief, which would naturally express itself in tears at the time of the departure of a loved one, would hardly be sufficient to explain these excesses. The fact that the wailing must be performed in a particular manner, at particular times, and in particular places would tend to show that we are dealing, not with a spontaneous emotion, but with an organized ritual. This fact becomes especially clear when we reflect that it is often the custom to hire professional mourners to set up the necessary wails. Moreover, if one studies the evolution of these cries, one will see that they tend more and more to fall into a definite cadence and rhythm, until at last we have the type of lugubrious discourse known as the dirge.

The most primitive wails that are set up at savage funerals consist of disorganized and unintelligible howling. After a time, however, distinct words are introduced. The sentences are usually addressed to the ghost. Their import is, first, an expression of profound grief; second, unmeasured and untempered praise of the one whose departure was so untimely; and, third, a plea that since, unfortunately, the death could not be avoided, the spirit should go to the place that has been appointed for it and should not remain behind to haunt those who are still in the land of the living.

In the light of the foregoing one will have no difficulty in understanding the evolution of what we call the "eulogy."

4

HUMAN beings are always afraid of the unknown. Ghosts, to be sure, are sometimes visible. Still, they are more frequently unseen, and therefore more terrible. They have an uncanny faculty, if we may credit the lore of universal superstition, of knowing the most secret thoughts that lurk in the minds of the living. On the other hand, this faculty is not reciprocal, so that, while the spirits may read our minds, we are not able to read theirs.

Among primitive people death is always caused in some

supernatural manner. The idea of "natural death" is as unknown to savages as is the theory of relativity or the concept of the fourth dimension. When an individual has
shuffled off this mortal coil, he will naturally harbour resent-
ment against the person who bewitched him and thus
brought about his passing. One of the reasons for the ex-
travagance of savage mourning-customs is the desire of the
survivors to impress upon the ghost the fact that they are
genuinely grief-stricken, that, far from desiring his death,
they had done everything in their power to avoid it, and that
accordingly, whoever might have worked the dire enchantment, the mourners are certainly without guilt. This is one
of the reasons why the custom has arisen to wear a particular colour (black in our part of the world) for a given period
of time. Some primitive folks simply turn their clothes inside out. This sort of thing not only acts as a demonstration
of overpowering grief, but also serves as a disguise. As the
bridal veil deceives the demon lover, so does the veil of the
widow deceive the ghost.

5

IT is noteworthy, however, that not all of the customs that
have grown up around the eternal mystery of death are of a
melancholy character. Consider, for example, the "wake,"
which is common not only in Ireland, but in certain other
sections of the globe. Some peoples also indulge in funeral
dances and games. After the body has been disposed of, it
is the custom for mourners and their friends to assemble
around a table and to eat. This is not, as people naïvely
suppose, due to the idea that, after the heart-breaking experience of the funeral, the bereaved ones will be hungry.
On the contrary, grief does not improve one's appetite.

That feast that follows a funeral is to some extent a relic
of what one might call "spiritual cannibalism." Among some
savages the eye is the seat of the soul, and when a rival

chieftain has been slain, the victorious ruler will eat the eye of his adversary. In ancient Rome the nearest of kin used to stand by the bedside of a dying man, in order to inhale his last gasp. Thus he acquired the virtues that inhered in the expiring soul.

It was once the practice in the highlands of Bavaria for people to eat what were called "corpse cakes" at funerals. The housewife prepared the dough for those cakes and then placed it upon the body of the deceased and allowed it to rise there. The bread thus acquired the virtues of the departed, which were transmitted to those who partook of the ensuing feast.

There is, however, another reason for the institution of the funeral feast. This is the notion that the ghost is still present, even after the elaborate precautions of the last rites have been duly taken. The spirit insists on being treated as one of the family. We have records of such meals where a special chair was set apart for the occupancy of the dead. Sometimes the ghost's portion was thrown under the table, or otherwise disposed of in a manner intended to indicate that it belonged to the one who had passed away. The idea was that, having partaken of the final meal, the spirit would be satisfied and would leave the realm of the living for ever.

The dances that in ancient times were widely associated with rites for the disposal of the dead were frequently obscene. The intention in such cases is easy to understand. By imitating through the mimicry of the dance the process by which life is generated, the dead were compelled to depart. The custom still has vogue among some peoples to sit upon the floor for a period of days after a funeral. The ground, of course, is Mother Earth, the principle of female sex energy. Contact with it will serve to avoid the haunting of those who belong, not to the kingdom of life, but to the kingdom of death.

The Irish wake and institutions like it are based upon

the theory that it is sinful to remain silent in the house of death. It is necessary, while the corpse is in the house, for everyone to remain awake, for if one sleeps, his soul may encounter the ghost in dreams and may thus be enticed away, much as if a bird flew into the window. Among some more primitive peoples where the wake is in vogue, there appears to be an idea that the dead take some part in the pastimes of the occasion. Still other people have been known to play games of chance during that period in order to determine the fate of the ghost. Will the spirit go to the realm of the blessed, or has it been supernaturally condemned?

There is, however, another side to this institution of the wake. Not only is it well to guard the living against the ghost, but it is also most fitting and proper to protect the spirit against the depredations of those demons who are always present in the house of death. Therefore the corpse must be watched, and various devices are employed to keep people from falling asleep, not merely because they fear the consequences to themselves, but also because they are solicitous about the welfare of the one who has passed away.

6

ALTHOUGH it is unquestionably true that the vast majority of funeral rites and customs have grown out of the universal fear of ghosts, it is also true that a number of practices were designed to benefit the departed rather than the survivors. For example, the Egyptian *Book of the Dead* describes at great length the journey of the soul through Amenti. This journey was fraught with many perils. To avoid each and every pitfall certain prayers were recited, certain hymns were sung, and special texts were inscribed upon the bandages of the mummies and the amulets that were entombed with them.

Until very recently in both India and China it was the proper thing for widows to burn themselves upon the pyres of their husbands. Obviously the widows did not perform this rite for self-protection against haunting. The purpose, on the other hand, was that of providing their erstwhile mates with their services as wives in the land behind the veil.

In remote antiquity it was a widespread custom to kill the wives, slaves, and favourite animals of an influential man, in order that these might attend him in the land of the shades. Tombs have been found in which large numbers of people have been thus sacrified in order that they might minister to the comfort of their departed lord. There have been reports of certain savage tribes whose chiefs were always eager to communicate with their dead parents. Even the most trivial details of their daily life were passed on to the next world. The method of effecting this communication was that of giving the message to a human being and then killing him, thus sending his shade ahead to the next world.

Thus the conventions that attach themselves to the disposal of the dead have arisen out of two ideas: first and foremost, the living must be protected against ghosts; second, the dead must be provided for and must have their wants gratified as far as it lies in the power of human beings to minister to the needs of the departed.

CHAPTER XII

The Tombstone, the Rock, and the Mineral Superstition

> *"I have careful records of about five
> hundred death-beds, studied particularly
> with reference to the modes of death
> and the sensations of the dying. . . .
> The great majority gave no sign one
> way or the other; like their birth, their
> death was a sleep and a forgetting. The
> Preacher was right: in this matter man
> hath no pre-eminence over the beast—
> 'as the one dieth, so dieth the other.' "*
> SIR WILLIAM OSLER

1

NOTHING is better known to students of the supernatural than the fact that the sun was once adored by all peoples as a god. That luminary was the great repository of sex energy. It was usually male and its function was to render the earth fruitful. So potent was this gigantic orb of fire that it was able to bestow children upon maidens who were exposed to its rays.

A number of myths, legends, and superstitions testify to the prevalence of this theory in the early days. For example, we have the Siberian story of a Khan who locked his daughter in an iron house in order to protect her from the advances of men. But one day she prevailed upon the old woman who was her jailer to permit her to go and see the world outside. No sooner had she left her prison than the "eye of God" fell upon her and she became a mother. Obviously the eye referred to is the sun.

In the class with the Siberian legend just mentioned is the Greek myth of Danaë, the mother of Perseus. The

father of Danaë locked her in a chamber for the same reason that actuated the Khan in Siberia. She did not escape
into the world outside, but Zeus managed to reach her in the
form of a shower of gold. Like the divine eye, gold symbolized the sun.

Because gold was suggestive of sunlight it was thought
to have magic potency. It was for this reason that gold was
used so frequently, not only in rings and similar objects of
jewellery, but also in the manufacture of sacred objects.
Especially among sun-worshippers was gold popular. Thus,
in ancient Peru the paraphernalia of devotion were for the
most part made of this metal.

If gold was a representative of the sun and hence possessed the mystic attributes of the luminary for which it
stood, so silver symbolized the moon and possessed female
powers. It is well known among readers of fairy-tales that
witches are immune to lead bullets. The magic of those
dreadful crones, however, will never avail against bullets of
silver. When one shoots a witch with a silver bullet, one
directs against her, not merely a physical, but also a spiritual
force.

Lead, on the other hand, is soft and is in no way suggestive of the mystic concept of love. Indeed, a pliable metal
has been associated with the very opposite idea in the curious lore of the supernatural. Thus, the notion was widespread among the ancients that a leaden arrow would destroy the love of a youth for a maiden. One will remember
that the arrows of Cupid were able to excite affection. Arrows of lead produced the very opposite effect. One may
understand, then, why the witch is proof against bullets of
lead; and one may also understand why she dreads a bullet
of silver even as she fears the fire.

It it interesting, in this connexion, that precious metals,
as repositories of life, are able to work miraculous cures.
Thus, according to a venerable British superstition, ring-

worm may be remedied by rubbing the afflicted part with silver.

2

In a general way it is true that metals and minerals stand in close relation to the supernatural world. In addition to the numerous notions people have entertained about the magic properties of metals, one might cite many instances of what we might call the "mineral superstition." A splendid illustration of this is to be found in certain current ideas about salt. It is bad luck to spill this commodity. Such spilling usually results in a quarrel, unless a counter-charm is employed to prevent so unfortunate a consummation.

Salt is of superlative value to humanity, as the loving Cordelia so beautifully testified. Still, there was a time when men were not familiar with its uses. (Perhaps they obtained their essential ration of chloride of sodium by drinking animal blood.) Until very recently there were natives of Australia who were ignorant of its uses. The discovery of salt marked an epoch in the history of mankind, and the mineral promptly took on magic properties. As a preserver its power was exerted on the side of life and creation, rather than that of death and destruction.

Plutarch refers to a vulgar notion to the effect that females among lower animals were able to give birth to young without the aid of a male, provided they licked salt. In other words, salt was so powerful that, like the shower of gold in the myth of Danaë, it was able to perform the physical (as well as the spiritual) functions of the male sex. The connexion between salt and the idea of love is clear from the fact that there are a number of savage superstitions which involve the bridling of the passions at a particular time and for a particular purpose—and in such instances frequently the abstinence is not only from the joys of love, but also from the partaking of salt. For example, there are certain Indians of Mexico who revere a species of cactus. Every year the men go on a long journey for the purpose of gathering this sacred plant. From the time when the men depart to the day of the cactus festival the Indians are very careful in their conduct. Among the restrictions which they impose upon themselves is that of complete restraint where human affections are concerned. Linked with this is the complete abstinence from salt.

Salt, in the view of superstition, has great medical value. It is used both to prevent and to cure illness. In the Book of Ezekiel we find a reference to the custom of rubbing newborn infants with it. And in the Second Book of Kings we read that Elisha, when told by the men of Jericho that a certain spring yielded poisonous water, asked that the people provide him with a new cruse, into which they were to put salt. He then cast the salt into the water and thus "healed" the fountain.

Salt is commonly used as an amulet; it is a protection against the evil eye. As a prophylactic against various forms of magic it is most powerful. For instance, one hears of a Russian maxim, "Throw salt on a gipsy as he (or she) departs from your house."

In Arabic countries today, when two people eat salt together, a mystic bond of union is effected between them. It is possible that, just as eating creates such a bond, the spilling destroys it unless the mysterious connexion between the friends in question is promptly rendered whole. This may be done by consigning a bit of the mineral to the flames, or it may be done (as in the current superstition) by throwing some over the left shoulder.

The fact that the spilling of salt is a cause of bad luck is but one illustration of the idea that a creator may be, in a sense, a destroyer also. There is good reason for this. The mysterious function of generation is frequently bound up with evil. This twofold aspect of the mystery of life finds its expression, not only in the salt superstition, but also through the myths, legends, and the like that go to form the basis of our knowledge of the supernatural and its history. Thus the mistletoe, unquestionably a symbol of generation, brought about the death of the good god Balder. The apple of love, primarily a creator, was responsible for the Trojan War and for the expulsion of mankind from the garden of Eden. In all parts of the world the serpent has been venerated as a creator, but was he not also the Tempter, the Evil One, the Destroyer?

For the same reason salt, in the lore of the supernatural, may be a force for good or for evil. To put a bit of salt on another man's plate is considered bad luck. As a countercharm against the spiritual evil thus caused, one may repeat the act and put a little more salt upon his plate. Possibly the best illustration of the relation that this mineral bears to both good and evil is to be found in the superstition that it is dangerous to give salt to a stranger and to let him carry it away. The reason for this is that salt is a repository of life itself, and if you permit the stranger to carry away your salt, he will be taking from you in effect a portion of your own life, your own strength, your own mystic virility.

3

If it may be said in a general way that metals and minerals are closely associated with the great transcendent supernatural, it is especially and most emphatically true that stones have been endowed with mysterious and even divine powers. Boulders and rocks of odd shapes have always been worshipped; meteorites like the Mohammedan Ka'aba have, of course, been objects of reverence; and stones with holes in them have enjoyed the adoration of multitudes. But this is not the whole story. Small rocks as well as large ones have been revered, puny and insignificant stones as well as gigantic and majestic ones.

While it is true that ordinary rough rocks have been worshipped, it is also true that an effort was early made to carve them into some semblance of the human form or of the most sacred parts of human anatomy.

As all art was originally part of the extensive ritualistic discipline by which men sought to effect contact with the supernatural world, so all sculpture was originally of the sacred variety. "Art for art's sake" is a phrase that has little enough meaning today, and such a judgment was not dreamed of in the ages gone by when no hard-and-fast distinction was made between the religious and the secular phases of human activity. The first crude attempts on the part of men to carve at least a faint resemblance of themselves upon the rocks were acts of piety—nothing more and nothing less. From such simple beginnings there slowly developed the practice of fashioning, with exquisite and well-nigh ineffable skill, gods and goddesses of stone.

Such was the early history of the sculptor's art.

4

THERE is no part of the world in which one does not encounter the remains of sacred stones. In England we have the famous circle known as Stonehenge. That show-place was apparently devoted to the worship of the sun, for it is so constructed that on Midsummer morn the rising sun falls in a direct line over the outlying stones and upon the central altar.

Nor is Stonehenge the only shrine of its kind. There are many remains of similar sanctuaries where the mystic ball of flame was represented by one or more stones. So close is the connexion between Sol and the rock that the word "heliolith," or "sun stone," is virtually a technical term in the science of comparative religions.

No better illustration could be brought forward of the mystic power formely ascribed to stones than is afforded by the age-old practice of wearing them as charms against evil

—especially against the evil eye. Out of that old custom there has developed the desire for jewellery as personal adornment. Certain gems used to be tied to the horns of oxen when the ground was being ploughed. This increased the fertility of the crop. The Greeks had a snake-stone that was effective against snake-bite. The resemblance of this object to the brazen serpent need cause no surprise, for they both stood for the same reality—the male creator.

In the Orient today, and particularly in China, Japan, and India, the stone pillar is one of the most essential features of temple architecture. In such instances the meaning of the upright emblems is frankly admitted.

Many of the sacred stones of the world are in the shape of pyramids. This was also a favourite shape among those people who adored the sun. The gigantic royal tombs of Egypt are among the wonders of the earth. They demonstrate the lengths to which people will go (if they are sufficiently superstitious) in order to rear colossal symbols of life to guard the gateway to eternity.

In the great temples of the Aztecs in ancient Mexico the altars dedicated to Sol were of this shape. It was one of the duties of the priests to slaughter on those altars the human victims demanded by the Sun as his divine due. The unfortunate people were bent backwards over the pyramids while the priests cut out their hearts and offered them to the god. When Cortez invaded Mexico and overthrew the empire of Montezuma, many of his followers were captured. Great was the horror and consternation of the Spaniards as they realized the part their comrades were destined to play in the ceremonies of the orb. It must be added, however, that the cruelties inflicted by the party of Cortez upon the natives were just as monstrous as that which the Spaniards suffered at the hands of the Aztec priests. When we consider that the subjects of Montezuma had not invited the invasion and were ready at first to welcome the strangers and pay them divine honours, till their hospitality was grossly abused, our feeling of pity for the victims of sun-worship is slightly mitigated.

5

THE relation of stone-worship to the development of mankind's spiritual institutions is not difficult to trace. The Bible records the existence of certain *"matzevoth,"* which certain righteous kings made a practice of destroying. The *matzevah*, as a matter of fact, was common, not merely in Palestine, but in Phœnicia and other Semitic settlements. The word is employed in modern Hebrew to connote "tomb-stones."

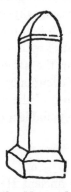

The Matzevah

The monuments to which certain biblical writers took exception were remnants of an earlier form of worship, which the enlightened seers and their followers had out-grown. Still, it is easy to understand how it happened that the altar arose as a development of the sacred-stone idea.

Since the monuments were regarded as embodying the divine principle of generation, it soon became the habit to honour them by placing offerings upon them. Sometimes wine was poured over them—in fact, this was a favourite method of showing reverence to any erect sign of sex. Food of one kind or another, grain, and animals slaughtered in their honour were given to them. The result was that the original upright shape of the stone had to be altered to receive the offerings, and the altar came into being.

But, as always in the evolution of conventions and spiritual institutions, side by side with the new stone objects, the old ones continued to be revered. The worship of the old monuments, however, gradually came to be abandoned by the progressive elements. It remained as the superstition of the masses. The advanced members of the communities worshipped at the altars; the retarded still continued their devotions at the *matzevoth*.

The first sacred stones were probably rough and natural. This is doubtless the reason why the first altars were constructed of stones on which "no tool had been waved." Following the altars came arks with stones (or similar objects) as their contents. So far the sanctuaries had been groves, under the open sky, but eventually came the houses of God, in which, however, because of the innate conservatism of all devout institutions, the symbolism of trees, stones, and arks usually remained.

6

THE famous Ark of the ancient Hebrews was a remarkable emblem. Above it were two winged cherubim, and within it were the two tablets of stone. According to one version, the rod of Aaron was placed "before the Testimony"; according to another view, it formed a part of the Ark's contents.

The "Aron Ha-eduth" or "Ark of the Testimony" was an object of inestimable power. It was habitually carried into battle by the worshippers, and the enemies of Israel were known to cry out in dismay when they saw it. They were afraid because the Jews were carrying their powerful divinity to do battle in their behalf.

When the Children of Israel crossed the Jordan, they

could discover no ford, but the priests who carried the Ark found themselves, so to speak, carried by it, and the people were enabled to cross the angry stream in safety. In like manner, when the Philistines had captured the Ark and, because of subsequent afflictions, desired to return it, they placed it upon a cart and attached two cows. So irresistibly were the cows driven by the holy object that they abandoned their calves and ran, lowing as they went, back to the camp of Israel. Thus, to carry the Ark was not really to bear a burden, for the divinity who resided within it guided and, if necessary, carried the ones who conveyed it.

Still, the Testimony was instinct with danger. On one occasion when it was being moved, the driver of the cart, one Uzzah, feared because the oxen stumbled, and he stretched out his hand to steady the precious cargo. At once he was stricken dead—he was punished for his temerity in seeking to assist the All-Powerful.

There were dangers that attached to sacred tablets of stone among other peoples also. Thus there is still extant a curse that was intended as a sort of protection for the tablets of the god Asher. ". . . To him, the one great god Asher, do I offer prayer and sacrifice and abundance of victims for his altars. Whoever shall injure the house of God, the sacred tablets, or hide them from God's people, his name shall be assigned to perdition, and he himself shall be cursed everlastingly. May his sovereignty perish, and his offspring not survive him; may his troops fly before their enemies, and famine and misery desolate all his lands; may no day of his life be joyous to him, and may his race be finally and for ever extinguished."

7

THE arks of other gods were similar in many ways to the Ark of the Hebrews. For example, the ark of Cypselus had above it a winged representation of Diana, holding in one hand a lion and in the other a leopard. In the same way, the ark of Osiris in Egypt had two winged and angelic creatures upon it.

Inside the Egyptian ark were the egg, the serpent, and the upright sign of sex. The ark that was carried by the Greeks contained the identical three items, all of them suggestive of the concept of creation. The implication would seem to be that the Hebrew Ark originally represented life in the same way.

This idea is borne out by the fact that the name of the Ark was "the Testimony." The Hebrew oath was regarded as something particularly holy, and accordingly it was sworn on the holiest part of the anatomy of man. For example, when Abraham wanted his servant to swear to do his bidding, he instructed him to place his hand "under the thigh," because an oath sworn upon so sacred an object would not readily be broken. Jacob took the same precaution when he required Joseph to take an oath.

Nor is this practice unknown today. In India there is a custom of certain priests to place their hands upon the holy part of Nanda, the sacred bull, before performing some ceremonies.

At the time of the Franco-Egyptian War General Kleber had occasion to suspect a certain Arab of treachery. The accused loudly protested his innocence, but it was evident that, in spite of his vigorous denials, he was suspected still. In his extremity and in his anxiety to prove his innocence beyond doubt, he threw off his clothing, and in this state he swore that he was guiltless.

The Latin word "*testis*" signifies both a witness and an anatomical organ. Apparently there was a time when the two were closely related in the minds of the people. Perhaps this will explain why David danced (in a state of nudity?) before the Ark. If the contents of the receptacle had been a literary document, that method of showing respect would have been distinctly unusual. But that was precisely the method of honouring a creative symbol everywhere.

In modern synagogues, the holy ark is always prominent. The contents of the modern ark among the Jews of today are scrolls of the Law. These scrolls are usually honoured by silver ornaments that contain little bells. It is noteworthy that bells have always figured prominently in the worship of creation. The bell has ever been a charm against the evil eye, and small bells are sometimes worn as amulets by superstitious people. The bell was used in the worship of Demeter, and the famous gong of Dodona was a historic charm. The Temple of Jupiter Tonans had bells hanging down to the door. Whatever may be the significance of the bell today, the outward part was once thought of as female, and the clapper as male. The object itself was a weapon in the war of Life against Death.

8

THE winged cherubim were at one time symbolic figures. Cherubim were common, not only in Palestine, but in other places. In the British Museum today are curious types of Assyrian cherubim, one of which has the head of a hawk and holds romantic emblems in each of its hands, while the other is not unlike the winged sphinx, having the body of a lion and the bearded head of a king. In the Louvre one may find a Phœnician cherub, which is likewise lion-bodied.

There is a Talmudic legend to the effect that the cherubim in the Temple used to embrace each other from time to time. This was a miraculous sign from Heaven and was intended to indicate the intense love that God felt for His people. The cabbala further developed this idea and taught that the love of the cherubim for each other was a representation of the union of earth and Heaven. Such a feeling with regard to this matter is to be detected in modern mysticism, for in

The Secret Doctrine, which is the great text-book of modern theosophy, the point is made that the wings of the angelic creatures above the Ark were symbolic of love.

It is at least likely that *The Secret Doctrine* is correct in this particular. That wings were sometimes used by the ancients to symbolize just such ideas is evident from the fact that there were wings upon the caduceus of Mecury and upon the dimpled body of the baby Cupid. To the modern eye Cupid, because he is a child, appears to be a most innocent and unsophisticated individual, but we know that he carries a quiver full of arrows and we are familiar with the symbolism of the arrow.

9

THAT the stone should be used to mark the resting-place of the departed cannot be surprising after what has preceded. At first blush it would appear as if the purpose of a tombstone is to preserve for all time the record of the fact that beneath it lie the mortal remains of a particular individual. But tombstones are older than the alphabet, and the earliest ones bore no inscriptions whatsoever. Jacob used stones to mark the site of Rachel's tomb; and again in the thirty-ninth chapter of the Book of Ezekiel we have a reference to a stone "sign" that was employed for a similar purpose. According to the First Book of Maccabees, Simon Maccabeus set up at the tomb of his father and brothers a stone marker, which consisted of seven pyramids.

Essentially the tombstone is but another example of what we have called in this volume the secret of the supernatural. It stands at the door of the tomb—the threshold that divides the world of the living from the abode of the dead. It protects the survivors against haunting, and, being a sign of life, it also guards the dead against those evil genii who have ever been associated with the realm of darkness, destruction, and death.

CHAPTER XIII

The Evil Eye

> *"Superstitions survive because, while
> they shock the views of the enlight-
> ened members of the community, they
> are still in harmony with the thoughts
> and feelings of others, who, though
> they are drilled by their betters into an
> appearance of civilization, remain bar-
> barians or savages at heart."*
>
> SIR JAMES G. FRAZER

1

AMONG the animals that possess supernatural power,
the hare is prominent. The Easter bunny still deposits
coloured eggs in the homes of credulous children. Occasionally the rabbit is a creature of ill omen. When the Thugs
of the East set out on one of their famous expeditions, they
used to watch the road to see if a hare crossed their path.
If one did, the enterprise was postponed. But as a rule the
bunny is a lucky animal. Its foot is especially valuable as a
charm.

The rabbit is famous for the large number of its offspring.
In a short time a single pair of rabbits will overrun a house
with progeny. For this reason the animal has been adored
by simple folks who saw in its fruitfulness an affinity between the creature and the gods of generation. Perhaps at
one time the hare was himself a god of creation.

But why is the foot of the rabbit particularly lucky? Why
not the head or the skin? There must be some significance
to the fact that the foot is the one portion of the animal's
anatomy that is regarded as effective in the war against the
myrmidons of Satan.

To understand the concept that lies at the bottom of the reverence for rabbits' feet, it is necessary to know something of the symbolism of the foot in supernatural lore. Human beings are inveterate worshippers of footprints. There is hardly a great prophet who has not (at least according to some tradition or other) left footprints behind him as relics for the adoration of his followers. The famous Buddhapada, or "footprint of Buddha," is curiously unlike the ordinary print of the human foot. In the first place, it shows a mark of the entire bottom of the foot. The arch of the normal foot is so constructed that but one of the metatarsal bones contributes directly to the impression, so that a print of an entire foot cannot be genuine, unless the god who made it was flat-footed!

Still, the prints are exceedingly common. The Mohammedans honour a number of them. One was left by the Prophet himself. But Mohammed was a comparatively recent character, and hence less honour is paid to his footprint than to those of no less ancient a personage than Abraham. That venerable patriarch has left marks which may still be observed in Mecca.

In the Harz Mountains of Germany one may see two enormous footprints in the rocks. In the days gone by, these were explained on the basis of a story. It seems that a certain baron had immoral designs upon a giant's daughter. The nobleman trapped the tall maiden and was on the point of subjecting her to his villainous will when the mother opportunely jumped from the sky and frustrated his diabolical plan. For many years the footprints left by the avenging mother were held sacred in Germany.

2

THE Scripture uses the word "foot" in an obviously symbolic sense. It is common among all people to veil an expression when to express one's meaning outright would be indelicate.

Thus we say: "If anything should happen to him," when we really mean: "If he should die." The substitute sentence is conventional, and the listener knows exactly what the speaker has in mind. Similarly, for the sake of modesty, certain scriptural writers wanted to disguise their discourse when treating parts of the body that are conventionally covered. When the Scripture speaks of "the water of one's feet," it has reference to a portion of the body other than the foot. When it speaks of "covering the feet" the reference again is not to the feet, but to that which requires covering. In Oriental lands to lay bare one's feet is a sign of the highest reverence. Moses removed his shoes in the presence of the burning bush. The hiding of one's feet from a sense of modesty would be as absurd in those countries as the covering of the head in the presence of ladies would be in the Occident. When a scriptural author speaks of "covering the feet," it is obvious to all students of the subject that he has something else in mind.

Among strictly Orthodox Jews today it is the custom at a certain point in the wedding-ceremony for the bridegroom to break a glass with his foot. As soon as this is done, the whole company cries out as loudly as possible: *"Mazel tov,"* or "Good luck." It is obvious that a custom of that kind must be an old one, and it dates from the remotest antiquity. Its symbolism is not hard to read.

If there was any time when the people required luck, that time was the occasion of a wedding. The gods in heaven were jealous of the joys of sex, and those joys had to be tasted gradually.

Living together on the part of two human beings always presents its spiritually menacing aspects. Innumerable devices have been invented by priests of different races to overcome this difficulty for people who desired to marry. One of the devices is the symbolic consummation of the marriage as a part of the wedding-ceremony. The glass is the sign of the female creator (to this day in India the female generator is conventionally represented as a hollow vessel). The groom shatters this symbol with his foot— also a mystic symbol. Then the people loudly cry out: "Good luck." Perhaps this shout scares away the demons.

In the sculpture and sacred art of ancient days one of the favourite themes is that of a god of fertility pressing his foot into the body of a woman, or into a lotus flower.

We begin to appreciate the hidden meaning of the rabbit's foot.

3

BUT we merely begin to appreciate it. The full significance of that charm (and charms like it) will not become apparent till we have examined the universally accepted superstition of the evil eye, and till we have discovered the profound influence of that superstition upon all human beliefs, institutions, and collective habits.

According to the belief of the ancient Greeks, there once lived a handsome youth named Narcissus. Although extremely attractive in appearance, he was never attracted to anyone else, so that he doubtless left a train of broken female hearts wherever he roamed. Nemesis, the goddess of justice, decided to punish the youth for this lack of feeling, so she decreed that he should fall in love with his own reflection in the water. The punishment proved so terrible that Narcissus pined away and died of grief. The water-sprites came to bury his body, but it had disappeared. In its place the naiads found a flower.

The story of Narcissus is an outgrowth of the feeling, present to this day in every part of the world, that it is dangerous to be pleased with oneself or to be praised by another. A Hindu mother will loudly proclaim that her child is wasting away, that it is ill, puny, and mentally deficient, not because she believes this to be so, but because to permit the gods to believe that the child is healthy or happy would be fraught with spiritual danger. An Englishman of the lower classes, if he must say something good of a friend, will add to his comment: "The Lord be with us." It is a widespread custom to knock on wood on such perilous occasions. When an ancient Roman had some good to say of anyone he admired, he prefaced the charm *"Præfiscini dixerim,"* which warded off evil effects. In modern Italy the magic clause is *"Si mal occhio non ci fosse,"* or "Let no evil eye have effect." Sometimes the expression in Italy is merely the pious *"Grazia a Dio."* If you see a good-looking child in an Italian street and admire it, the nurse is likely to counteract the poison of your praise with the words: *"Dio la benedica."* In like manner the Turk concludes his praises with *"Mashallas,"* "God be praised." Superstitious Jews will affix to compliments the potent word *"Imbeschrien"* or *"Unberufen."* Each of those words seems to mean the same thing: "You are not invited." This is an invitation to Evil to stay away.

The dangers attendant upon praise are many. But most of them are in the form of mystic emanations from people's eyes. In the view of superstition, all the organs of the body give forth emanations which are brim-full of possibilities for harm, but the most sinister (because most powerful) darts are those that come from the eye. One illustration of this is to be found in Egyptian mythology. The father of the gods was Ptah. The gods sprang from his eyes. But men, not requiring such potency, sprang from his mouth.

In the timid estimate of superstitious folks, the spiritual world has always been more productive of evil than good. Accordingly, the supernatural force of the eye was more often malicious than otherwise. In fact there is no belief in a benign eye, unless we place in that category the idea of Plutarch that love is sometimes produced by the fascination of the organs of vision.

One of the great works of Perseus, the Greek hero, was

the slaying of the gorgon Medusa, whose hair was composed of live snakes and whose eye was so terrible that it turned to stone everyone and everything it looked upon.

The people of Brazil relate an old story to the effect that a hunter once killed a bird whose eye was so powerful that one look was sufficient to kill anything it beheld. The hunter, of course, kept out of the bird's range of vision when he performed this noteworthy feat. Having dispatched the creature, he carefully severed its head, which he used thereafter as a weapon. At one time, however, his wife was handling the head, and, not being aware of its power for harm, she accidentally turned it upon her lord and master. Instantly the gallant huntsman departed for the realm of the dead. In her amazement and terror the good wife turned the head upon herself—and she promptly joined her ill-fated spouse.

The Hindu conception of Saturn takes the form of a wicked and vindictive divinity named Sani. When the wife of Siva gave birth to the child Ganesa, the parents celebrated by inviting the deities to a feast. But they forgot to invite Sani. So ungovernably angry did the neglected deity become that he went to the divine party and looked at the babe. No sooner had the malicious glance fallen upon the child than its young head fell off. Not a moment was to be lost. The gods were horrified and wanted to repair the injury. It was beyond their power to repair the original head, so they compromised by cutting off the head of an elephant and substituting it on the neck of the infant god. The story is supposed to explain why it is that Ganesa is usually represented with the head of an elephant.

This is but one version of a universal folk-tale. In our story of "The Sleeping Beauty" the same idea is present. We have the birth, the feast, the neglected fairy, the curse of death, and its mitigation so that the child would not die, but sleep for a century.

Most bad luck is ascribed to the baneful influence of the eye. Our word "ill" is a contraction of the word "evil," and it is a hold-over from the days when all sickness was thought to be a result of fascination. Our women are still accustomed to blacking their eyebrows, and it is generally assumed that this arose out of the feeling among men and women that such blacking was æsthetic. As a matter of fact, the darkening of eyelids is still practised in some places where its original efficacy as a charm against the evil eye is frankly understood and admitted. First came the supernatural charm and then the idea that it was æsthetically desirable. The same development has taken place in the case of jewellery. One thing is clear. The blacking of eyelids served a double purpose. In the first place it protected one against the darts that were shot from the eyes of others, and in the second place it protected one from casting the baneful emanations oneself.

Not all people whose glances are harmful are themselves malicious by disposition. All unwittingly people kill or maim or injure by their glances. Just as in the Middle Ages the ecclesiastics were sure that a woman might be a witch without either her knowledge or consent, so people might hurt their own beloved by looking at them. Fathers have been known to kill their children by a glance. Shepherds have destroyed their own flocks by the power of the eye. Cattlemen have caused their own cows to refuse to give milk.

The evil eye was present not only among men and women, but also among gods and animals—every sort of being that was able to see. We have seen how it was exercised to the detriment of the elephant-headed son of Siva. Juno was notorious for her evil eye, and the primary purpose of Mercury's caduceus was to serve as an antidote against it. It was essential that the messenger of the gods be shielded against Juno's darts at such times as he was carrying messages between her enemies.

The serpent and the fox were specially characterized by the evil eye. Other animals had it also. Above all, the hideous attribute belonged to Juno's sacred bird, the peacock. The feathers of this bird were "full of eyes" and they were all powerful for harm. To this day, people refuse to have peacock feathers in their houses, for fear that death will enter with the ill-omened plumage. Moreover, the hare, like the serpent, was noted for the magic power of its eye. In Ireland the hare was once so feared for this reason that on May Day the pious used to round up large numbers of rabbits and slaughter them, in order to rid the countryside as far as possible of the spiritual menace they bore.

But it happens (in view of superstition) that a creature with the evil eye may be a charm against the force that emanates from the eyes of others. For example, hunchbacks were noted from time immemorial for their possession of the evil eye. But a hunch-back was also an antidote against the ethereal poison. For a long time there was a certain hunch-back who used to take his station before the Casino at Monte Carlo, in order to permit people to touch him at so much per touch. This brought luck to the players, and he did a large business. The nature of the good fortune bought by the superstitious players at Monte Carlo was that of a counter-charm against the mystic emanation that dealt, not only financial loss, but also destruction and death.

Since the hare was so closely connected with the evil-eye theory, it is easy to understand why it was selected to bear a counter-charm against its own fell magic. This is why a credulous person, even in the twentieth century, will occasionally carry a rabbit's foot in his pocket. He may be ignorant of the whole dramatic history of his practice and may be totally unaware of the complex symbolism involved; yet he derives solace from the feeling that he owns a magnet that will draw "good luck" in his direction, and will frighten "bad luck" away.

4

MOST of the charms, amulets, talismans, and formulas that have been designed to bring luck were intended in the first place as shields against the darts of the evil eye. But since these darts are themselves representatives of the force of death, the amulets, charms and so on have been originally connected with the idea of life. As a rule they have been representations of one kind or another intended to symbolize the parts of the human body that were looked upon as repositories of life—visible representatives of the divine power of creation.

If it was true that brides and grooms have always required protection against the eye, so, for obvious reasons, did the soldiers who went forth to battle. Spears and javelins bore a menace of course, but the menace was a visible one and hence not nearly so terrible as the eerie and uncanny supernatural powers the soldier had to face. Therefore it was never sufficient for him to have purely physical defensive armour. Far more important was the spiritual armour that every soldier carried for himself, and that every regiment or legion carried for the collective benefit of its members. The institution of the mascot is hoary with age. And there is splendid reason for this. The soldier sets out deliberately to face death. The wizards of the other side will direct their enchantments against him, and the evil eyes of his opponents will be trained upon him. To ward off such supernatural adversaries he must employ the mystic power of life.

This is the reason why the Roman legions carried before them real serpents upon a pole. The shields and hats of soldiers in the past were always decorated with emblems of a mystic character, and even in the late war the German hordes wore upright spear-heads (male) upon their heads. The entire "science" of heraldry, which concerned itself with the devices worn by knights in the Middle Ages, included few, and perhaps no, symbols that cannot be shown to be developments of either the male or the female symbol. Either the helmet showed an upright object like that of the Germans during the war, or it showed the crescent, the virgin moon of Isis, which is also the mystic head-dress of Maia, the virgin mother of Buddha, and is the halo of Ishtar, Hathor, Artemis, and Diana. It is the sacred sign of Mohammed today.

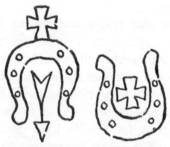

The Horseshoe Idea in Heraldry

One method of attaining protection against the evil eye was that of suspending an emblem of motherhood above one's door. The Arabs of northern Africa used to put up over their holy places the real parts of a cow or other female animal. In ancient Yucatan or Peru there were temples with arched doorways, and at the tops of the arches were engravings of the female creator. Up till recent times there were churches in Ireland, notably Cloyne Cathedral, County Cork, over whose doors was a sculpture of a nude woman pointing to herself. Thus we see the process of development which has culminated in the nailing of a horse-shoe above the door. The strength of motherhood as a weapon against the force of destruction may be inferred from the statement of Pliny that if a storm was about to come up, it might be dispelled by any woman who would merely uncover herself before it.

5

WITH all the varied devices that people have thought of from time to time, superstitious people have never felt safe from the power of the evil eye. A man may wear an amulet and may be in a building which is protected by a horse-shoe; still, if he suspects fascination, he will take additional precautions. Thus he may make the "fico," as it is called in Italy. "Fico" means "fig." The sign is made by closing the fist and allowing the thumb to protrude between the index and middle finger. This is supposed to be suggestive of masculinity and hence is a charm. Another protection is to make an oval with the thumb and index finger. This is the female symbol. From ancient times it has been the custom to hold an obscene emblem before anyone suspected of exercising witchcraft or sorcery. His power disappears at once. The same expedient was effective as against devils.

It was the proud habit of Roman generals to parade before the grateful public when they returned after a victory. But this put them literally before the eyes of the people—a situation that was obviously dangerous. To avoid fascination, the generals put an obscene figure before their chariots. The figure became the god Fascinus, who doubtless earned his name from the use to which his images were put. From that obscene god we derive our English word "fascinate"—a word so loverlike in its implications, and, alas, so reminiscent of the evil eye.

CHAPTER XIV

The Amulet

> *"So in the Libyan fable it is told*
> *That once an eagle, stricken with a*
> *dart,*
> *Said, when he saw the fashion of*
> *the shaft,*
> *'With our own feathers, not by other's*
> *hands,*
> *Are we now smitten.'"*
>
> ÆSCHYLUS
> (TRANSLATION BY PLUMPTRE)

1

THERE are those who say that the wearing of jewellery is at bottom a means of demonstrating one's wealth. Even the decorous and gentle-mannered, according to this view, take the opportunity that is afforded by the existence of jewels of showing their fellows that they can afford to waste their substance. The jewel itself adds nothing perceptible to one's well-being beyond the satisfaction it gives as palpable evidence of superfluity of wealth.

Beyond doubt there is some truth in that contention. An imitation pearl may bear so close a resemblance to the genuine article that no one but an expert will be able to detect the counterfeit. Still, the average individual wishes to own a "real" gem. If the worth of the object lay in its beauty, then the difference in value between two practically indistinguishable "jewels" would be negligible. Since it is not, we may conclude that the real value of jewellery is based (in part at least) upon its ability to excite admiration and envy.

But the habit of wearing jewels, and the æsthetic judgment that they help to render one personable, arose in the first place out of the fear of the supernatural. Bracelets, necklaces, rings, and "charms" go back to a time when such objects were practical in and of themselves. They were valuable as potent shields against witchcraft, sorcery, magic, and the evil eye.

One of the most powerful gems, according to the lore of superstition, is the diamond. According to one authority, if a diamond is placed upon the head of a sleeping woman who is true to her husband, she will be magically impelled to caress that loving spouse. In addition to the diamond, honourable mention must be given to the jacinth, the sapphire, and the carbuncle, which careful parents used to suspend from the necks of their children. In the event that such gems could not be procured, a piece of amber was frequently employed.

Especially powerful as talismans were stones that were cut to resemble (or which naturally resembled) certain mystic animals. For example, the scarab, or sacred beetle, which was reported by the superstitious to have no female of the species, was always potent as a charm. To wear a stone image of this beetle was to be well armed against the evil eye. In like manner a frog, cut in amber or made of gold, was effective. The frog, in fact, possessed truly marvellous powers. According to one account, if you remove the tongue from a living frog and place this tongue upon the heart of a woman who is sleeping, you may then ask any question and the reposing woman will give you true answers. And as for the toad, everyone knows that it bears in its head a precious jewel. What is not so generally known today is the fact that if anyone manages to secure such a gem from the head of a toad, he will be the fortunate possessor of one of the most potent amulets known to superstition.

In addition to animals, certain plants are effective as

amulets. Garlic is such a plant. Some Hindu women today
wear a cross engraved upon a fig-leaf. It has long been the
custom for women in India to wear a fig-leaf charm from
the day of their marriage. In the eighteenth century there
was quite a storm when Catholic missionaries attempted
to induce the women to wear the cross instead. The result
was a compromise, so that the matrons now wear a combination—the cross engraved upon the fig.

Strings of beads are themselves effective as amulets, but
their efficacy is increased if a special charm is hung upon
them. Roman youths wore a disk called the *bulla*, which
represented the sun, while the crescent was worn by
maidens. These symbols were also favourites in the British
Isles, and they are used at present in southern Italy.

Amulets are almost personal necessities in some parts of
Italy. Sometimes they are in the form of the fico; sometimes they take the form of the oval hand; sometimes they
are diminutive representations of the hunch-back. There
are other devices also, but they all serve the same purpose.

During morning worship, Orthodox Jews wear upon their
heads and arms little objects called phylacteries. These are
boxes containing sacred texts. The boxes are attached to
straps by which they are bound round the arm and on the
head. Presumably they fulfil the command: "Bind them as
a sign upon thy hand, and let them be as frontlets between
thine eyes." But the winding of a strap round one's arm
or forehead is in primitive religion one of the rites of
serpent-worship. So in the case of the may-pole, the winding
of the ribbon round the pole is strangely reminiscent of
primitive snake-rituals.

2

THE wiles of the spirits of darkness against animals and
plants were always as effective as those against men and
women. It was therefore necessary to call the force of

life into play to protect these beings. In certain parts of
Java when the rice is about to blossom, the planter and
his wife strip themselves and run round the field unclad.
Following this, they embrace each other under the open
sky.

In Transylvania it is feared that the birds will eat the
seeds unless care is taken to scare away the powers of evil.
The method of doing this shows a curious and unsatisfactory
combination of a low and a high culture. The farmer goes
naked round the field, after which he piously recites the
Lord's Prayer. In some places this is varied by having the
wife of the farmer, candle in hand, go through the ceremony.

In Central America in the early days, when the seed was
planted, the natives scrupulously indulged in caresses. This
sort of thing was regarded by the priests as an act of piety.
There were even certain officials whose duty it was to perform this act just at the time when the first seeds were
planted. Customs of this kind might be multiplied and
examples cited from all over the world.

3

It is scarcely possible to overstate the importance that
primitive people ascribed to loverlike rituals and to objects
which they regarded as suggestive of the power of creation.
It happened not so long ago that the Dutch troops abandoned
an old cannon on the island of Java, at a place called Bata-
via. The cannon instantly become a forceful god, to whom
rice and other offerings were regularly given and to whose
service a number of priests devoted themselves. Of course
the new divinity was like the Roman Priapus, and it was
his special concern to cure such evils as barrenness. Women
who desired children dressed themselves in their finest
raiment, garlanded themselves with flowers, and sat all day
long astride the abandoned gun. The worship of this god

continued for some time and the priesthood waxed fat on
the profits. But the cult was destined to meet a sudden end.
In 1876–7 the Dutch Government removed the divinity,
which happened to be its property, and the worship ceased.

Incidents of that kind demonstrate that the sacrifice
offered by Roman brides to Priapus was something more
than a sop to the jealous god. It was also a means of trans-
mitting to the bride the magic properties inherent in the
idol.

But it was even more. It was a gift to the girl of power
to resist evil in general. Henceforth she was luckier than
she would have been without the aid of the ceremony. She
could battle with the force of death, since she was imbued
with the power of life.

The evolution of the amulet or luck piece can be traced
in the art of Pompeii and Herculaneum. In the museum at
Portici one sees an ancient sacred vase on which is shown
a woman in the act of embracing the huge symbol of sex.
Another vase shows a vender of small sex-images offering
them to women for sale. He carries a basketful.

Thus we have first the adoration of the physical creator
itself. Then we have the worship of the symbols that represent generation. Next come the small images that are
to be worn for luck. Finally we have the highly conventionalized symbols, the rabbit's foot, the horseshoe, the
triangular abracadabra, the *bulla,* the suggestive hand, the
serpent ring, the crescent. . . .

4

THERE are, of course, many amulets that bear no relation
to the idea of love. Since sacred animals can cure diseases,
the teeth, horns, etc., of such animals are effective as talismans. If this is true, how much more powerful are relics
—that is to say, the teeth, bones, and even hair—of saints!

Even pictures or statues of holy men possess power to avert evil.

We have also the binding or constricting amulets. The simple ring, the jewelled bow-knot, and the knotted string are examples. These confine the demons and prevent them from harming the bearers. Among primitive people knots are used both to cause and to cure illness. The Koran mentions this practice. In 1572 it was found that a witch who was about to be burnt at Saint Andrews was wearing a knotted cloth. This was instantly removed, for in all probability Death would not have been able to conquer her if the constricting charm had been on her person. Timid cattlemen have been known to carry locks round the herd to prevent the beasts of prey from committing depredations.

Then too we have the repository of evil used as a sort of inoculation against its own mischief. The little brooms that are sold at carnivals and are used to tickle people at Hallowe'en are outgrowths of this idea. The broom was the vehicle of a witch; therefore it was employed as a prophylactic inoculation against witchcraft. The miniature of a hunchback is a similar "charm."

There are countless physical objects that are believed to be repositories of spiritual power. They may be used for protection against devils. Many Roman Catholics wear about their necks the Carmelite scapular, of which it is said: "Whoever wears the scapular until death will be preserved from hell."

CHAPTER XV

The Magic Formula

*"One hour of justice is more than
seventy years of prayer."*

MOHAMMED

1

THE most dreaded vehicle of spiritual malice is, of
course, the evil eye. But there are other methods of
fascination besides that which emanates from the organs
of vision. For example, there is the touch, which is everywhere used for magic purposes. The laying on of hands is
a world-wide method of curing disease. Up till recent times
the kings of England cured scrofula by their royal touch.
In every religion provision is made for blessing people by
placing the hand upon the head of the person to be blessed.
When a rabbi is ordained, the officiating celebrant places
his hand upon the head of the youth; and the idea is that
Moses thus laid his hands upon Joshua, and he upon his
successor, and so on, so that the mystic virtue has descended
through the touch from the time of Sinai to the present
day.

As is to be expected, however, fascination through touch
is usually more pregnant with evil than with good. The man
with the evil touch is as greatly to be feared (albeit he is
not as unbiquitous a menace) as the man with the evil eye.

It may be that this idea arose somehow out of actual
observation of the facts of nature. The electric eel fascinates
its prey by purely physical contact, and other animals seem
to have a similar power. The following passage from Dr.
Livingstone's account of his travels in Africa will illustrate
the kernel of truth in the fascination superstition: ". . . I

heard a shout. Starting and looking half around, I saw a lion just in the act of springing upon me. I was upon a little height; he caught my shoulder as he sprang, and we both came to the ground below together. Growling horribly close to my ear, he shook me as a terrier dog does a rat. The shock produced a stupor similar to that which seems to be felt by a mouse after the first shake of a cat. It caused a sort of dreaminess, in which there was no sense of pain nor feeling of terror, though quite conscious of all that was happening. It was like what patients partially under the influence of chloroform describe, who see all the operation but feel not the knife. This singular condition was not the result of any mental process. The shake annihilated fear, and allowed no sense of horror in looking around at the beast. This peculiar state is probably produced in all animals killed by the carnivora, and, if so, is a merciful provision by our benevolent Creator for lessening the pain of death."

2

JUST as one could send out waves of mysterious influence either for good or for evil through the eye or touch, so the voice possessed a special magical charm. Perhaps even this idea has a slight basis in actual fact. In one of the novels of Wilkie Collins the author makes the following statement: "Among the hundred thousand mysterious influences which a man exercises over a woman who loves him, I doubt if there is any more irresistible to her than the influence of his voice." And has not the poet observed:

> Music has charms to soothe a savage breast,
> To soften rocks, or bend a knotted oak?

Mythology is full of heroes and demigods who had power to fascinate by the voice. Orpheus could charm the very rocks by the sweetness of his music. Circe changed Ulysses and his men into swine by the magic of her words. The sirens' wondrous song was so powerful that sailors were drawn to the singers as irresistibly as iron filings are drawn to a magnet. Even the creation of the world was effected through the voice of God. Reality was called into being when the words were pronounced: "Let there be light."

The magic power of the voice is usually greatest when the words used are grouped in certain mystically potent formulas. We have, for example, the story of Simeli Mountain, in which the poorer of two brothers learned that a certain hill would open up and reveal a cave full of treasures to anyone who would say: "Open Sesame." The hill would close again when the formula was pronounced: "Shut Sesame." The richer and more greedy of the brothers then discovered the same secret. He used his knowledge to enter the cavern and he closed the mountain behind him. But unfortunately he forgot the magic words, and though he did his best to call them to mind, and in his extremity invented a number of phrases, nothing would avail. It was impossible for him to escape except with the aid of the command: "Open Sesame." Thus he remained a prisoner till the robbers came who claimed the treasure, and they punished the prisoner for invading their premises. The instances of magic formulas in folk-lore are beyond number.

3

THE study of magic words would hardly be complete without reference to the superstitious import of nomenclature. A savage will carefully avoid telling his real name to a stranger, because the knowledge of a person's cognomen might easily be used to bewitch its owner. Therefore, the savage usually has two names—a real one, which is a secret, and a make-believe one, which he tells to others.

The names of gods in ancient times were known only to the priests, for an enemy might use the name to bewitch the god and thus to destroy the people whose bulwark and protection he was. Sometimes in warfare spies were sent out to learn the deity's real name, so that the official magicians of the besiegers might make use of the information. The four-lettered title of God (YHWH) in the Bible was never repeated to anyone, but was known and used by the high priest alone.

The fairy-tale of Rumpelstiltzkin is interesting in this connexion. Once there was a poor miller's daughter who was commanded by the King to spin a roomful of flax into gold. She was shut up in the room, and, being unable to obey the order, she started to cry. A little man then appeared, and he offered to work the miracle in the girl's behalf if she would reward him. She gave him her necklace, and he spun the flax into gold. The next night the King put the maiden in another room and gave her the same command. Again the little man showed himself, and in return for a ring he performed the difficult task.

On the third night the girl was confronted with the same problem. But she had nothing left to offer to the little man. He thereupon suggested that she promise him the first child that would be born to her. She agreed, and in the morning the King received his gold.

So happy was the monarch that he married the miller's daughter, and in due course a child was born to the couple. The Queen had forgotten all about the promise, but the strange man came to demand the baby as his right. The poor mother was horrified. She offered riches as a substitute, but the creature insisted upon having the child. Finally he agreed to forgo all payment if the Queen should discover his name within three days.

The Queen spent the first and second of the days trying to guess the man's name. She sent heralds throughout the realm and bade them collect all the names they could find and report to her. But when the man came to conduct the examination, his own name was still unknown to the distraught mother. On the third day, however, the messenger had good tidings. He had seen a small individual dancing before a fire and singing as he danced:

> "Today I bake, tomorrow I brew,
>   Then, little Prince, I will come for you;
>   For no one knows, no matter his fame,
>   That Rumpelstiltzkin is my name."

When the man went before the Queen, she began to guess a few names, to each of which he said: "No." Then she said: "Is your name Rumpelstiltzkin?"

"A witch has told you. A witch has told you," the poor man exclaimed. In his excitement he stamped his feet and threw his arms wildly in the air. So vigorously did he gesticulate that he flew into pieces. The discovery of his true name had wrought his destruction.

4

SINCE the voice was so powerful, it was but natural that it should have been employed in the pursuit of luck.

Among the American Indians there used to be certain eloquent persons whose duty it was to preach to the fish. In the evening the red men would assemble on the banks of a stream to listen while the preacher exhorted the denizens of the waters. The theme of such discourse was always by way of invitation to come and be caught by the particular tribe that employed the speaker instead of by a rival tribe. "A good preacher," says Frazer, "was much sought after, for they thought that the exhortations of a clever man had a great effect in drawing the fish to the nets."

This sort of thing is a step in advance of the old practice whereby the words were not employed for persuasion, but for magic compulsion. Pliny says that he personally knew of a case in which, through the skilful use of incantation, an olive orchard which belonged to a Roman knight changed places with a parcel of land on the opposite side of the road. The two pieces of ground crossed the road and substituted themselves for each other—all because of the magic fascination of the human voice.

The preachers to the fish represent a transition between those who used magic formulas to compel the powers of nature to grant their wishes, and the moderns who have reached a higher plane of culture and address prayers to the God of heaven. The preacher to the fish used his voice, it is true, to fascinate the finny creatures, but he did not rely upon a formula, nor yet on the magic timbre of his tones. He relied on a combination of these with his own powers of persuasion and eloquence.

Prayer today is an attempt to influence the All-Highest, to the end that He will alter His divine purposes in the interest of the petitioners. The idea is not present that the prayer must of necessity be answered. The petition may be effective and it may not. Such is the theory of most modern religionists.

In the early days, however, those who employed the spoken word in their attempts to enter into relation with the supernatural world acted upon a different theory. Prayer began, not as a request, but as an incantation. It was originally an attempt to compel nature to do the bidding of the magician, who used for this purpose his power of fascination through the voice. Primitive prayer was an endeavour to fascinate God.

5

As with the magic touch, there is a grain of truth out of which the idea of fascination through the voice may have grown. Hypnotism is a real enough phenomenon, yet the force of suggestion that it employs consists at bottom of words. Psychoanalysis is a perfectly scientific method of curing certain diseases by the sheer power of words. People have been made ill by words. It is a common incident for people to lose their appetites (a purely physical reaction) because of something they have heard.

It is barely possible that the whole superstition of fascination through the voice, and the whole evolution that has grown out of it, have sprung from the realization that words and music do influence human life. Certainly it is true that speech is no insignificant factor in the growth of civilization.

CHAPTER XVI

The Crescent, the Star, and the Cross

> "*Nature speaks in symbols and in signs.*"
>
> JOHN GREENLEAF WHITTIER

1

IT would be distinctly erroneous to say that the symbols of the great world-faiths today are in any sense conventional representations of generation. Looking at the cross from the point of view of Christianity, or at the star from the point of view of Judaism, or at the crescent from the point of view of Mohammedanism, one must conclude that not one of those emblems is indicative of anything save the highest ideal of the faith for which it plainly stands.

This book is devoted to a study of the conventions and beliefs of primitive society, and a review of the facts that throw light on man's earliest and most painful efforts to grope his way to truth. Now, it happens that each of the symbols here considered has been adored from the remotest antiquity and by diverse groups of people. In the words of Dr. Inman, "The devout Christian believes that all who venerate the Cross may hope for a happy eternity, without ever dreaming that the sign of his faith is as ancient as Homeric Troy, and was used by the Phœnicians probably before the Jews had any existence as a people; whilst an equally pious Mohammedan regards the Crescent as the passport to the realms of bliss, without a thought that the symbol was in use long before the Prophet of Allah was born, and amongst those nations which it was the Prophet's mission to convert or destroy."

Let it be understood, then, that when we speak of those

emblems in this chapter, our reference is always to the pre-Mohammedan crescent, the pre-Jewish star, and the pre-Christian cross.

2

SYMBOLS like those which were once in common use are rarely invented in these days, and when they are, the purpose behind them is no more profound than that of gratifying our whimsical taste for that which resembles the antique. There are designs—on wall-paper and decorated furniture, for example—that are frankly meaningless, and one would regard with amusement any individual who should seek to discover in them any hidden meaning that the draughtsman intended to convey. But when one goes into a store where Chinese or Japanese objects are exposed for sale, one sees on every hand elaborate designs every curve and angle of which was originally intended to convey a message—and still does convey that message to the initiated.

As Lafcadio Hearn has phrased it, "Art in Japan is so intimately associated with religion that any attempt to study it without extensive knowledge of the beliefs which it reflects were mere waste of time. By art I do not mean painting and sculpture, but every kind of decoration, and most kinds of pictorial representation—the image of a boy's kite or a girl's battledore not less than the design upon a lacquered casquet or enamelled vase—the figure upon a workman's trowel not less than the pattern of the girdle of a princess —the shape of a paper doll or wooden rattle bought for a baby, not less than the forms of those colossal Ni-O, who guard the gateways of the Buddha's temples. . . ."

The reason why such elaborate symbolism is no longer used in the Occident is that among us printing is a cheap process and the majority of the people are able to read and write. Of course, letters are symbols as truly as the dragon

and the peach, but the alphabet is so much more effective
as a means of conveying ideas than are the conventionalized
signs of earlier days that the former has replaced the latter.

The alphabet, however, did not spring into existence full-
grown like Minerva from the brain of Jupiter. Letters arose
out of picture-writing, which at first was not conventional,
but consisted of rude attempts actually to depict the objects
that writers desired to describe. But, when the objects
to be indicated were common, the tendency was for recognized signs of them to develop. One could doubtless find
many examples of this process in the evolution of the conventional ideographs of China.

Even letters at first had a complicated symbolic value.
Take for instance the well-known mystic alpha and omega.
The alpha was originally written $\measuredangle$. It was a sign of the
ploughshare, which cuts into the ground to assist in rendering Mother Earth fruitful. This mark was likewise the sign
of the ox, and one will note that it bears a resemblance to
the head of that animal. The ox was both honoured and
feared in the days gone by, because of its supernatural
powers. It is still prominent in astrology as the constella-
tion Taurus. The omega, Ω , on the other hand, is the
crescent, the virgin moon of Isis, the mysterious sign of the
horseshoe.

Is it necessary to add that such conceptions were highly
spiritualized in Hebrew and Christian usage? The Jews
attached special significance to the combination of the alif
and tau (the beginning and end of the alphabet) as in the
fourth word of the Hebrew Scripture. A similar concept of
totality is found in the Apocalypse, where the Alpha and
Omega refer expressly to "the First and the Last."

3

IT is not true that all of the signs known to mankind were
originally concerned with the idea of life. Thus the owl

has usually been regarded as a type of wisdom, the wolf of
want, the raven of despair, and the fox of cunning.

But still the fact remains that most of the early representations were loverlike in character. This is by no means an
indication of widespread impurity or lechery. The Greek
and Roman matrons who became so wild at the feasts of
Bacchus were neither wild nor savage on other occasions.
If they performed rites of that character, they did so because they thought that their god required them and because
they were convinced that their prime duty was that of align-
ing themselves with the spiritual forces of Life in the ceaseless cosmic battle with Destruction and Death. They knew
of but a single method of effecting that alignment. They
acted for truth and righteousness, albeit according to their
lights. Can anyone do more?

If the symbols that have come down to us were once
concerned with the mysteries, that is because those mysteries were profoundly important to our forbears—on them
hinged not only their own prosperity, but the very integrity
of the earth, the succession of the seasons, and the ways of
the stars in their courses. Thus the cock is an emblem of
the sun. In former days people were not conversant with the
facts of modern astronomy, and many of them shared
the illusion of Chanticleer that, should he neglect to crow,
the sun would be powerless to rise.

4

THE crescent is a very ancient sign and appears in many
connexions. In one case, a goddess with child is depicted
upon a large crescent, thus signifying the idea of purity or
virginity. We have one picture of a large crescent floating
upon a vast expanse of water. Above it is a dove carrying
a branch, and the whole picture is encircled by a rainbow.
The conception in that case is similar to the idea behind
the story of Noah and the Flood. The ancient inscriptions

and sacred designs on which the crescent occurs are beyond computation.

The Old Conventional Idea of the Union of Sun and Crescent

Mysterious Hieroglyphs involving the Crescent Idea

The six-pointed star, or double triangle, is likewise of indescribable antiquity. It is to be seen in the sacred lotus, and it consists of two parts, the male triangle pointing upwards like a pyramid, and the one pointing downwards, which is female. In India today the double triangle is used as the holy sign of Siva and Sakti. The male triangle represents the god, and the female one stands for the goddess.

Nor was the six-pointed star limited to the East even in the early days. It was one of the emblems revered by the American Indians before the invasion by white men. An exact copy of what is called the "shield of David" is to be found in the Temple of the Sun at Uxmal in Yucatan. The sun in that ruined temple is sculptured in stone. The Sri Iantra is an ancient Hindu emblem. It was placed on the ground, and a particularly sacred image was stationed in the central circle.

The Sri Iantra

5

STRANGE as it may seem, the Jews once revered the cross. The proof of this is to be found in the Book of the Prophet Ezekiel, where the sacred tau is specifically mentioned as a sign to be inscribed on the foreheads of the people. The word is sometimes translated "mark," but the Hebrew word is "tau," which was the name of the simple cross.

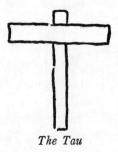

The Tau

The swastika is to Buddhism what the cross is to Christianity, and the crescent is to Islam. Moreover, just as the shield of David is really a cross (since it consists of two crossed triangles), so the swastika is a variant of this universally beloved, feared, and adored emblem. Sometimes it appears as a simple outline, but at other times one finds it accompanied by numerous symbols, which speak the language of love. Outside of Buddhism this emblem appears as a lucky sign (卐 or 卍), which is known to superstitious people the world over.

The Simple Swastika

In addition, however, to the swastika, the symbolism of the Buddhist religion includes a form of cross that bears a striking resemblance to the emblem we know as the cross of Christ.

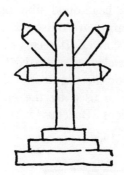

Buddhist Cross (Thibet)

6

WHEN the Spanish conquerors came to America, they were amazed to find that the natives knew and worshipped the cross. In the same way, modern readers may be surprised to learn that the cross was used as a religious sign and particularly as a marker for the resting-place of the dead by a people who preceded the Etruscans in Italy. Since the Etruscans were on the ground before the Romans, one may appreciate the antiquity of the symbol. In the ruined city of Palenque in Mexico there is a slab of stone on which there is a picture of a cross being worshipped by two people. One of the worshippers is offering a child to the holy object.

At Bombay in the cave of Elephanta there is a relief that shows the artist's conception of the slaughter of the babes at the time of the birth of the Hindu Saviour, Krishna. The executioner is standing before the tearful and entreating mothers, and over his head is the cross.

Stranger still is the fact that ages before the days of Christianity the crucifix, or cross with a deity upon it, was widely adored. Buddhist crucifixes are to be found in India and are centuries pre-Christian. In the State of Chiapas in Mexico there is a hollowed-out figure of a god on the cross. He wears a head-dress like that of the Egyptian sphinxes, and his arms are outstretched. But the figure is concave instead of convex. It seems that the sculpture was a mould into which clay was pressed to make uniform emblems for the use of the people.

The cross was also used by the ancient Greeks for religious representations. Bacchus wore a ribbon of crosses upon his head.

The Head-dress of Bacchus

In Babylon the conventional method of writing the name of the god Tammuz was the sign of the heart and cross, thus:

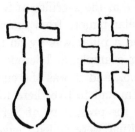

The Mark of Tammuz

In short, this emblem has been honoured from the earliest times, and among practically every people known to historians.

7

IT is hardly necessary to indicate that the pre-Christian crosses represented nothing so inspiring as the tragic episode of Calvary. They were instead outgrowths of the sacred-pillar idea. The column forms a part of virtually every temple that has ever been erected to gods anywhere. Originally the pillars were separate from the temple buildings proper; then temples were built with towers before them; finally the two structures were combined, so that to-day we have mosques with minarets pointing upwards, cathedrals crowned with spires, and churches with steeples directing the eyes of beholders towards heaven.

In front of the temple of Solomon were two pillars, called respectively Jachin (it stands) and Boaz (in strength). In this connexion one might mention that all Syrian temples had pairs of columns in front of them. This merely shows that Solomon followed the fashion of sacred architecture that was prevalent in his day. Originally the theme of that architecture had been derived from the universal idea of the struggle of the Creator with the Destroyer.

The worship of pillars was carried on in a fashion as complicated and as ritualistic as any other form of devotion. We are aware of the sacrifice of Saint Simeon Stylites, who lived on a pillar remote from the world. But the practice of living upon a pillar was by no means originated by Saint Simeon. For example, at Hieropolis there was an immense erect symbol, and it was the custom for a priest to mount that emblem and to live there for seven days, praying the while for the prosperity of Syria. The priests who performed that ritual were called *"engutheoi"* or "near to God."

8

THE adoration of the pillar was a pagan practice and is not to be confused with the rituals of the higher religions. Still, it has survivals that may be observed in the customs of modern times. Thus the may-pole is a hold-over from the days when such rites were part of the accepted spiritual practice of the people.

The original ceremony of the may-pole was one that may well shock the sensibilities of cultivated folks. It always involved the horror of human sacrifice. It was by no means a children's exercise, and it was not designed to please the watchers by its cheerful pageantry. The wisest men of the community participated, instead of the children, for much depended upon the ritual. Such important matters as the management of the ceremonies which were sacred to the powers of fertility could be entrusted to no incompetent or immature hands.

It is noteworthy that one feature of modern May Day celebrations is the dance of the participants round the pole. Each child holds in its hand a ribbon that is attached to the top of the symbol, and the object of the dance is to braid the streamers in a symmetrical design. But the use of streamers round a pole is familiar to students of comparative religions. We have noted, for example, the straps that Orthodox Jews still wind round their arms every morning, and we have remarked that in ancient days these straps were probably intended to represent the serpent. In modern Africa the natives frequently attach serpent streamers to sacred trees and poles.

The connexion between the idea of the snake and that of the pole may be observed from a serpent goddess who is found in Yucatan. Her image is described as "hewn out of a block of basalt nine feet high. Her drapery and arms were formed of snakes, her feet were tiger's claws, and on her sides were the wings of a vulture, whilst she wore as necklaces human hearts, hands, and skulls. . . ." At the shrines of this goddess were pillars marked with cabbalistic signs of one kind or another, mostly symbolic animals.

The ceremonies that used to be indulged in on May Day leave no doubt of the intention with which they were instituted. In the English celebrations the devotions began on April thirtieth. The men and women together journeyed to the wood to select a tree for the village. During the night they indulged in orgies, like those held in honour of Bacchus in the days of Greece and Rome. When ready, the pole was placed in the middle of the town, and then began the invocations, both prayerful and magical, to the powers of life. Human sacrifices and the union of the selected King and Queen of the May marked the joyous event.

9

IN the course of time the pillar became changed into the sacred tower, much as the rude stone evolved into the altar. Not that the old pillars were abandoned; but side by side with them were the new symbols—much higher and more suggestive of mystic potency than the old. In many places today there are either towers of that type or their ruins. Especially in ancient Ireland were the towers worshipped, and we still have their mute evidence of the old practices that used to flourish in the Emerald Isle.

Originally the towers were located in front of the temples of the gods and were nothing less than special repositories of the divine creative energy. On top of the tall structures it was customary to place one of the received emblems of generation. Among the favourite signs used for this purpose were the cock, the fish, and the arrow. These are still conventionally employed as weather-vanes, the custom having been retained, but secularized.

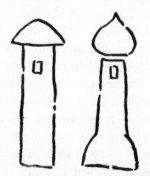

The Round Towers of Ireland

The rooster is especially favoured as a vane, and therefore indicators of the direction of the wind are sometimes simply called "weathercocks." The connexion of that fowl with the sun is clear.

Some people have not inclined towards the tower idea. The Mohammedans use the minaret today, but they favour the great hollow dome. The Jews occasionally use steeple-like effects in their temples, as in the Strassburg Synagogue, but as a rule they, too, prefer the dome. In the days gone by, before Judaism or Christianity as we know them today were thought of, the dome was female, as the minaret was male. Both were spiritual weapons to be used in the interest of life.

10

WHILE one can appreciate the urge to revere the cross of Calvary, it is not so simple to understand the origin of the pre-Christian emblem. To say that it arose from pole-worship will not solve the difficulty, for the question remains: How? The pole is not a cross and is not suggestive of the cross. How, then, did the symbol first come to be adored?

One of the most primitive methods of making fire was by the use of the wooden fire-drill. A piece of soft wood was placed on the ground and held in place with the foot of the operator. A hole was bored in this block, and in the hole a stick of hard wood was rapidly rotated. In order to turn the stick, it was necessary for a transverse beam to be employed. This drill was one of the earliest inventions of the human race.

That the object should have been revered is not strange. The manner of its use suggested power to unschooled minds, and the mysterious reality that sprang from it was in itself worthy of reverence and awe. Long after other and more effective methods of making fire had been devised, the drill was retained for religious and similar uses, just as candles have been retained among us for devout exercises long after the invention of the electric light.

In Europe during the Middle Ages the drill was used for the manufacture of "need fire" which was a magic flame through which cattle were passed for protection against demons and enchantment. The famous Midsummer fires that were kindled regularly by the European peasantry for similar superstitious purposes would have lost their efficacy if they had been lit in an ordinary manner.

11

AMONG the crosses that have been venerated by mankind one of the most important is the well-known *crux ansata*, the handled cross or "key of life" of the Egyptians. This emblem was usually held in the hands of deities.

The "Key of Life"

Like the double triangle, the "key of life," was a mystic representation of the two powers of creation embracing each other. One hint that this is so may be derived from the very name, "key of life," but a stronger hint is afforded by the myth of Osiris, which proves at least that such an object was the sort of thing the Egyptians were naturally given to adoring.

The myth is essentially as follows. The goddess Nut (the sky) was faithless to her husband, who in a rage hurled at her the curse that her child would be born on no month of no year. But it seems that Nut had a further liaison with Thoth, with whom she used to beguile the hours playing draughts. Thoth usually won at these romantic matches, and he managed to win one seventy-second part of every day. He put these all together, and since, according to the story, the Egyptian year then consisted of three hundred and sixty days, the sum of the parts was five complete days. He generously added the five days to the year, and so it happened that Nut's son was able to be born, for those extra days were not properly part of the cycle, and were not counted in the curse.

In spite of the fact that the young Osiris was brought into the world under such questionable circumstances, his own life was more than irreproachable. Indeed, he was the favourite god of the Egyptians, as the beautiful Balder, for whom the Norsemen wept, was the darling of the North. If the myth is to be believed, the people who dwelt in the fertile valley of the Nile knew nothing whatever about crops, and their sole diet was the flesh of their fellow human beings. But Osiris taught the people the arts of agriculture.

Osiris had an enemy in the person of his brother Set, or Typhon, the Egyptian Devil. That jealous divinity surrounded himself with a party of conspirators, and they constructed a coffin which exactly fitted the body of husbandry's father. The box was a beautiful one and was coveted by all beholders. On the occasion of a certain feast, Typhon offered to give this casket to whomsoever it should fit perfectly. One after another the guests tried it, but the dimensions of the box did not tally exactly with their own. Finally Osiris lay in it, whereupon the wicked plotters slammed the lid shut, cemented it down, and cast it with its precious contents into the waters of the Nile.

Now, Osiris was married to his sister Isis, who ruled Egypt in his stead in order that he might have time to go about among the peoples of the earth and spread the arts of civilization. When Isis heard the terrible news of the death of her husband and brother, she went into mourning and became wretched and inconsolable. Unhappy and restless, she went in quest of the body, and in the course of her search encountered some marvellous adventures.

In the mean time the casket was washed out to sea, and it finally reached land at Byblus, in Syria. At once a tree grew up and enclosed in its trunk the coffin and the body. The King of the land saw the tree and admired it, so he had it cut down and used as a pillar in his palace. In some way Isis heard of this; so she journeyed to Byblus, sat down beside a well, and met some maidens from the royal household. Through them she gained admission to the palace, and (precisely like the disguised Demeter) she was appointed by the Queen as a nursemaid for the baby Prince.

When a goddess finds herself in this sort of situation, she usually proceeds to use some celestial magic on her charge in order to render the infant immortal. Also she is likely to be discovered by the babe's mother and thus to be forced to throw off her disguise and reveal her divinity. Isis was no exception. As soon as it was learned that she was indeed a goddess, she begged for the pillar, which was of course given to her, with the compliments of the kingdom. She took out the coffin and thus rescued the body of her beloved.

But Typhon was not to be so readily outwitted. When Isis went on a visit to her son Horus, whom she had conceived in a miraculous manner so that her virginity had not been impaired, the murderer stole the body, cut it into fourteen pieces, and distributed the parts throughout the land so that they might not easily be found and put together again.

Just how Isis managed to find the sacred pieces is not clear from the original accounts, because there was apparently some difference of opinion among the myth-makers on that score. The fact is, however, that she did find them. Ra then took pity on the widow and sent gods down to bind them together in the form of a mummy. That is supposed to be the origin of the custom of swathing bodies in linen. As Osiris was resurrected through that device, so his followers hoped to share his immortality by following the same practice.

Unfortunately, however, the body of the god was not complete. The holiest part had not been discovered. Therefore Isis made him a new one out of wood. That object was always present in the celebration of the great Egyptian mysteries. Reverence was paid to it. It was the creator. Was it the "key of life"?

12

WHETHER or not the *crux ansata* was originally intended to serve as a conventional symbol of the body of Osiris, the fact is that it was an object of veneration, not only throughout Egypt, but elsewhere. The "key of life" was abandoned with the greatest reluctance by the people, even after conversion to higher and nobler faiths. This sort of conservatism is to be noted in spiritual matters generally, but especially in those items of ritual and symbolism that concern the dead.

Thus it happens that even among the early Christians the *crux ansata* was occasionally used to mark the resting-places of the departed. Along with other signs, one finds it on tombs in the catacombs of Rome. There it is in the consecrated ground where the martyrs lie buried beneath the Immortal City.

CHAPTER XVII

The Fear of the Dark and the Legend of Santa Claus

"Even they who worship other gods worship me, although they know it not."

FROM SPEECH OF KRISHNA,
IN THE *BHAGAVAD-GITA*

1

OF all the characters in the supernatural drama, there is none more winning and more gentle than the amiable Santa Claus. His followers, it is true, are children; but there are thousands of little folks who regard him as the most distinguished individual in the universe. There is no such thing as fear of him, for it is well known that he would never inflict harm upon any living being. He is merely a big genial immortal, who cheerfully devotes all his time and energy to the task of making others happy.

Santa owns a workshop at or near the North Pole. There he manufactures toys and desirable objects of various sorts for gratuitous distribution among children. Every year at yule-tide he harnesses his reindeer to his famous sleigh and sets out to visit the homes of countless boys and girls. In theory his policy is to leave presents for good children only; but, as a matter of fact, when the time for decision actually comes, he usually pushes far from his mind the harsh demands of strict justice. He is so large-hearted that he finds it impossible to contemplate the disappointment even of the wicked.

The good man from the North leaves his gifts in specially provided places. The large and bulky presents he ranges round a tree, which has previously been carried into the house, and which is decorated in a colourful manner for the occasion. There are always lights on this tree. Small candles were once used exclusively, but coloured electric bulbs are coming into vogue.

Santa does not deposit all of his presents at the foot of this illuminated indoor tree. Over the fireplace the stockings of the children are hung as receptacles for the smaller of the supernatural gifts. It is well that they are placed in that particular spot, for Santa Claus has a peculiar habit. He never enters the homes of his little hosts by way of either the door or the window or the skylight. His entrances are most unceremonious and most delightfully informal.

Invariably he comes down the chimney.

2

THE full name of Santa Claus is Saint Nicholas. The tradition is that this Saint was Bishop of Myra, in Lycia. He lived a noble life, although, alas, he fell a victim to the fanaticism of men like the Emperor Diocletian. He was persecuted and tortured. He was a martyr to his faith.

It seems that in the time of Saint Nicholas there lived a poor man who had three daughters. It was, of course, impossible for the girls to find husbands, because they had no dowries whatever. In despair the father was on the verge of sending the maidens into the streets to earn their sustenance in a disgraceful manner, when Saint Nicholas kindly provided the dowries.

Because of this act of generosity (so runs at least the traditional explanation) the custom arose for people to give presents secretly on the eve of December sixth, which is the day of Saint Nicholas. In some countries this is still the custom, though in America and elsewhere the practice has been transferred to Christmas.

Unfortunately, the good Saint Nicholas has left behind him no footprints on the sands of time. True we have traditional stories about him, but trustworthy historic records are one and all strangely silent where he is concerned. Thus, it is said that he was present at the Council of Nicæa. But his name does not appear in the roster of those who took part in that gathering. Saint Athanasius was acquainted with the great bishops of the period in question, but he did not seem aware of the existence of Saint Nicholas.

But although from the cold view-point of purely secular history there is no reason to suppose that Nicholas, Bishop of Myra, ever lived, he is widely invoked. He is the protector of children and also of merchants, sailors, travellers, and scholars. Hundreds of churches have been erected in his honour. He is (or was) the patron Saint of Russia.

He is our Santa Claus.

3

THE rites of Saint Nicholas were not always so innocent as they are today. Up until very recently the sixth of December ushered in what was called the "Feast of Fools." In ancient Roman times the month of December was sacred to Saturn, and during the month the notorious Saturnalian revels were celebrated. These sacred ceremonies of Saturn included feasting, dancing, unrestrained indulgence in joy, the giving of presents, and a strange exchange of places by masters and slaves.

The Feast of Fools followed the exact pattern of the Roman Saturnalia. The great dignitaries of the Church were temporarily deposed, and in their stead untrained boys wielded spiritual power. In some places the revels were presided over by the "Boy Bishop." In other places the celebrant was known by such names as the "Abbot of Unreason" or the "Lord of Misrule." The wildest orgies were freely permitted. As time wore on, the moralists in the Church became more and more shocked at the excesses of the feast, and some of their indignant fulminations are still extant. But the revels were popular and they lingered for centuries.

The Feast of Fools was celebrated in France as late as the year 1645.

4

IT would be rash to identify the personality of Santa Claus with that of the god Saturn. Still, it is evident that Santa is a pagan immortal—perhaps, indeed, he is a compound of several divinities.

Why does Santa place his large and bulky gifts at the foot of a tree? Why is the tree brought indoors? Why is it always illuminated? Above all, why does Saint Nicholas come down the chimney? He is a portly creature, and it would surely be more comfortable for him to enter homes by the door. But the narrow flue remains his one and only means of ingress and egress.

The tree with the lighted candles upon it is obviously a relic of the yule-tree, which featured the celebration of the Teutonic feast of yule (or *juul*). In midwinter, when the days were the shortest in the whole year and when it looked very much as if the sun was in danger of extinction, this festival of fire gave strength to the luminary through the power of imitative magic. Nor is this a leaf from ancient history. In some places of Central Germany the ceremony of the yule-log lasted till the middle of the last century.

The details of the yule rites varied in different localities. Sometimes the log was fitted into the base of the hearth, so that it burned ever so slowly and was not completely consumed when the year was over and the time arrived for another section of consecrated wood to take its place. At other times it was merely charred in the fire and then removed, to be replaced during thunder-storms as a protection against the destructive proclivities of the elements.

The virtues of the yule-tree were many. Ashes from it, if strewn over the crop, would prevent mildew, and such evils as were known to result from supernatural opposition to human prosperity. Placed in the water that the cows drank, the wood rendered the animals fruitful. As a charm against certain types of ill fortune, it was well to keep the mysterious object under the bed. Some people retained the magic instrument in the house all the year long and then lighted the new one from a burning fragment of the old. When the tree was in the house, the Devil himself was powerless to work mischief within its walls.

We are now in a position to explain some of the quaint habits of Santa Claus. We understand, at least, why he comes and goes by way of the chimney and why he arranges gifts round the Christmas-tree. In part he is the spirit of the yule-log, which was once burned upon the hearth. Does this not account for his association with the grate, the chimney, and the illuminated indoor tree?

5

THE reader is familiar with the mystic significance of trees in the strange lore of the supernatural. But why should one burn the sacred log? Is there any occult relation between the flame and the blessed emblem of masculine power? Has fire a mystic significance? Is there any special reason for kindling sacred lights at the time of the winter solstice?

It is hardly to be accounted a mere coincidence that the Jews celebrate a feast of lights at the same season of the year. The occasion is the festival of "Dedication," and, according to the Jewish tradition, the rites were instituted to recall the triumph of Judas Maccabeus, when he drove the Syrians out of the Temple and rededicated the holy edifice to the service of the Lord. When this took place, it was found that there was but one day's supply of pure oil on hand to keep the perpetual lamp burning. It required eight full days to find more of the requisite fuel. But in the mean time the light miraculously continued to burn. The supply that under ordinary conditions would have sufficed for but twenty-four hours kept the holy flame alight for one hundred and ninety-two hours. Therefore, every year, observant Israelites kindle one light on the first night of the festival, two on the second, and so on, until on the eighth evening eight candles are burning.

But the Jewish and Christian and Norse feasts of light coincide with others of a similar character which were also celebrated at the same season of the year. Curiously enough, the ancient Christians used to observe the anniversary of the birth of Jesus on January sixth. December twenty-fifth was regarded by the followers of Mithra as the nativity of the sun. It was the policy of the early Church to permit the people to retain their pagan customs, but to reinterpret them more acceptably. In this particular instance what happened is clear. Frazer quotes a Christian writer, a Syrian, who summed up the story in the following words: "The reason why the Fathers transferred the celebration of the sixth of January to the twenty-fifth of December was this: It was a custom of the heathen to celebrate on the same twenty-fifth of December the birthday of the Sun, at which they kindled lights in token of festivity. In these solemnities and festivities the Christians also took part. Accordingly when the doctors of the Church perceived that the Christians had a leaning to this festival, they took counsel and resolved that the true Nativity should be solemnized on that day and the festival of the Epiphany on the sixth of January. Accordingly, along with this custom, the practice has prevailed of kindling fires till the sixth."

6

MITHRA was born in a cave (according to the Persian story), in a state of obscurity and poverty. A few shepherds only were present to welcome the god, who had come to bless mankind and the world. For a long time the babe lived in the cavern, till at length he received the sacred mark, familiar to us as the sign of the covenant with Abraham. Then, and not till then, did he leave the lowly abode that offered him his first shelter. When he went out into the open, he appeared as "a shining pillar of light."

There were, according to Mithraism, two great powers in the cosmos, one Light and the other Darkness—which is but another way of saying that one was Life and the other Death. Mithra aligned himself with Life, and he devoted himself to fighting the battles of the Sun. The crowning achievement of his life was the slaying of the mystic bull, whose blood fertilized Mother Earth and caused her to bring forth corn. This is graphically represented in the pictures that were once used in Mithra's mysteries. In some of the sculptures no blood flows from the wound inflicted on the bull by the hero. Instead, stalks of corn are dropping from the sacred cut.

Mithra's holy day was Sunday. On that day work was forbidden to his worshippers, except such labour as was particularly helpful to the crops. The law of Constantine which went into effect in A.D. 321 was an attempt on the part of the Emperor to combine the practices of Mithraism, which had been his faith, and those of Christianity, to which he had been converted. The law read: "Let all the judges and townspeople, and the occupation of all trades rest on the venerable day of the Sun; but let those who are situated in the country freely and at full liberty attend to the business of agriculture; because it often happens that no other day is so fit for sowing corn and planting vines: lest, the critical moment having been allowed to slip, men should lose the commodities granted of Heaven."

Especially sacred to Mithra, however, was the day of his

nativity. On that day, and also on every Sunday, the worship included a number of ritual items. Most important among these was the practice of eating the flesh and drinking the blood of the bull. Whoever performed this rite was brought closer to the divine hero and approached nearer to salvation.

There is little room for doubt as to the real origin of the Mithraic feast of the winter solstice. In a general way it is the fact that all of the early rituals that marked that significant anniversary in the sun's career were intended as magic devices to induce the orb to renew its life. The connexion that the ancients believed to exist between the rays of the luminary and the idea of rebirth may be learned from the old custom of Egypt and Syria. The priests went into their caves, and promptly at midnight they rushed forth with the cry on their lips: "The virgin has brought forth! The light is waxing!" In Egypt the new-born flame was actually represented by the image of a babe, which was shown to the worshippers in the course of these midwinter rites.

7

THE sun was usually regarded as something more than a fiery body that gave warmth to the earth. It was the seat of male energy, and its function was to fructify Mother Earth and to cause her to bring forth living things. In so far as sacred lights were representations of the sun, they too partook of this mystic potency. Therefore, in addition to their effect as charms to bring back the dying Sol, they worked wonders as symbols of life.

Among the great fire-festivals of Europe was that of May Day. We have learned the general nature of that occasion and have noted how it degenerated from an anniversary pregnant with significance to a mere children's observance.

The true inwardness of May Day may be inferred from such customs as that which prevailed till fairly recently in Russia. At least as late as 1855 it was the habit for maidens of the lower classes to meet in some lonesome spot to light their fire. They would then jump over the flame, taking turns. It occasionally happened that men were discovered near enough to permit them to watch these mystic rites. When that happened, the girls were so enraged that they killed and sacrificed the offending peepers. The observances were secret ones, and intruding males were thought to be justly punished.

But where was the harm if the men did watch? The harm lay in the meaning of the ritual. Leaping through fires, sacred ones, is a widespread practice, and is always indulged in for the same reason. The fire, being a representative of Father Sun, is charged with generative potency, some of which may be acquired by the leapers. Among the Celts, to cite one example, it was the custom to pass cattle through the May Day fires. This rendered the animals fruitful and it also endowed them with some virtue against witchcraft. In other words, the May Day flame possessed the identical power that resided also in the charred log of yule.

8

THE ceremonies of the may-pole are at least æsthetic. The dances may be beautiful, and the pageantry may be impressive. But what shall we say about Hallow-e'en? Removing other people's gates, annoying neighbours, starting fires, and soaping windows have little to commend them on an æsthetic score. The fact is, however, that the original intent of the strange ritualism was practical. In pagan days Hallow-e'en was an important religious event, and its purpose was the familiar one of enlisting the aid of Life as man's ally.

Originally, All Hallows Even, or Hallow-e'en, was one

of the annual occasions when all the ghosts of the departed returned to visit their former abodes. That there were such occasions was well known among the superstitious, and there were others when no spirits of that sort were allowed to walk in the land of the living at all. On Christmas Eve, for instance, no ghosts were suffered to be abroad; but on Hallow-e'en they were everywhere. Similarly they were all out on May Day, or on the night preceding (which is known as Walpurgis-night).

In addition to the spirits of the dead, the witches were all out on those occasions. They rode through the air on broomsticks or they were mounted on black cats, which were transformed into coal-black chargers for this purpose. The human servants of Satan went at such times to their famous sabbaths, or diabolical conventions. The fairies, gnomes, and elves were all abroad on such fateful evenings, so that, especially at Hallow-e'en, it was literally the fact that Pandemonium had broken loose.

The situation was a serious one for all good people. The eerie malignity of ghosts is well known, and on evenings like those we are considering, that wickedness was combined with all the evil of the whole force of hell. Still, it was necessary to use tact. To insult the ghostly visitors would add fuel to the flame of their vindictiveness. On the other hand, the witches and their kind were openly at war with all good folks, so that no one ran any risk of further infuriating them by a frank acceptance of the demoniacal challenge. The task of the community was twofold. On the one hand, it was necessary to play the tactful host to the ghosts, and on the other, to engage in mortal combat with the unseen, and therefore doubly terrible, subjects of Satan and Lilith.

In the face of all this, it is not easy to explain the spirit of levity and hilarity that is bound up with the occasion today. Still, it is well to remember that, in the normal evolution of convention, it sometimes happens that games which were used in the first place for the purpose of divining the future will be transformed into games played for amusement alone. Now Hallow-e'en was a time when divination was indulged in. For instance, in the Scottish highlands, people used to dive for apples and a sixpence to determine the future. Whoever could recover either an apple or the sixpence with his mouth (it was not permissible to use the teeth) was destined to be lucky. It is possible that the light-heartedness now connected with the anniversary is to be explained on the basis of the fact that divination was once practised at that time.

9

IN waging any war, whether against fairies or palpable men of flesh and blood, it was essential to use magic. In dealing with the wraiths of the departed, one was never wholly safe, unless armed with amulets and charms.

The particular embodiment of sanctity that was actually employed on Hallow-e'en and May Day was fire. On the latter occasion the paraphernalia necessary to spiritual safety included also whips. Of course, it is obvious that, in addition to any mysterious force that might have reposed in the flames and lashes, they were both effective in scaring the demons away. In the good old days witches were familiar with burning and flogging, so that the sight and heat of the fire, the smell of the smoke, and the ominous cracking of the whips, all tended to fill them with horror and helped to induce them to depart.

That some such simple idea was, at least in part, responsible for the ceremonies is clear from the nature of the rites. Not only were fires kindled, but burning hoops were rolled downhill, and flaming disks were thrown into the air. If any witches were overhead on brooms or happened to be riding by on transformed cats, they faced serious danger. So on the eve of May Day boys sometimes assembled and cracked whips. As far as the sound was heard, the country was cleared of witches. It would be possible to explain all of this on the basis of the idea that the intention was to frighten the evil beings by suggesting to them the thought of torture.

Nevertheless it is well to remember that there was a time when it was thought that creative power resided in both whips and fires. The flame and the lash figure among the symbols of many faiths. Sacrifices were always burned on the altars of gods. Vesta and goddesses like her maintained sacred fires, and they were very particular about their care. In the Temple at Jerusalem the Jews kept the perpetual light, which consumed nothing but "pure olive-oil," and the olive has been a sex symbol from the earliest days of which we have any record.

The whip, while it is not so universal a religious symbol as fire, is nevertheless far from rare among the well-known instruments of devotion. The flagellants of the Middle Ages were monks who carried straps and publicly flogged each other as they promenaded along the roads. At the feast of the Lupercalia in Rome the youths stripped themselves and took in their hands thongs of goat-hide, in order to whip all the girls they might meet. Nor did the maidens shrink from the whippings. They gladly and eagerly submitted to that chastisement with an object that possessed the virtue of life and conferred a mysterious benefit upon those with whom it came in contact. The sculptures and artistic representations of many peoples show gods holding in their hands "quickeners," which were merely whips, types of the serpent and the magic wand.

The whip is snaky in shape. It is sometimes identified

with the serpent, and its significance in comparative religions is the same. We still speak of a certain variety of lash as a "black snake." Abnormal psychology knows a type of degenerate who is so weighted down with racial memories that he identifies the whip with the object for which it stood in the crude symbolism of long ago.

10

THE use of fire on such occasions as Walpurgis-night and Hallow-e'en offers a clue which may enable us to understand why it is that human beings are so frequently afraid of the dark. There are at bottom two reasons for this universal fear; one is physical, and the other is spiritual. From a purely material view-point, there was ample cause for the terror our fathers must have felt in primitive times when darkness set in. The jungle awakens in the night, and many beasts of prey go forth in search of food. Luminescent eyes peered at men out of the blackness, and one never knew when one's body was to be converted into food for a carnivorous creature.

But combined with this physical cause was a spiritual one. To this day, in the homes of the superstitious, ghosts walk at night, and the air is filled with devils, if not witches. "Vampires," or blood-sucking ghosts, used to rise and imbibe the life fluid of sleeping persons—always at night.

Still, one may well wonder why it is that the night is more terrible than the day—that is to say, why the spirits of harm are active in darkness rather than in the light.

It is important to remember that, as a rule, primitive folks regarded the Sun and the Earth as man and wife. Although the divine astronomical pair required each other for the production of living things, still each alone could transmit power. For instance, it was notorious that the Sun could render a maiden fruitful and could even become the father of her child. Sometimes this was regarded as a blessing, and we still hear the occult expression: "Happy the bride the sun shines on." Some people, however, were afraid of this quality of sunlight, and a canopy was held above the heads of the bridal pair to prevent impregnation on the part of the god. To this day Orthodox Jews employ such a canopy at all weddings, even when they are solemnized at night.

The Earth also could work wonders through its power of generation. The Greeks knew of a giant named Antæus who was the darling of this All-Mother. When he was thrown to the ground, Earth renewed his vigour and he was therefore practically invincible in a wrestling-match. Heracles finally conquered him by holding him in the air and strangling him where his divine mother could not fill him with her mystic strength.

Canopies were not merely used by brides and grooms, but also by kings. Some monarchs are allowed neither to touch the ground with their bare feet, nor to have the rays of the sun shine directly on their heads. The sultan of Morocco has a sacred umbrella held over his head whenever he ventures out of doors. The mikado is so holy that he is never exposed to the direct rays of the sun and he never touches the ground.

This curious prohibition applies sometimes to young girls who show signs of maturing into womanhood. Such maids are sometimes hung in hammocks in the dark, and sometimes they are suspended in dark cages. One reason why the mistletoe was so mysterious is that the shoot is always between the earth and the sun. It is shielded from both.

The reason for all this is not far to seek. There was a time when holiness and love were one and the same. Now, holiness is always full of danger. If the earth or the sun came in contact with the maturing girl or the king, the results would be disastrous to all concerned. The sun might die, the earth become barren, the king languish, and the maiden wither up into a mere skeleton.

11

IF ghosts wandered at night rather than by day, this was because they could not stand the light of the sun. They were exorcized by the sexual energy the luminary contained. The devil who served Faust was named Mephistopheles, a word derived from the Greek, which means (freely translated) "the one who does not love the light." The forces of Life were always those of light; and the powers of Darkness were always those of death. Ahura-Mazda in Persia was the deity of goodness, while Ahriman was the Devil. This distinction was widespread, and it is so still.

The sun was a blessing to man in two different ways. In the first place it afforded physical sustenance by making the crops grow, the herds prosper, and the women fruitful. In the second place it caused the demons to flee in confusion.

Under those conditions it is hardly strange that among every people there is an obvious coincidence between the principal devout exercises and the seasonal crises of the sun. Summer and winter, spring and fall, are each ushered in with special ceremonial observances, and the solstices are always occasions for rites.

These rites generally included the kindling of holy fire. Many of them are still feasts of lights.

12

SACRED fire differed from ordinary flame. The distinction between them is made in the Scripture, where we are told of the punishment of two men who inadvertently introduced the wrong kind on the altar of Yahweh. To this day people use candles exclusively for holy purposes in spite of the convenience of such modern inventions as the electric light. In the same way, no matter what devices were invented in the past, the religionists of yore clung to the friction method, or to some equally mysterious one.

The worshippers of the Aryan god Agni use fire on the occasions of birth, marriage, and death. The Parsees put flame at the head of corpses. It is the custom of many peoples to put candles at that place for mystic reasons. Sometimes the candle is said to be symbolic of immortality.

Still there were some fire-worshippers who held all flames sacred and made no distinction between sacred and profane fires. The Medes, for example, never put out any conflagration, for such an act would have been tantamount to putting a stumbling-block in the way of the god of life. It would have amounted to giving aid and comfort to the god of darkness, the Adversary, the force of death.

13

WE are now in a position to understand why the yule-log was periodically burned. We also have a partial clue which will help us to understand the reason why Santa Claus, who is in a sense the spirit of yule, is so genial, so loving, and so merciful. But Santa is a composite personality. In so far as he is built up of elements that were contributed by the Norse peoples, he is an embodiment of the yule and the log. But southern strains have been blended with northern in the formation of his personality. He is in part the spirit of Saturn, in whose honour the Romans used to observe, during the month of December, the feast of the Saturnalia. For the present it will be necessary to take leave of Santa, at least until we have had some opportunity to review the facts with reference to the romantic Roman feast of December and to note the effects it has had upon subsequent customs and conventions.

In the mean time we must not forget that the ideas of early man with regard to the importance of fire were based upon a substructure of truth. All civilization is founded on fire. It has been a great ally of man in his struggle against the dangers and horrors that have beset him. It has enabled man to invade cold countries and to dwell in them in comfort. It enables him to cook his food, and he is the one animal that is able to do so. In short, it affords power.

Perhaps our fathers did well to recognize the glory that fire contained. Perhaps they were gifted with something like prophetic insight when they ascribed to it a mystic force—the force of life. They were not radically wrong when they sought to acquire power from it. Their mistake was one of method. They tried to obtain the virtues of fire by leaping through it, by making painful contact with it, by offering sacrifices to it, and even by feeding it with the precious flesh and blood of their own kind.

The story of civilization might well begin with the words: "In the beginning there was fire." To the animal that discovered its uses all things were added. In time it came to be identified with life itself. As Yahweh was jealous of the knowledge that came to man through the eating of the apple, so the gods of Olympus were enraged when Prometheus stole the flame from on high and gave it to humanity.

Unconsciously we still recognize a subtle connexion between the idea of fire and that of life. One recalls the immortal metaphor of the Bard of Avon:

> Put out the light, and then put out the light:
> If I quench thee, thou flaming minister,
> I can again thy former light restore,
> Should I repent me; but once put out thy light,
> Thou cunning'st pattern of excelling nature,
> I know not where is that Promethean heat
> That can thy light relume.

CHAPTER XVIII

The Carnival and the Saturnalia

"The boast of heraldry, the pomp of
pow'r,
And all that beauty, all that wealth
e'er gave,
Awaits alike th' inevitable hour:
The paths of glory lead but to the
grave."

THOMAS GRAY

1

FOR the most part the devotion accorded to a symbol of life in the days gone by was of a joyous nature. The Dance of the Gods bubbled over with effervescent hilarity. Thus in the north of Europe men and women used to be tied together, and together they danced about a pole. The Europeans also indulged in a ceremony of heaving a maiden into the air. After the heaving the men and women piously kissed each other, and it was understood that the result of this process was luck.

But there is a sad aspect of this devotion. The adoration of a symbol of life frequently involved the slaughter of human beings. In the worship of poles, for example, it was sometimes the custom for human victims to be executed upon them by way of sacrifice either to the god or to his wife. Such sacrifices were offered both to Father Sun and Mother Earth—and for the same reason. Both the father and the mother divinities were concerned with creation, and it was not possible for them to dispense life continually, unless occasionally they were enabled to replenish their supply of the precious substance. That substance was animation, and accordingly it was necessary for them to receive from time to time some of the life they were in the habit of distributing.

As a matter of fact, this is the foundation of most sacrifice. Unless the god receives the first-fruits, he cannot continue to function. In the case of the gods of life, it was necessary that human beings be slaughtered in their honour. Thus, among the Dravidians the Earth required not merely human meat, but quivering flesh, warm from the body of the consecrated victim. Similarly in Mexico the Sun demanded hosts of human beings, who were bent back over the symbolic pyramidal altars, while their hearts were deftly torn out by the priests. In quite the same way the European fires demanded human flesh on such occasions as May Day and Hallow-e'en. If those fires had been merely intended to burn the witches or to frighten them, it would have been superfluous to feed them with living men. But they were repositories and distributors of life, and as such it was essential that they receive this offering on a principle similar to that of the first-fruits.

There was, however, another reason for human sacrifice. Among numerous peoples the god himself had to die, in order to prevent his growing old and feeble and thus causing the world itself to grow old and feeble likewise. All over the earth we find relics of ceremonies in which the deity was represented by a man. The man ruled for a while in splendour, but at a particular time he was deliberately killed and his place taken by a younger and stronger individual. Strange as it may seem, this sort of thing was the root from which the institution of monarchy has sprouted. The usual history is as follows: First, the king is the god who is slaughtered in order that his life may be mystically renewed. Eventually there arises a king who is strong enough to prevent the execution, and the ceremony is altered so that a mock king is killed instead. In this process, which has repeated itself countless times in different sections of the globe, the king loses his divinity. He is a god no longer—but he rules by divine right.

2

ONCE upon a time, so the ancient Romans believed, there lived a good King of Italy whose name was Saturn. Like the Egyptian Osiris, he taught his people the arts of agriculture, instituted laws, and established the most glorious and most halcyon civilization the peninsula had ever known.

Saturn was more than a king. He was a god of husbandry, and accordingly while he was incarnate in the flesh, the crops grew in abundance. Moreover, all property was held in common; everyone was satisfied with his lot, and there was no quarrel in the land. There was no slavery, and there was no tyranny. Warfare was unknown. The calm and peace of Eden suffused all of Italy. The age of Saturn was the golden age—the mythical time when the hard world of the senses was a dreamy and luxurious paradise.

Exactly how the divine King was translated to the halls of the gods is not clear. But it is known that he suddenly vanished from the haunts of men, and the age of gold came to an end. The people, however, did not forget the merry monarch who had come to earth to confer upon them so many blessings. Numerous shrines were devoted to his service; the month of December and the seventh day of every week were held sacred to him; and every twelfth month the whole population gave itself over to the joyous celebrations of his holy festival, the Saturnalia.

3

THE Saturnalia might serve as a splendid example of the sort of worship we have ventured to call the "Dance of the Gods," Essentially it was a revel, a magnificent collective carouse on the part of the devout. But it was more than this, and because of its other features which throw so much light on the story of the supernatural, it deserves a special chapter for its elucidation. Not only did the annual feast of Saturn involve the reversal of status on the part of masters and slaves, not only did it include the election of a temporary monarch whose every whim was scrupulously gratified, regardless of how degrading and how disastrous it was to the purity of others; but the feast culminated in genuine tragedy. At the close of the festivities the mock king was required to step to the altar and cut his own throat.

Though the details of the Saturnalia are shocking to the tender sensibilities of moderns, it must be remembered that the entire festival was at one time a species of sacred drama. The levity, the universal and unrestrained happiness, the licence granted to bondsmen, the feasting, the dancing, and the drinking were all intended to portray the paradisiacal conditions that prevailed when Saturn himself walked among men. The temporary king represented the god, and if he enjoyed boundless privileges in that consecrated role, his rights were no greater than those accorded to other human representatives of divinity, such as the Pharaohs of ancient Egypt, the priests of Bel, and the Incas of Peru.

But all of this glad carousal came to an abrupt end before the week was over. The drama closed with the bitter scene of human sacrifice. The man slaughtered was not a mere victim dedicated to the god, but was the god himself, or, what amounted to the same thing, his official representative.

In the course of time the tragic feature of the ceremony came to be omitted. In its place certain symbolic gestures were made—as if the king were going to be killed. But far from the city, in the outlying districts where the progress of culture was slow, human impersonators of Saturn were dispatched every year.

We have an authentic record of such a sacrifice as late as

A. D. 303. Perhaps the hideous custom lasted longer than that, in the remote and inaccessible sections of the Empire.

4

IN different parts of Europe today it is the custom to hold certain annual carnivals of one kind or another. Some of the celebrations are extremely elaborate, so much so that they frequently attract the camera men of the cinema. When the picturesque parades are depicted on the screen, it is probable that many observers fail to appreciate the development of the rites or to understand the meaning of the curious symbolism. Much of the latter is doubtless interpreted as mere drollery, born of the fertile brains of clowns and professional entertainers. Perhaps some such idea is present in the minds of most of the participants also, for many of them must be quite unaware of the history of the strange processions, and of the hoary antiquity to which they may be traced.

If the folk-ceremonies of Europe were nothing more than theatrical productions, intended to amuse, or perhaps to inspire, the populace, why should the same gestures be repeated year by year, and why should the same designs be employed again and again? If it is entertaining to watch the motions of gigantic manikins, does not the jest lose its savour after a while for people who, from childhood, have witnessed the identical puppets parading in the identical manner once every year?

The fact is that folk-ceremonies, however humorous they may appear in this age, were once sacred rites, to be compared with such dramatic representations as the mysteries of Eleusis, the weeping for Adonis, and the joyous Saturnalia.

Consider, for example, the gigantic marionettes, to which allusion has just been made. They originally represented the colossal demons who, according to the idea once prevalent in the north of Europe, were the rightful owners of the soil which human beings dared to cultivate, and upon which they built their homes. It was necessary to propitiate those supernatural landlords and to induce them to permit men and women to remain as tenants on the land. The parades were among the methods used to gain the goodwill of the demoniac proprietors of the ground. Originally, the ceremonies were not amusing at all. They were matters of great moment and were doubtless conducted with all the solemnity due such significant occasions.

In Rome, both at the Bacchanalia and the Saturnalia, disguises were worn. Certain celebrants covered their faces with masks, and their bodies with white clothes that resembled the attire of a corpse. As a matter of fact, the people thus dressed were intentionally disguising themselves as ghosts in order to propitiate a particular group of spirits, who themselves were originally ghosts. From this sort of thing the modern pastime of masquerading has developed.

5

IT so happens that in many of the folk-carnivals of Europe, which take place on the Sunday before Ash Wednesday, the custom exists of pretending to kill the king, or chief celebrant. Sometimes the honoured personification of the spirit of the event is an effigy, which may even sit upon a throne for its brief day of glory. But in the end it is destroyed. Sometimes it is burned upon a pyre.

It is obvious that these carnival celebrations are lineal descendants of the Saturnalia. But the question remains, why were they shifted from December to the Sunday before Ash Wednesday?

The answer is that when the Christian religion was carried to the lands in question, the Church made a most laudable effort to stamp out all pagan religious institutions. But this was difficult, because the inborn conservatism of the people prompted them to retain the ceremonies and feasts to which they had been accustomed from of old. Accordingly the Church proceeded to invest the popular celebrations and folk-rituals with a Christian meaning. Wherever this was not possible, the alternative was so to arrange the religious calendar that there would be no time for pagan celebrations. This was done so effectively that the old feasts were pushed aside—there was little opportunity to observe them. They were bunched together, so to speak, and were observed when the calendar permitted. The custom thus grew of celebrating the old revels on a particular night, although in former times the celebrations had been spread over a number of days. In the course of time this insitution became famous. Such is the story of the European carnival.

6

IT must not be imagined, however, that the Saturnalia have left no traces in the merry celebrations that are associated with the month of Decembe.. The Abbot of Unreason, the Lord of Misrule, the Boy Bishop, and other rulers of the mediæval Feast of Fools were all, though doubtless unconscious of the fact, impersonators of Saturn. Until recently, as we have discovered, these were occasions of boundless joy, in which people did not hesitate to give themselves over to the wildest excesses.

Among the European winter festivities of former days was the Feast of the Ass, which was finally stamped out in the fifteenth century. Sometimes the ass was introduced in the revels of the Feast of Fools, but there was also a special festival observed in honour of that animal. In the form in which we know it the whole thing was a sort of burlesque, but, as with other conventional days of merry-making, its origin must have been connected with a serious form of worship.

The celebration of the Feast of the Ass at Beauvais was much as follows: The prettiest girl in the community was

placed upon an ass. The girl held a baby (or a doll). There
was a procession from the Cathedral to the Church of St.
Étienne. Mass was then recited, but when the time came for
the congregation to respond, the people called out the ejaculation "Hinham" (which was equivalent to "He-haw") three
times.

The origin of the Feast of the Ass is not known. It was
probably a pagan rite that survived from Greco-Roman
times. One can understand the romantic features of the festival when one considers that the ass was sacred to Bacchus.

7

THERE are winter revels in modern times that remind one of
the old Roman celebration of the Saturnalia. At these affairs
it is the habit to throw confetti, which calls to mind the real
grains of wheat or barley that used to be thrown for magical
purposes. The pointed hat, now used in fun, was originally
the head-dress of a free man, but slaves were suffered to
wear it during the Saturnalia, as a mark of their temporary
freedom.

It cannot be doubted that Santa Claus contains within
himself some of the qualities of the merry Saturn. Certainly
the genial immortal who devotes himself to the manufacture
and distribution of presents bears a resemblance to the Roman deity who presided over the golden age.

CHAPTER XIX

The Queue of Heaven

The Queen of Heaven

> " . . . *How gladly would I meet*
> *Mortality, my sentence, and be earth*
> *Insensible! how glad would lay me*
> *down*
> *As in my mother's lap!"*
>
> JOHN MILTON

1

ACCORDING to the second chapter of Genesis, Eve was not created as part of the original plan of God. Only after He had made Adam, did it occur to Him that it was not good for the man to live alone. A helpmate was necessary. One by one the animals were inspected with the end in view of discovering a fitting companion for the father of mankind. But those lower beings were all inadequate or undesirable, though Adam gave them the names that they bear to this day. Therefore God put his creature into a deep sleep, extracted a rib from him, and fashioned Eve.

The woman thus was not part of the plan, but was, as someone has suggested, an "afterthought." Nor was she an auspicious afterthought. She it was who succumbed to the fatal temptation of the snake, and through her wiles Adam also fell from grace, thus barring himself and the whole human family from the lazy and (it must be confessed) ignorant pleasures of a tropical Eden.

In like manner, the Greek gods gave Pandora as a present to the man they had created. The woman was instructed under no circumstances to open the box that was entrusted to her care. But curiosity, apparently looked upon as a distinctly female trait, overcame Pandora, and she lifted the lid. Instantly all the troubles that have since afflicted humanity escaped and spread themselves all over the world. It was impossible to imprison them again in the casket. Had it not been for this ill-starred gift of the gods, human life would been halcyon, without care and without evil.

On this point the myths of the whole world are unanimous. The world was created for man and not for woman. The female was proffered as a gift to her lord; and she was a gift that he soon discovered was decidedly faulty. According to the Babylonian account, men even returned the gift, and God took the woman back. Then the husband was lonely and asked again for his wife. This shuttling back and forth continued for a while, till the creator in his wrath refused to receive back his present. "You cannot live with her and you cannot live without her" was his divine comment. So he punished the first man for his vacillation by forcing him to retain his wife and compelling him to live in the same world with so inferior a creature.

The various faiths of man have continued this tradition, which dates back to the remotest antiquity. The Mohammedans look forward to a graded heaven, where the faithful will not merely eat and drink, but will enjoy the company of ethereal maidens. Still, it must be remembered that the heavenly girls are specially designed for the pleasure of the elect. Earthly women will not be admitted to the paradise of Islam.

The regular morning prayer of Orthodox Jews contains a clause: "Blessed art Thou, O Lord, King of the universe, who has not created me a woman." When a female worshipper is reciting her morning prayer and comes to that passage, she substitutes for it the admirable formula of pious resignation: "Blessed art Thou, O Lord our God, King of the universe, who has created me according to His will."

The Church of England, in its traditional marriage-service, formulates its estimate of woman in the following words: "For after this manner in the old time the holy women also who trusted in God adorned themselves, being in subjection to their own husbands; even as Sarah obeyed Abraham, calling him Lord; whose daughters ye are as long as ye do well, and are not afraid with any amazement."

2

THE science of biology clashes directly with mythology as represented, let us say, in the story of Pandora. Contrary to the idea that man was created first and that woman was merely a gift to him (called into being by a sort of divine mistake and intended as a servant of the male), the fact is that the lowest forms of life are really female, if they may be regarded as having any sex at all. Certain it is that animals on the bottom rungs of the ladder of evolution exhibit powerful females and puny males—when they reach the stage at which there is a division betwen the sexes. It is the habit of the spider mother to eat her tiny and insignificant spouse after he has rendered the one service he is capable of performing. The male bee is the drone, whose position in the hive is that of both pariah and victim.

But as evolution goes on, we find the male increasing in virility and in importance. Thus among polygamous cattle the bull is the master of his herd, and in the curious social stratification that has recently been found to exist in the barn-yard, the rooster is always the ruler and the privileged leader.

The story of the evolution of the sexes is the story of a struggle between them, in which the female has gradually been worsted. Little wonder is it that man, triumphant at last, should declare himself supreme by divine right and should assert that his supremacy is rooted in nature—that it is part and parcel of the scheme of creation itself.

There is, however, another reason why the weaker and fairer sex has been consistently degraded in the various institutions that humanity has called into being. Originally, as we have seen, the savages who inhabited the world did not understand the true significance of manhood and womanhood. Their ignorance of nature in general extended to the field of generation, and they had not the slightest idea of the relation between love on the one hand and creation on the other. Finally, however, the observations of gifted individuals produced the first great heresy—namely, that love is the kiss of life.

At once this function, so strange and so transcendentally important, became an object of worship; all human beliefs and institutions were revolutionized; and reverence and adoration were directed towards the great god of increase. This did not, as might be supposed, give added dignity to the position of woman, the mother. On the contrary, the effect of the discovery was the very opposite. It was imagined that the important function of procreation was that of the male, and that the duty of the female was merely to harbour and nurture the life that had been planted by her spouse. Thus the seed is planted in the ground, and while the work of Mother Earth is important, still, at best she feeds and succours the life that has been given to her.

The result of such theorizing on the part of early man was a worship, not of sex in general, but of masculinity, looked upon as the sole cause of creation. The earliest symbols of life are male, such as the oak-tree, the stone, the serpent, and the erect pole. But in time further observation made it plain that motherhood was also potent in this matter of generation, which, indeed, resulted from the two forces acting together.

3

THE outgrowth of this development was the calling into existence of three kinds of divinities. The first deity in every part of the world was the father, but soon there appeared also the goddess and the divinity who was at once male and female.

The earliest goddesses were abnormally powerful (as had been their male counterparts), and their power was manifest in their bodily formations. Thus the Ephesian Artemis was the All-Mother, and the manner in which she was represented may be inferred from her name, "Many-breasted Artemis."

Artemis of the many breasts probably did not spread her worship among the early Norsemen. Yet the Norse goddess Isa was characterized by the same strange bodily formation, which attribute was intended, as in such goddesses everywhere, to indicate that the divinity in question was the All-Mother.

Possibly the most interesting mother in the whole history of the supernatural is the Chinese and Japanese goddess Kwan Yon, whose name is variously spelled, Qwaon, Kwan-wan, etc. She has a thousand arms, in every one of which she holds a different symbol of sex. Like Venus, a type of whom she undoubtedly is, she rose from the waves; and she sits upon a lotus. Sometimes she is a mermaid. Sometimes babies grow out of her whole body; her fingers and toes and entire form simply exude the little creatures.

Kwan Yon was sought after in marriage, but she refused to be wed. Because of this she found it necessary to descend into hell. She might have remained there for ever, were it not for the circumstance that the light of her radiance filled the nether regions with glory, and hell became as heaven— to the infinite disgust of its diabolical ruler. The King of hell therefore sent her back to the upper realm on a lotus flower.

By this time her father was an old and feeble man, and Kwan Yon was touched with a feeling of commendable pity. She took flesh from her holy arm and employed it to rejuvenate and invigorate her parent. It is not difficult to notice the similarity that obtains between the career of this goddess and the life stories of gods like Attis and Osiris, and goddesses like Persephone and Ishtar.

Among the symbols that Kwan Yon holds in her hands are the whip or quickener, the ark of life, the sacred flame, the winged sun, the tree of life, and the pendant cross.

4

MANY of the symbols that are sacred to this mother are not female at all, but male. The candle, the whip, the flame, the sun, for example, are signs of the father, just as the lotus, the ark, and the fish are signs of the mother.

The reason for this seeming confusion is that motherhood and fatherhood are interdependent. The continuity and increase of life depended upon the union and co-operation of both of these mystic forces.

The mother holding in her hands the signs of the father represents a beginning of the conception that flowered in the notion of the divinity who was at once father and mother. These deities are of two kinds—the god with female characteristics, and the goddess with male attributes. Brahma is a god, but for the purpose of creating the world he added another sex unto himself. This feature is conventionally represented among his devotees by showing the deity seated upon a lotus.

If male gods sometimes showed female attributes because they were creators, so for the same reason goddesses sometimes bore the characteristics of the male. Adonis was occasionally both man and woman; and Astarte was now and again both woman and man. Even Venus, the queen of beauty, and the recipient of the golden apple, was occasionally part man. To show this she was represented as bearded. The Venus at Cyprus had a beard, but wore the clothes of a woman. The Venus at Paphos had not only a beard, but also other qualities of a man.

The worship of a god who was womanly, or of a goddess who was manly, was always the most obscene, and from our point of view the most degenerate, the world has ever known. It was a common thing for the priests of the Queen of Heaven to sacrifice their manly strength, not merely by abstaining from marriage but by injuring themselves with knives during the bloody rites in honour of the goddess. At some of the ceremonies men used to disguise themselves as women, while women disguised themselves as men, and under cover of those "sacred" masks the worshippers indulged in excesses, which hardly lend themselves to description in terms of decency and delicacy.

Of course, it must be understood that the worship of Adonis and that of the Queen of Heaven were both thoroughly moral and proper according to the lights of the people who engaged in them. Such rites must have contained at least the germs of higher development, for from such crude beginnings the grandest and purest spiritual expressions in the world have slowly evolved. This is surely indicated by the fact that the title "Adonis," which is the appellation of Tammuz, is really the same word as "Adonay," which is still used in the temples of the Jews as a name of God. And as for the sacrifice of the right to have children, it is a simple matter to trace its subsequent development and to note its presence, albeit in modified and spiritualized form, among us today.

5

THE Queen of Heaven was not a lonely goddess, worshipped in one isolated section of the globe. Her temples dotted the earth, and her altars may be found wherever human beings have felt the urge to bow down before the All-Mother. The Queen was not merely the Venus of antiquity; she was also Io, Isis, Astarte, Ishtar, Mylitta, Maia, Juno, Diana, Artemis, Hera, Rhea, Cybele, Ceres, Frigga, and a host of others.

Although those goddesses were mothers, they were none
the less virgins (or many of them were). Diana was noted
for her romantic adventures; yet she was a virgin and was
honoured as such. Juno was usually not undefiled in this
sense, but once every year she bathed at a certain fountain,
and the waters restored her virginity. Isis was the sister-wife
of Osiris; still, when she became the mother of Horus, she
did so in a mysterious manner. She was a bird hovering over
the body of her deceased husband, and thus she became a
mother.

In this connexion one may remark that the religious art
of almost every people shows among its most sacred representations the mother and child. Sometimes included in
these sculptures are other symbols, as in the famous ones of
Isis, Horus, and the Fish.

CHAPTER XX

The Fish and the Mermaid

"It is only the ignorant who despise education."

PUBLIUS SYRUS

1

AMONG the inhabitants of the supernatural world some are (in form) half human and half animal. Satan is a well-known example. He does not bear a perfect resemblance to man, for he has the leg and hoof of a goat, and the horns of a bull. The god Pan and his subjects the fauns and satyrs were similar in appearance to Satan. The centaurs were composite creatures, part man and part horse. All such beings were symbolic. They indicated originally certain ideas connected with the mystery of love.

One of the most picturesque of all the dwellers in Fairyland is the mermaid. She is half maiden and half fish. Today she is regarded as an imaginary person, and even children usually doubt her reality. But she was once important among the immortals, and she lingered as a genuine supernatural long after the advent of the higher faiths.

Thus it is recorded that in the year 1440, during a flood in the Netherlands, some girls who were rowing a boat met a mermaid. They lifted the strange creature into their skiff and conveyed her to the town of Edam. There the child of the sea received a domestic education. She wore woman's clothes. Moreover she was religious, for whenever she passed a sacred emblem, she performed her devotions.

In the year 1531 (so runs another tradition) a similar being was found in the Baltic Sea. She was sent to the court of King Sigismund of Poland. There was little opportunity to observe her habits, for she died, alas, after three days.

2

ALTHOUGH the mermaids of modern times were little more than curiosities, they were descendants of illustrious ancestors. Time was when they were mother goddesses, and doubtless in the days of their ascendancy they assisted in the divine task of giving life and light to the world.

There were also gods who were mermen, similar to their better-known sisters, but of the male sex. Some of the fish gods were more fishy than mermaids; they had legs and human heads, but the rest of their bodies were piscatorial. The great Anu, to cite one example, was such a divinity.

It was by no means degrading for a deity to be thus represented. On the contrary it was a signal honour to be thus closely linked with the function of creation.

It is significant that, in the art of the early Church, one finds the fish used as a symbol of the Saviour. In fact, no less pious a soul than Saint Augustine said of Him: "He is the great Fish that lives in the midst of the waters."

3

SACRED animals abound in all parts of the world. Obviously, there is always a reason why a particular species is deified and adored. Either the creature is so shaped that it suggests creation, as does the snake, or it is powerful and virile, like the bull, or it has many offspring, like the hare. The fish is a great layer of eggs. Some species lay so many eggs that if almost all of them were not somehow destroyed and prevented from developing into full-sized adults, after a few generations there would be a dearth of fin room in the ocean.

The egg, of course, has always been sacred to the mother goddess. Since the fish is the greatest of egg-producers, it has been everywhere elevated to divinity. It was a symbol of motherhood in general and it was always sacred to Venus, under whatever name and in whatever place that divinity has been adored.

Now, it happens that Friday was the holy day of Venus; in fact the day derives its name from Frigga, the Venus of the North. Historically, there have been two ways of honouring the sacred creature on the day devoted to the service of Venus. One was to abstain from eating it, and the other was to eat it—reverently and sacramentally. There have been savage folk who never ate fish (perhaps there still are). Such people have been known to walk beside a fish-laden stream in time of famine and to die of starvation rather than offend the All-Mother by devouring her holy animal.

But the custom of abstaining from the flesh of a sacred animal is usually bound up with the further custom of eating that flesh on certain specific occasions. The idea is the same that lies at the root of cannibalism—namely, that the devouring of anything tranfers its properties to the eater. Thus, if you devour the heart of a slain enemy, you acquire his courage; and if you consume certain other sections, you assimilate his power and virility. In some places the liver is recognized as the seat of the soul, and there to eat the liver is to add strength to your own soul.

If one consumes the flesh of mere man in order to acquire worth-while characteristics that once belonged to the slain, is it not more practical to eat the flesh of a god and thereby to become like him? Frazer lists a number of such practices among primitive people, and we may infer the details of the rituals from such section-headings as "Killing the sacred ram," "Killing the sacred turtles," and "Killing the sacred bear." Under each of those heads Frazer describes a rite, sometimes of a most elaborate nature, that involves the slaying of nothing less than a deity, in order that the worshippers might take unto themselves the properties of the most powerful beings they were able to conceive.

Since among all peoples the most desirable characteristic has been that known as luck, and since this is at bottom fullness and abundance of life, it has usually been the practice among primitive folk to eat the flesh of gods who were concerned with the mysterious function of generation.

Forlong tells of some friends of his who caught a turtle in India. They were not permitted to keep it. The women of the community appropriated the animal and used its holiest parts to make a potion, which increased their fruitfulness. But as a rule the sacred animal is never eaten except on the most solemn occasions, and then only in the most apologetic ritual manner. Thus there is a ritual for the eating of the flesh of the sacred bear, which includes the setting up of the bear's head on a table, and the offering to the head of a part of the creature's own meat. This sort of thing is common among simple and undeveloped people.

In this connexion it is worthy of mention that the fish was associated with Friday back in pagan days. Thus offerings of fish were given every Friday to Frigga, the Venus of the North.

Frigga was the Goddess of fertility and marriage.

For ages, people have been given to the practice of imitating the fish in their devotions. The priests of Nineveh used to wear on their hands a sort of mitre, which was designed to represent the mouth of the fish. This hat had a circle on each side to portray the eye.

Sometimes the fish was used as a sacred mark to represent a particular divinity. A conventional emblem of Ishtar took the form of an upright fish. It was roughly outlined—somewhat in the following manner:

It is well known that in the evolution of religions the conceptions that men form of gods change radically from time to time. Thus a deity may have been originally a fish and may then have developed into something quite different. Amon-Ra of Thebes was originally a ram; then he became a manlike being with a ram's head. Zeus was once an oak-tree; then he became the thunderer who threw darts at oaks. Dionysos began his career as a goat and a bull; later those creatures became sacred to him, while he himself acquired human form.

Sometimes the god changed his aspect completely, but occasionally he (or she) became half animal and half human. One of the greatest of the gods of western Asia was Hea (or Hoa). He was a snake deity, the husband of the sea, and to him all fountains, wells, pools, and streams were sacred. But before Hea was a snake, he was half man and half fish.

4

THE mermaid of fable was usually a lovely creature, and sometimes she lured sailors to their doom. She was not merely charming; she was irresistible. And as she was radiant, so was she heartless.

Just how this idea came into being it is hardly possible to state with any degree of accuracy. Still we know that there were many temples of Venus which were located on high places overlooking the sea. We know that those sites were selected in order that tired and lonely mariners might see them from afar. The temples were sanctuaries, where girls surrendered their purity and devoted the price of their shame to the institutions and to the priests of the Queen of Romance.

Perhaps those maidens were the sirens—the ladies of the deep—the mermaids who tempted sailors and lured them to destruction.

CHAPTER XXI

The Mystic Numbers, Three, Seven, and Nine

*"The philosopher aspires to explain
away all mysteries, to dissolve them
into light. Mystery on the other hand is
demanded and pursued by the religious
instinct; mystery constitutes the essence
of worship, the power of prosely-
tism. . . ."*

HENRI-FRÉDÉRIC AMIEL

1

THE Koran speaks of certain sinful persons "who puff into the knots." Such a reference requires explanation, and so an Arab commentator points out that the people indicated are given to the practice of tying knots and then blowing into them in order to work magic. No less a person than the Prophet himself was enchanted in this manner. A Jewish magician tied nine knots in a cord, which he proceeded to deposit in a well. Fortunately, the Angel Gabriel told Mohammed where the string was hidden, and so, with the help of Ali, he retrieved it. He then pronounced some charms, and at each charm one of the knots opened of itself. The Prophet had been rendered ill by the enchantment, but as knot after knot untied itself, he became gradually better, till at last the spell was broken and he recovered his health completely.

The magic power of knots is well known in superstition. They may render a man ill, by constricting his power; and, on the other hand, they may cure illness, by binding the demons who are afflicting the patient. But why did the wicked man who enchanted Mohammed take pains to tie nine knots? Why not eight, or ten?

A study of magic, witchcraft, sorcery, and the like will reveal the fact that certain numerals have a mystic power in and of themselves. Therefore these numbers are used for the casting of spells. Even today, in the concourse of mystics, people ponder over various numbers, some of which they regard as lucky, and some of which they fear as unlucky. This is what is known as the science of "numerology."

In the course of the ages many numerals have come to have supernatural significance ascribed to them. But there can be no question about the fact that of them all, three, seven, and nine stand pre-eminent.

2

THE number nine is used by primitive people both to cause and to cure illness. We have observed how the nine knots in the hidden cord resulted in harm to the person of Mohammed. On the other hand, during the Middle Ages, Englishmen used to cure a sty by taking the hair from the tail of a black tom-cat and applying it nine times to the eye of the patient. It is important to remember that this ceremony was effective only in the event that it was performed on the first night of the new moon.

There may have been several reasons why nine commended itself to human beings in prehistoric days as a mystic numeral. In the first place, it is the product of three threes. The sanctity of three has been recognized in all ages and among practically all people. Why this was so we shall have an opportunity to consider.

But there was another reason why nine was filled with mystic power. It is a number that is, so to speak, inseparably bound up with the creation of human life. On the eve of the Passover it is the custom among the Jews to recite a certain madrigal of numbers, in which each numeral is associated with some item of spiritual importance. One is associated with one God, two with the two tablets of stone, three with the three Patriarchs, and so on. In the traditional rendition the number nine is quite properly associated with the sacred stream of life.

It may be in place to add that when people have advanced far enough to make use of the decimal system for purposes of calculation, they must notice a peculiar fact about the number nine. The sum of the digits of any multiple of nine is either nine itself or some multiple of nine. Thus two nines are eighteen; and one and eight are nine. Three nines are twenty-seven; and two and seven are nine. This might be continued indefinitely.

3

WE have noticed that in the magic cure for sties the ceremony had to be performed on the first night of the new moon. The association of the moon with magic is well known, and one might add that the weaker of our two luminaries is particularly concerned in the mystery of the number seven.

The month, according to the lunar calendar, is divided into four periods of seven days each. According to the Scripture, God created the world in six days and rested on the seventh, so that the whole of reality is formed on the scheme of a seven-day period. Everyone will acknowledge that, among people who do not have our Bible, the institution of the sabbath is built up on the worship of the moon. But even in the Bible it is noteworthy that the terms "new moon" and "sabbath" are regularly used together, as if they were somehow connected.

The mystic importance attached to the number seven has resulted in the rise of other institutions besides the sabbath. Every seventh year, for example, was a sabbatical year, which was a "year of release" in ancient Israel, during which the ground was allowed to lie fallow. The fiftieth year was the jubilee, when land that had been sold reverted to the family that had originally held it, and native slaves were set free. It is said that the Ten Commandments were given on Mount Sinai seven weeks after the departure from Egypt. In this case, and for this important event in the history of the world, seven times seven days were counted. In the early days of Christianity the reverence for seven was manifest. Thus, in formulating the cardinal virtues of the new faith, the four virtues of Plato (wisdom, courage, temperance, and justice) were used as a basis. To them were added three more (faith, hope, and charity), so that the total was seven.

To step from sacred tradition to the realm of superstition, the force of the number seven becomes even more noticeable. If a babe is born in the seventh month, it is thought to have a greater chance of surviving than if it is born in the eighth month. There is no basis in fact for this supposition. The one reason for the idea is that the number seven is lucky. In the same manner, it is well known that the "seventh son of a seventh son" is a born magician. Such a man is thought to be simply suffused with supernatural power.

4

BUT of all the numbers in the infinite scale none has been more universally revered than three. When one studies the historic symbolism of the supernatural, one is struck with the constant recurrence of that number. Such items as the tripod and the trident are more than common. In China the sign of the three takes the form of a three-legged bird. In India we have the three-wheeled chariot.

Many Gods hold in their hands small objects in three parts, or else they extend three fingers aloft while folding two into the palm of the divine hand. The mystic hand of Buddha, which is used as an amulet in the Far East, is quite unlike the ordinary human appendage. The thumb and little finger are exactly alike and curve outwards: the whole hand is symmetrical, showing the three middle fingers flanked on each side by a smaller auxiliary.

In reciting the priestly benediction after the ritual manner, the pious Jew extends his fingers in such a way that the number three is apparent. The thumb is extended; the index and middle fingers are held together as one; and so are the ring and little fingers. Some people are not able to hold their fingers in this manner, and in such a case the Hebrew binds his digits in the proper way with the fringe of his praying-shawl. The Christian also shows the sign of the three in offering a benediction, by folding under his little and ring fingers, and extending only his thumb, index, and middle fingers.

While the Greeks recognized nine Muses (three times three), they knew of exactly three Furies, three Graces, and three Fates. "Many-breasted Artemis," the Greek All-Mother, sometimes had three bodies, in each of which she held romantic symbols. The plurality of bodies in this case was to show that she was the mother in all three realms of reality—the air, the earth, and the water (or underworld). The identical idea was carried out in the threefold Babylonian godhead as represented by Anu, Ea, and Bel, and in the Assyrian godhead as represented by Asshur, Anu, and Hoa. The Buddhists make use of the sacred number in their conventional grouping together of Buddha, Dhamma, and the Church; the Brahmins bind together the divine personalities of Brahma, Vishnu, and Siva.

Such combinations as those just indicated are well known. But even among the less developed and less widely recognized cults the number three appears in connexion with the basic organization of the supernatural world. Take, for example, the Whydah in western Africa. The threefold godhead of those simple people includes the tree, the serpent, and water. Of these the serpent is probably the most important. Serpent houses abound, and they are the finest that the natives take the trouble to build. The snake has his priests and his priestesses, who minister to him and attend to the sacred details of his ritual.

5

IT would be rash to offer an explanation of the origin of the idea that the number three is mysteriously powerful, and to insist, as some students do, that it is the one and only true explanation. Perhaps some hint may be derived from the three bodies of Artemis. Possibly the number may have suggested to early man the division of matter into gas, liquid, and solid. It is more likely that the mystic three is connected with Mother Moon, because she was always supposed to have a most uncanny influence upon the destinies of everything and everybody. To this day there are thousands of superstitious people who feel that their fate is somehow linked up with the full moon, the waxing moon, and the waning moon. Certainly that fact had something to do with the mystic three, because among the ancient supernatural groups of three one of the most prominent was that of the moon, the snake, and the hare.

The moon is a supreme mystery to the mind of the superstitious. In the past it was usually regarded as female; it was Astarte, the Queen of Heaven, the divine mother. The Moon was the wife of the Sun, and from the union of the pair incalculable blessings resulted for humanity.

But the situation was a bit complicated because of the fact that there was a man in the moon. There are various reasons why the moon was a mother rather than a father— her clocklike regularity for example. But the man in the moon had to be otherwise explained. In Greenland the moon is not a mother, but a father; and the sun is the mother. This is contrary to the usual interpretation, and it is doubtless based upon the people's poetic observation of the face in the lesser light. Moreover, the luminaries are virulent and hateful in their manner of carrying on a cosmic war between the sexes. The moon, in Greenland, is the enemy of women, while the sun is the great hater of men. When there is an eclipse, the darkness is due to some incident in the sex war, and accordingly men hide when there is an eclipse of the sun, and women hide when there is an eclipse of the moon.

6

A NUMBER of scholars feel that there is another reason why the number three is instinct with mysterious power. The first god of creation to be recognized by primitive man is, as we have demonstrated, the male generator. This consists of three outward parts. A study of early symbolism involving the mystic three will show that this fact was not totally absent from the minds of those who first drew the emblems. The three parts of the creator form a unit from which power proceeds. Since life was the great object of primitive desire, hope, and worship, and since it was the core of the great cosmic mystery, the number three itself very early became an embodiment of all that was desirable. It was certain; hence it was life and luck.

CHAPTER XXII

The Men who Invented Sin

*"The essence of good and evil is a
certain disposition of the will."*

EPICTETUS

1

LOVERS, as a rule, shun publicity. They want to be left
alone in the moonlight and to shut out of their lives for
the time being the rest of the world. Since this is so, one
might imagine that if a swain and a damsel are beloved of
each other, this should be a matter of indifference to everybody else, unless, of course, other complications, such as
jealousy, are present. Even the question as to whether or
not the love-affair is being carried on in a licit, or socially
approved, manner, does not directly affect anyone other
than the parties immediately concerned. The fact remains
that people are very much on the alert in this matter, and a
private love-affair between a boy and a girl is likely to be of
profound interest to a wide circle of people.

It is a fact that, in the event that a love-affair between a
man and a woman is not of the type which the law recognizes
as proper, the tendency is to blame the female more than
the male. True, this tendency is not nearly so marked now
as it was in the past. In Bible times, for example, it seemed
the natural thing for Judah to be indignant at the immoral
conduct of Tamar and to decree her punishment, until he
learned that he himself was the father of her child. The
thought that he was as worthy of punishment as the girl (assuming that the two were equally guilty of committing the
identical sin) never occurred to people in those days. But the

feeling is still prevalent that the sinful maiden is more to be shunned than the sinful man, or, better yet, that an act which is sinful when a girl performs it is something to be passed over with amused tolerance when a man performs it.

It is quite significant that this strictness with regard to romance is universal. Among every group of people, and in every part of the world, the difference is felt between one type of love, which is regarded as proper, and others, which are looked upon as improper. The exact contents of the judgments differ, of course, from place to place, and have differed from age to age. Some savages comport themselves in a manner that is highly disgusting to civilized folks, but even the lowest and most primitive of human beings have some sort of law or set of customs to regulate the love life. If this were not so, one might conclude that one set of people, and one set alone, discovered the difference between right and wrong. But since the distinction is always present, in no matter what group one studies, the fact becomes clear that the reason for it must be somehow rooted in the nature of man himself.

Where did the idea first arise among the most primitive peoples that there were types of affection between men and women that were lawful, and others that were wicked? Why is it that romance is so full of possibility to arouse righteous indignation even in the breasts of people who are in no way affected by the private lapses of lovers? Why is it that people whose thoughts are usually inclined towards contemplation of the supernatural still concern themselves so insistently with love, so that they will pay more attention to questions like divorce and birth control than they will to questions relating to violent crime and corruption? What is the origin and history of the feeling that the wayward woman is more blameworthy than the wayward man? Why does the woman pay?

2

THE violent indignation that breaches in the moral code engender in the breasts of perfect strangers goes back to the early conception that such things did concern the whole community, and for a most practical reason. If two people were indiscreet, innocent parties were almost certain to suffer in consequence. Take, for example, Sodom and Gomorrah. The people of those cities were guilty of a type of conduct that was hateful in the sight of God. Because of the wrath of Heaven, those communities were miraculously destroyed, and it is safe to say that had there been any solitary righteous man in one of those places in addition to the specially favoured family of Lot, he would have been annihilated in the storm of fire and brimstone that must have rained alike on the just and the unjust.

As a matter of fact, this idea is still widely current among people to whom the supernatural world is as real a factor in the life of men as it ever was. Great calamities like the earthquake and fire in San Francisco, the sinking of the steamship *Titanic,* and the floods of the Mississippi were laid to wrathful interference on the part of Providence with the natural order—the object being to punish whole communities for the iniquity of some of their members.

The progress of enlightenment, however, has narrowed this notion very materially, and there are comparatively few people left in the civilized world who seriously believe that earthquakes or floods or icebergs are deliberately sent to afflict associations of people in order that wholesale supernatural vengeance may be satisfied.

But even if we should grant that the moral lapses of lovers might cause whole communities to lose favour with the Power that governs the world, the question would still remain, why are the private lives of human beings of such supreme interest to the inhabitants of the supernatural world? Why are the gods worried because a youth and a maiden love each other, but neglect to enter the state of matrimony? If this sort of conduct does not directly affect other human beings, how much less ought it to be, strictly speaking, the concern of the supernatural world?

3

THE first thing to remember is that men and women are predisposed to favour the idea of marriage, because that institution is so deeply rooted in nature. There is marriage among the birds and among the apes; and there is systematic marriage, albeit polygamous, among the cattle. A study of prehuman marriage reveals that it is a biological system that obtains in those species in which the period of helpless infancy is long, or in which few progeny are born to each couple, or both. Among salmon there is nothing resembling marriage, for the reason that the female lays so many eggs that even if almost the entire batch is destroyed, the species can still be continued.

It is quite probable that, in the course of evolution, some types of animal life did come into existence in which, though a period of helpless infancy was part of the individual life-history, and the number of progeny was small, the instincts to mate and remain in loving union for a relatively permanent time did not manifest themselves. Such types must have died out. We are the descendants of countless generations of those living beings who did exhibit those instincts. Mankind came upon the world stage with an inherited disposition to favour the institution of marriage—not necessarily the marriage of one man to one woman, but the living together of parents for a time sufficiently long to enable the adults to rear the children to maturity. Even in the instances where one woman had a plurality of husbands, there was always some adequate provision for the rearing of the young.

4

BUT this inherited predisposition is by no means sufficient to account for the strong feeling that there are two kinds of romance, one legal and proper, and the other illicit and execrable. Whenever one finds a sense of righteous indignation as powerfully developed as it is in this case, one may feel sure that it is rooted either in strong economic considerations or in man's extensive superstitious proclivities. There is ample proof that both forces have operated here.

At one stage of human development there comes into being what is known as "marriage by purchase." Women used to be looked upon as property, and they were so regarded in many particulars until very recently indeed. The girl was at first the chattel of her father, who sold her at the proper time to the man who became her husband. From that time she passed into the possession of a new master, whom it was her bounden duty thereafter obediently to serve. Sometimes this ownership extended beyond the grave, and she was burned at her husband's funeral or otherwise executed in order that her soul might serve his soul in the world beyond the veil.

It happens that a pure damsel is always more valuable in the sight of a man than one whose charms have already been the property of someone else. This may be due to the inborn vanity and egotism of the male, but to whatever cause one might assign it, it exists as a fact to be reckoned with.

If, prior to the marriage of a maiden, she was the lover of a man, and if her charms had been given to a stranger, her bride price fell. She was therefore guilty in the judgment of primitive people of depriving her father of that part of her value which constituted the difference between what her price would have been had she remained pure and what her price actually was in her unchaste condition. At first the blame for this theft was cast on the girl alone, and while she was punished with dire and merciless chastisement, her equally guilty lover went free.

It soon came to be recognized, however, that a share of the guilt for this misappropriation of property belonged to the male. Still, the idea never took root, and has not till this very day, that the measure of his delinquency was precisely as great as his partner's. That is the real reason why the natural indignation against the unmarried mother does not extend with equal force against the unmarried father. The bride price is a thing of the remote past, but the feelings engendered by the old system of "marriage by purchase" persist in the racial memories of men and women in our own age of enlightenment.

5

In addition to the vanity of men, lovers in the early days had to consider the demon lover and the divine lover. The lovesick devil, seeing his beloved in the arms of a mere man, would stop at nothing in order to wreak his diabolical vengeance upon his successful rival. Besides, the gods of heaven whose goodwill was essential to human prosperity, used to be lovers of no mean ardour. How could a man ever be certain that in embracing his beloved he was not poaching on the sacred preserves of a god?

Nor did the danger end there. Human beings are afraid of the unknown. Sex has always been the greatest of mysteries; with all our intricate modern research, it is so still. It is easy to understand, therefore, that, even if we left the demon lover and divine lover out of the picture for the time being, there would still remain some peril in romance.

We have a hold-over from that conception in the universal superstition that whenever a man embraces a woman, he is weakened in consequence. No amount of investigation on the part of the learned has succeeded thus far in convincing the common man that this is not so. The reason why people first believed that sort of thing in the dim days of prehistory was that strength was linked up in their view with life. That is why cannibals eat the holy parts of their enemies in order to acquire their power. Since vigour resided in man's creative faculties, the use of those faculties involved the using up of his strength. At least once during his lifetime every good Mohammedan makes a pilgrimage to Mecca. When he is engaged in this most sacred duty, he must refrain from the joys of human love. At that time he must be strong.

But romance involved also the dissipating of spiritual strength, or, better, it involved the terrible danger of coming into close contact with something holy. All peoples have somehow entertained the theory that whatever was holy was dangerous—therefore taboo, untouchable. You could not look upon God's face and live.

In the Book of Exodus we are told that Moses wanted to see the glory of God. But this was impossible. The average man could not see the Lord at all, but Moses was granted a special privilege. He was told to ascend the mountain and to take his station in the cleft of a rock. Then, when God was ready to reveal Himself, He placed His hand upon the cleft, so that Moses could not see His face, but when He had passed, He removed the divine hand, and Moses saw the hind parts of the Deity, but the deadly (because holy) face remained invisible.

Among some people on a lower plane of culture than the ancient Hebrews, the king is the god. In such a case it is death to touch the food or the clothing of the royal person. If such a king is thoughtful, he will burn his clothes when he is ready to discard them and will likewise destroy the leavings of his table. Stories are told by travellers among such folks somewhat as follows: A king had left some of his food after a meal by the wayside. A savage then happened along and tasted of the remnant. The white man thereupon told the poor fellow that the food was holy, whereupon the innocent person writhed in torment and actually died—all because of his knowledge that he had made contact with divinity.

The demon lover and the divine lover were not the greatest dangers that attached themselves to human love. Over and above them was the sanctity of romance itself. A man and a woman might have been irresistibly drawn to each other (what psychologists technically call "romantic love" is fairly new, but the mysterious chemistry of loving attraction is as old as the animal kingdom), but it behoved them to be wary in the presence of the force of creation.

6

IF the impulse that leads to love were less fundamental and less powerful a constituent element of human nature, it is possible that the stupendous fears of men would have wiped affection out of the human race and would have destroyed mankind. Even as high-minded and advanced a thinker as Saint Paul said that his own manner of life (celibate) was best, and that marriage was, so to speak, midway between the ideal existence and sin. The only reason why men who found it impossible to resist temptation were advised to found homes was that "it is better to marry than to burn."

Still, with all its dangers, and in the face of the hostility of the whole supernatural world, man has continued to love and to mate, albeit in fear and trembling. Since it seemed necessary to walk into the valley of the shadow of death in order to gratify a basic and instinctive urge, there grew up in every part of the world certain magic ceremonies designed to render the love life less perilous. The important feature of marriage, in the view of primitive people, was never the contract, but was always the ceremony. To pronounce certain formulas, to make certain motions, to be aided by friends in the ritual manner—these were the important items in the marriage relations; these gave that relation its sanctity.

The primitive wedding-ceremonies, out of which the later ones have developed, were built up with two ends in view. The first was to deceive the supernatural lover, and the second was to inoculate the couple against spiritual evil. Just as the modern physician gives his patient a mild case of cowpox in order to immunize him against the greater danger of smallpox, so the early medicine-man prescribed a mild contact with spiritual evil, in order that the client might become accustomed to it and be stronger for the task of fighting it off.

Some of the methods of inoculation against the dangers of romance were both simple and innocent; others were neither. It is still the habit of lovers to exchange locks of each other's hair. A swain is likely to wear the charm next to his heart. Or it may be a piece of jewellery, a pendant, a ring, perhaps a ring broken in half so that each lover may retain a portion of a single object.

For ages lovers have worn such objects. All married folks use the ring in the ceremony. A person's belongings, particularly something that has been close to his body, are, in superstition, somehow endowed with a part of his soul. Magic used to be worked through such objects. The lock of the maiden's hair contained part of her personality, and as such it was dangerous to the man who wore it. But he braved the peril in order to accustom himself to this spiritual evil, so that when the marriage was finally consummated, he was better able to fight off the baneful effects of his commerce with sanctity.

But other methods of inoculation were, from our point of view, less innocent. After the marriage ceremony it is customary for the groom to kiss his bride before the assembled company. Nowhere is this regarded as either immodest or vulgar. It is, on the contrary, the conventional thing to do. It is expected. There seems to be a feeling, and one, it must be confessed, that has the facts on its side, that the ceremony would be incomplete without the kiss.

Now the kiss is sometimes a substitute for greater ceremonial intimacy. At yule-tide one is privileged to kiss any girl who stands beneath the mistletoe. In the old Temple of Mylitta the maiden who sat beneath that sacred plant was thereby giving a sign that she was ready to sacrifice her purity to the goddess. In like manner, the ceremonial kiss that follows the wedding-ceremony is all that remains of a former practice of public inoculation against the dangers of contact. The fact that it was done in public, with the moral support of the company, naturally added strength to the couple, and an element of safety. For who does not know that it is safer for a number of people to enter a spiritually perilous place (say a haunted house) than for one person to brave it alone?

7

In former times a love union outside of wedlock was nothing less than a great social menace. Even if the guilty people themselves managed to escape for a time from the consequences of their deed, who could say that evil was not brewing for the whole tribe? Indeed, the punishment might have actually begun prior to the discovery of the crime. Had not so-and-so died? And was it not well known that all death was the result of either witchcraft or the wrath of the supernatural world? Was not so-and-so ill—that is to say, possessed of devils? Clearly the guilty pair merited the blame for all the evil that had come upon the tribe. Vengeance alone demanded their punishment. But expediency demanded it too. Possibly if sufficiently dire punishment was meted out, the spirits would relent. Maybe they would lift the curse from the people.

Is it any wonder, in the light of these facts, that people whose temperament inclines them towards the supernatural are so easily roused to ire when they contemplate the vices of romance?

In the words of Crawley, "It may be confidently assumed that individual marriage has been, as far as we can trace it back, the regular type of union of man and woman. . . . The common idea . . . [is] that marriage was ordained to prevent illicit intercourse; this, of course, it does prevent, but it invents it first. Taboo and law when they sanction a human normal practice produce the possibility of sin. . . ."

CHAPTER XXIII
The Master

> *"Yet each man kills the thing he loves,*
> *By each let this be heard,*
> *Some do it with a bitter look,*
> *Some with a flattering word,*
> *The coward does it with a kiss,*
> *The brave man with a sword."*

OSCAR WILDE

1

IF both gods and devils have from time to time fallen in love with human maidens, if the incubi have condescended to mate with women, and the succubi with men, it is quite as true that there have been innumerable men and women who have literally fallen in love with supernatural beings, imaginary perhaps, but real enough to them.

The basis of the Dance of the Gods was the primitive theory of imitative magic. Ritual romance was an effort to enlist the aid of the principle of life in the eternal battle with death and destruction and desolation. But it is also true that even before the connexion between love and life was understood, there were certain loverlike rites indulged in for their own sake, perhaps because they were at one and the same time thrilling, joyous, and mysterious.

It is a commonplace of psychology that people are most likely to turn their thoughts towards the supernatural at those ages which mark crises in the development of their creative powers. Among most people this fact is recognized and allowed for, and therefore at the age of puberty, twelve or thirteen, the boy is initiated or confirmed into the mysteries of the faith he is expected to adopt and espouse.

Religious faith offers a variety of satisfactions. If the

world has been unkind, the believer may hope that the other
world will be kinder. If the worshipper is poor, perhaps
poverty is a delusion, or a chastisement of love that prepares
God's favourites for the enjoyment of bliss for evermore.
If a man is suffering in any way, and for whatever reason,
faith provides a blessed avenue of escape into the supernatural world, where the frustrated will realize their dreams in
gladness and where the weary will find rest.

Nowhere is frustration so poignant as in the sphere of
romance. People have been known to become mentally un-
balanced because of disappointments in that field of human
interest. It is well known among psychiatrists that when a
man or a woman is unattractive and cannot find a real outlet
for the desire to be loved, the grief is so considerable that it
sometimes drives the afflicted soul literally to distraction.

If one cannot have what he desires, if he is balked in the
effort to achieve whatever is essential to his happiness, the
next best thing is for him to escape from reality entirely
and to imagine that he has it. The supernatural world is a
convenient sanctuary for those to whom the real world has
nothing satisfactory to offer. If an impressionable and sensitive woman has no lover, she may (if the supernatural is
sufficiently real to her) find herself a demon lover, or even a
divine one. Was not the fair Sara in the Book of Tobit beloved of the devil Asmodeus, and were not Europa and Io
beloved of the King of Olympus? Did not the sons of the
gods come down to embrace the daughters of men, and does
not the Scripture assure us that the offspring of such unions
were the giants who at that time walked upon the earth?
Why should she, too, not abandon this unappreciative world
and remove to Fairyland, the dream-world, the supernatural?

2

Now, a person might be emotionally starved, not because he
is unattractive or because his marriage is unfortunate or

because he has been disappointed in love, but because his nature is an abnormal one and his impulses and desires are perverse. Such creatures usually find it very difficult to adjust themselves to the cold world, and the supernatural is their only salvation.

While there are many types of abnormal wish that cannot conveniently find gratification in reality, the two outstanding ones, because they are the most astonishing, are first the desire to inflict pain, the impulse towards purposeless cruelty, and second the opposite desire to be a slave and to suffer pain at the hands of one's beloved.

To a certain extent all love partakes of the nature of both of those ambitions, which are curious only when they are exaggerated and in those personalities in which they are dominant to the exclusion of other wishes. Thus there are those who torture the ones they love, and find in that monstrous activity their chief source of joy in life. They seek mastery and are frequently not satisfied with the mere infliction of physical pain, but must inflict mental pain as well. They will not merely whip or slash their unfortunate lovers, but, if possible, they will do these things in public; or they will browbeat their ladies fair in the presence of strangers.

Then too there are those who are so constituted that they derive romantic pleasure only from the state of slavery. They constantly want to fall down and adore the heartless objects of their affection. They want their lovers to beat them, to torture them, to maim them, to insult them. In such pain they find satisfaction, for injury is the supreme pleasure to such perverse creatures.

Curiously enough, both the masters and the slaves find gratification in the supernatural world. There are certain fairy tales which provide them with a dream life, and, among practically all peoples, there are certain features of the spiritual life which not only give them the satisfaction they crave, but lend to that satisfaction the sanction of Heaven.

3

THERE is a strong probability that the famous fairy-tale of
Bluebeard arose out of the unhappy career of Giles de Rais,
who was executed in 1440. Whether this is so or not, it is certain that the story did not develop out of thin air, nor did it
rise, like Aphrodite, from the sea. There have always been
such individuals, who have murdered their loved ones and
have been impelled to commit the most hideous of crimes
by the inexorable force of their inborn desires.

Giles de Rais was no obscure individual. He came from a
prominent family in Brittany, and he achieved the eminence
of Marshal of France. But, as happened frequently in those
days of superstition, he who had risen to a post of distinction
was accused of commerce with the Devil. The specific charge
was that he had abducted some hundred and fifty women
and children, had viciously abused them, and had then sacrificed his victims to Satan. On this charge he was duly tried
and convicted. Amid the bitter curses of the cringing, superstitious (and lustful?) mob Giles de Rais was hurled into
eternity.

It is freely acknowledged in our day that the sin of actual
commerce with the Devil is one which has no reality outside
of the imagination of human beings. Still, the belief that such
crimes were actually committed gave opportunity to the
real Bluebeards to satisfy their lust for cruelty. The belief
afforded to such people a pious excuse on the basis of which
they could justify to themselves as well as to the outside
world the tortures they heaped on the heads of the miserable
accused. Nor did they merely achieve justification. They
covered themselves with piety and glory. Did they derive
pleasure from the sight of the burning witches, from the
smell of their roasting flesh and the sound of their agonized
wails? Then this was positive proof that they were carried
away by the spirit of the sacred occasion; that they rejoiced

in the suffering of the damned, even as God and His saints enjoyed it. The joy that the elect derive from the sight of the pain that is inflicted on the erring for ever is beautifully described by Jonathan Edwards, as follows:

"The saints in glory will see how the damned are tormented; they will see God's threatenings fulfilled, and His wrath executed upon them. When they see it, it will be no occasion of grief to them. . . . The Scripture calls this wrath God's fury and the fierceness of His wrath; and we are told that this is to show God's wrath and to make His power known; or to make known how dreadful His wrath is, and how great His power.

"The saints in glory will see this and be far more sensible of it than we can possibly be. They will be far more sensible how dreadful the wrath of God is and will better understand how terrible the sufferings of the damned are; yet this will be no occasion of grief to them. They will not be sorry for the damned; it will cause no uneasiness or dissatisfaction to them; but on the contrary, when they have this sight, it will excite them to joyful praises. . . ."

According to the theory of Jonathan Edwards, it was God and not the damned who decided, before the birth of the soul in question, what its destiny would be. God created the world, put Adam in the garden, and foredoomed him to sin, so that all of his descendants, with the exception of the very few persons whom He saw fit to cause to believe right doctrine, might be damned for ever to all the tortures of hell. And yet, though this punishment was to last for all eternity, the sight of it all did not excite pity among the elect few, but it was rather a source of godly satisfaction, and the blessed were excited by their view of perdition to praise the Author of it all.

So gentle a soul as Martin Luther recognized the difficulty presented by the idea of eternal damnation. Luther solved the problem in the following manner: "This is the acme of faith, to believe that He is merciful who saves so few and

condemns so many; that He is just who at His own pleasure
has made us necessarily doomed to damnation; so that, as
Erasmus says, He seems to delight in the tortures of the
wretched and to be more deserving of hatred than of love. If
by any effort of reason I could conceive how God could be
merciful and just, who shows so much anger and iniquity,
there would be no need for faith" (*De servo arbitrio*, I, sec.
23; translation taken from Lecky, *History of Rationalism*).

4

STRANGE as it may seem, the impulse that leads people to
practise cruelty is a fundamental constituent of the love instinct. Cruelty and love do not appear to go together, for
what normal mother is deliberately tyrannical where her
children are concerned, and what loving husband is intentionally abusive to his wife?

Still, even in these cases a close study will reveal that the
affection manifested is by no means devoid of the element of
racial memory of old-time cruelty. When a mother fondly
says of her offspring: "I could bite him," is this just an un-
important and meaningless metaphor, or has it some psychological significance? When a youth says of a maiden:
"I could eat her," does this startlingly cannibalistic pro-
nouncement cover a deeper, albeit unconscious, feeling?

Awhile ago, in the Zoological Garden of New York City,
there was a tiger of the type known as a jaguar. Since it is
not good for tigers to live alone, the authorities procured
a female of the species, and, in order to accustom the two
to each other, placed them in adjoining cages. The courtship
began forthwith. The swain would sidle up to the cage of his
beloved and would lick her paws through the bars. Every
possible sign of devotion was manifested, and the keepers
finally reached the conclusion that the time had come when
the betrothed couple might meet each other more intimately.

The door between the two cages was opened and the bride

stepped over the threshold of her bridegroom's chamber. Thereupon he pounced upon his dear wife and ate her up!

This story may seem strange to laymen in this field. But it will not seem peculiar to either biologists, animal psychologists, or keepers of zoological gardens. It was doubtless because of fears that such would be the consummation that the two were confined in adjoining cages before being suffered to meet each other more intimately.

The warlike features of romance in the lower reaches of the animal kingdom are well known to scientists. The kiss is often accompanied by fierceness and snarling and gory strife. Do we not begin to see, then, that such ejaculations as "I could bite him" or "I could eat her" are not nearly so innocent as the speakers of such lines imagine them to be?

5

IF the supernatural world is to minister to the requirements of people whose love life has been thwarted in the sphere of reality, it is hardly surprising that the needs of the congenitally cruel are gratified in the realm of make-believe. The story of Bluebeard and tales like it, however they arose, are to be explained as social day-dreams, through which the monstrous impulses of humanity find an outlet.

But it is especially true that the supernatural world permits cruel persons to return to reality, since it affords them a reason for venting the blood lust on their fellows. The Inquisition is a case in point. Today, when the influence of the supernatural is not so strong as it was during the dark ages, people still organize lynching parties, and they convince themselves at such times that their lust is at bottom a passion for righteousness, and their inquisitorial tactics a sacrifice to justice. In the days gone by, the unseen world with its sanctions and its demands afforded a far better excuse and a more powerful urge to cruelty.

One hears much, for example, about the "car of Juggernaut." It is said that beneath its wheels worshippers used to be killed for the glory of the divinity. In fairness, however, it must be admitted that, while there may have been some fanatics who thus committed suicide under the chariot of that god, still such sacrifices were not regular parts of his worship.

The truth of the matter is that there is no god named Juggernaut. There is, however, a Hindu deity whose name is Vishnu, who is the second person in the well-known Hindu Trinity. According to the believers in that god, he has appeared on earth in many different incarnations, one of which was that of Krishna, the saviour. The god has a number of different names to signify his different characteristics; and one of them is Jagannath, which, in the Western World, is usually pronounced (and spelled) Juggernaut. The temple dedicated to him under that name is built in a suggestive shape, having a conical tower which rears its apex one hundred and ninety-two feet in the air. The mystic number three is also recognized in the structure, for the image of the god inside is always accompanied by those of his brother and sister. During the summer there is a festival, in the course of which the statues are placed in cars and transported to the summer home where they take up their abode for the season.

While demented pilgrims may from time to time cast themselves beneath the wheels of the car, the god does not approve of the practice. Jagannath, as might be inferred from the symbolism of his temple, does not like death. It is the rule of his service that if a worshipper drops dead during the devotions, the ritual is stopped at once, while the edifice is cleansed from the pollution that the Grim Reaper always leaves in his ghastly train. The story of the car of Juggernaut is a gross exaggeration.

6

IF public opinion has been unduly severe in the case of Jagannath, it has been singularly mild in its estimate of the Hindu sect known as thuggee. In fact, few people in the Occident are aware of the nature of the rituals in which the followers of that amazing religion used to indulge. Still, it is possible to infer something concerning the character of those rites from the fact that the cult has bequeathed to us our English word "thug." (In like manner, our word "assassin" is derived from the name of the sect of the Persian prophet Hasan.)

The Thugs (or Thags, as they are sometimes called) were the worshippers of the goddess Kali. The wife of the immodest god Siva, usually known as Sakti, has many names, and Kali is one of them. But, as the reader is aware, a goddess changes her attributes radically when she is known by another name. Kali is still worshipped in India, though thuggee itself has been stamped out (not without the greatest difficulty) by the British East India Company and the English Government. The goddess is a hideous being with four hands, in one of which she holds a severed human head!

Kali is a blood-thirsty divinity. It is her will that all human beings, with the exception of her own elect, be destroyed. At one time, so runs the myth, it was her practice to slaughter (or to have her priests slaughter) as many men as possible. In fact, she inaugurated this carnage soon after the creation of the world. But Vishnu objected to this, and he ordained that from every drop of human blood that fell to the ground another human being would miraculously spring. From Kali's point of view this decree was abhorrent, because the more blood she managed to spill, the larger did the hateful population wax.

But Kali hit upon a scheme. She instructed her elect in the art of strangulation, so that men might be killed without bloodshed. Women were never killed by Thugs, because the patroness of the sect was female. The goddess undertook to dispose of the bodies herself, provided that her worshippers kept their faces averted while she did so, for it is always improper, not to say dangerous, for any mortal to look upon the face of a deity.

For a while the plan of Kali was carried out and all ran smoothly enough. Men were strangled and robbed; the population grew smaller; and the treasure of the goddess began to swell. In the course of the devotions following each murder, the faithful turned their faces away and the corpse was disposed of. But a certain Thug permitted his curiosity to overcome him, and to his surprise he saw Kali in the act of eating the human sacrifice.

Since that time the goddess has never deigned to show herself in person to mortal men. In punishment for the disobedience of that one man the Thugs were commanded to bury all the corpses themselves. For this purpose they used a pickax, which became the symbol of Kali herself. Divine services were offered to the goddess before every murderous excursion, and a part of the regular ritual was the adoration of the mystic pickax.

It might be imagined that a sect of that kind was really bent upon gain and not upon salvation; and that the urge to murder and steal was of the earth and not of the supernatural. But when the British set out to conquer thuggee, their experience did not bear out any such idea. It was no simple matter to catch a Thug, but when one was apprehended, he did not shrink from the doom that awaited him. On the contrary, he went to the gibbet in a spirit of fanatical transport and the highest joy. Was he not, in his own estimation, one of the elect? Was he not blessed of Kali, the wife of Siva? Was he not going to his death as a martyr in her service? Was he not bound straight for paradise?

The Thug would grasp the rope, put it round his own neck,

and leap into the air with the gladsome shout: "Victory to
Kali." Great men have been known to contemplate death
with fear and trembling. Not so the typical Thug who went
to the scaffold. He achieved the ideal of the poet who would
have us approach the grave

> Like one that wraps the drapery of his couch
> About him, and lies down to pleasant dreams.

7

IT is possible to deride such anti-social believers as the
Thugs and the Assassins, and one may spurn them as ignorant and superstitious savages. Such a view is, however, decidedly superficial and distinctly out of harmony with the
facts.

The greatest of the leaders of the Assassins was Hasan
(or Hassan) Sabbah. While it is true that his leadership
was gory and murderous, it is also true that he himself was
a theologian of repute. Al Ghazali, who stood in the front
rank among the theologians of his day and section of the
world, wrote a refutation of Hasan's theories. This at least
shows that the controversial powers of the Assassins' leader
were not beneath the notice of Al Ghazali.

The Assassins believed that the Koran was not to be taken
literally. The literal meaning of the text was a sort of cur-
tain behind which the truth lay. They laid much stress on
the virtue of obedience, which resulted in rendering their
ruler the most perfect example of an absolute despot one
can imagine.

The exact derivation of the word "assassin" is not known,
but the most plausible theory is that the original name was
"Hashishim," or "drinkers of hashish." This was a drug
made from the hemp plant, which there is reason to believe
the members of the sects were in the habit of imbibing, perhaps to acquire courage for some dangerous adventure.

In this connexion, Marco Polo speaks of a certain valley
that he claims was used by the Assassin chief as a make-
believe paradise. The contour of the valley was such that a
man unescorted and unguided would not be able either to
enter it or to leave it. When the leader had selected a man
for an unusually perilous mission, he drugged the chosen one
and had him carried into the valley. There, when the sleeper
awoke, were beautiful maidens, whose sole business it was
to entertain him and to minister to his comfort. The next
step was for the man to be drugged once more and returned
to his home. When he awoke this time, he was informed that
the ruler had sent him to heaven in order to afford a fore-
taste of the joys that would be his for all eternity should he
obey his leader implicitly.

There can be no doubt about the fact that this charming
tale reported by Marco Polo is a myth, and that no credence
is to be placed in it whatever. Still, there must have been
a reason why the legend arose in the first place. Unquestionably the reason is that the followers of Hasan were
so thoroughly obedient, and so willing to brave dangers, that
some explanation seemed necessary. The explanation was
furnished by the story of the make-believe Elysium.

If the Assassins are to be regarded as a sect rather than a
mere band of murderers, this attitude is even more in order
towards the Thugs of India.

The conduct of the Thugs was based upon a philosophy
that is both exalted and subtle. The theory was that the
gods were high above mortals—that their thoughts were not
our thoughts nor their ways our ways. Now, such considerations as "good" and "evil" have reference to human conduct, or to that which affects humanity. The distinction between right and wrong is a human one and is utterly beneath the notice of the gods. Verily, according to those think-
ers, all our good deeds are but as a filthy rag, and mere
morality cannot lead to salvation. To be of the elect, to be

listed among the few favoured of Heaven, one must obey
the injunctions of the spiritual world. One must obey, moreover, with the full knowledge that the divine will may be
unintelligible to finite minds.

Still, this philosophic justification will hardly serve as an
explanation of the origin of the practices it was invented to
excuse. Those cruel rituals did not have their source in
philosophy, but in human nature. Thuggee and cults like it
may rightly be regarded as expressions of that human impulse which forces lovers to be harsh and tyrannical at times.

Such cults are but examples of the use to which the supernatural world is sometimes put by the will to mastery.

8

NOWHERE does the master emerge so resplendent as in the
discharge of the duty (often expressly recognized as such)
of religious persecution.

The unbeliever was hateful in the sight of God; therefore
he ought to be hateful in the sight of the godlike. Besides,
among many persecuting groups the man who was mistaken
in his ideas about the supernatural was doomed to eternal
punishment of a sort far more intense than any which mere
human beings had the power to devise or to inflict. If the
erring were permitted to spread their pernicious doctrines,
the danger to the community must have been inestimable,
for the danger was directed not against mere earthly life,
but against the immortal souls of the people. Any practice
that would serve to stamp out so damnable an evil as theological error was not merely just and proper, but was thought
of as worthy of praise. This is the argument that exalted the
Inquisition for so many years and is used to this very day
by apologists for the Holy Office. When Charles V determined to abdicate the throne and retire to the monastery
at Yuste, he turned over the reigns of government to his
son Philip II and gave him strict instructions (as any mon-

arch might have done under similar circumstances) to do everything in his power to advance the cause of the Holy Inquisition. The cruelty of that institution was thought of as really mercy, for in stamping out the deadly contagion of heresy it diminished the sufferings and added to the eternal sum of happiness that was in store for humanity.

But in addition to heresy, there was always at hand the visible kingdom of Satan on earth. That monarch had his own followers who actually believed that they had bartered their souls for the working of some devilish magic. And besides those who entertained that conviction, there were countless others who were suspected of selling themselves to the Prince of Darkness in return for some favour such as the restoration of youth, as in the well-known legend of Faust. On all sides were witches and sorcerers, who were subjects of Satan and by that same token enemies of God and His people. To ferret them out and to destroy them were the two foremost duties of good and pious folks. When a witch was apprehended and her unholy compact with hell was demonstrated to the satisfaction of the judges, it was meet and proper that she be made to suffer. Not only did justice demand this, but her pain might serve as a deterrent to some other individual, who might otherwise have entered into a similar alliance.

The characteristics and most intimate habits of witches were well known during the dark ages. It was a favourite device of a witch to change herself into a wolf and to prey upon the flock of her God-fearing neighbours. This was the crime of lycanthropy, for which countless women went to the stake. It was a precarious crime to commit, for if it happened that a part of the seeming wolf's body was cut off, it automatically changed itself into the corresponding part of the witch's body when the inevitable transformation back to human shape took place. Many subjects of the Devil were detected by that circumstance, if we may trust the solemn records of the courts. Thus it happened that a husband was out in the field when he espied a wolf. Totally unsuspecting, he pursued the animal and managed to cut off a front paw. One may imagine his surprise when next morning he found out that in his pocket was not a wolf's paw, but (according to his testimony) the bloody hand of his lawful wife. He was not permitted to divorce his wife in those days, but the belief in the supernatural served him effectively in place of that right.

Among the methods of detecting witches was that of finding the "insensible spot." There was always one spot on the body of a subject of Satan (though its exact location varied in different individuals) which was not sensitive to any kind of pain. If a needle was inserted at that particular point, the person would not shriek, for the excellent reason that he (or she, for it was usually a woman) would not feel it. Accordingly, if one was suspected of witchcraft or sorcery, it was possible to determine the fact of guilt by stripping the suspect and pricking him (or her) in all conceivable spots. Some people were specially skilful in the art of thus confounding the children of hell. This art was developed in Scotland into a recognized profession, and the good people who followed it were known as "prickers."

But even with all the splendid and intricate technique that was called into being for the important purpose of detecting the damned, it was frequently a troublesome task to force a confession out of a suspect. We have a record of a certain Dr. Fian who was known to be guilty of raising the wind by black magic. Put to the torture, he confessed, but before there was time to execute him, the wretch retracted and had to be tortured all over again. Among other items, the bones of his legs were broken into tiny fragments, and yet so strong was his unspeakable loyalty to Satan that he refused to acknowledge his guilt. Finally, says the righteous chronicler, "his nailes upon all his fingers were riven and pulled off with an instrument called in Scottish a turkas which in English we call a payre of pincers, and under every nayle there was thrust in two needles over even up to their heads. . . ." Still, and the chronicler regretfully records it, the Devil had so deeply "entered his heart" that he remained obdurate in his denial, and it became necessary to burn him without the satisfaction of the confession.

9

IT may seem strange to assert that much of the righteous in- dignation of the chronicler and of the executioners and tor- turers whose persevering efforts he took such pains to describe was at bottom mere perversity. Still, this view is substantiated by the fact that at times of mass cruelty, even of a pious character, romantic activity is great. It is the habit of persecuting mobs to dishonour the maidens whom they discover in the ranks of the erring. At the time of the Span- ish Inquisition the reverend gentlemen of the Suprema (or supreme council) used to squabble in a most undignified manner over the possession of female slaves who were con- fiscated with the property of heretics. It is noteworthy that such squabbles did not take place over the male slaves.

If there is need to find other illustrations of the use of cruelty in the making of favourable contacts with the super- natural world, one may adduce the presence of the whip as an almost universal religious symbol and as a part of the paraphernalia of devotion. The whip was the "quickener," a sign of the male sex, and many gods in different parts of the world hold it in their hands.

At the feast of the Lupercalia in Rome, the youths used to strip themselves and take thongs of goat-hide, with which to whip the girls they passed as they ran through the streets. This rendered the maids magically fruitful, for here again the whip was the "quickener," the giver of life.

In the Shinto religion there is the feast of the first full

moon of the year, on which occasion the youths used cere-
monially to whip the young maidens. The same ceremony,
or a similar one, is popular among certain modern farming-
communities in Europe. There is also a custom in the Upper
Palatinate of striking a bride as she advances from the door
of the church to her seat.

The roots of that kind of ceremony lie deep in the hidden recesses of human desire.

10

HUMAN beings are meat-eaters, like the lion and the wolf,
the serpent and the owl. Instinctively the meat-eater seeks to
gratify his two basic impulses, to eat and to love. Both are
forms of hunger, and both are closely related. It is no accident that we speak so glibly of "the hunger of love." The
sight of suffering in a living being appeals to a certain side
of the meat-eater's character. It means the death of another
being (or the impending death of the poor creature). It
means food.

But man seeks to rise above that primeval horror, and, in
a general way, it is true that he succeeds in doing so. He
cannot root the age-old desires out of his nature, but he can
transform them and make them serve noble ends. Thus he
can make of the urge to mastery the estimable characteristic
we call "ambition." Or he may derive a sort of symbolic and
vicarious satisfaction from participating in competitive ath-
letics or from interesting himself in prize-fighting, bull-
fighting, and the like. But there are some persons in the
course of whose development something goes wrong, and
they do not transform their bestial natures into something
higher. They are almost literally tigers in human skins.

Still, such a monster is different from the normal man in
degree rather than in kind. Scratch the gentleman, and one
may find the tiger underneath. That is why lynching is still

popular, and it is the reason why the news of a hanging is read with such avidity by the gloating populace.

Since this urge is present in all men, however they may hide it from themselves, it is necessary for it to find some outlet. One of the outlets is provided by the supernatural world. The Thugs found it there, and so did all those who flattered themselves that they were serving the inscrutable ends of Heaven when they persecuted unoffending men, women, and even children for their opinions.

CHAPTER XXIV
The Slave

> *"There are men to whom the most precious and best thing in their lives appears to be some disease of their soul or body. They spend their whole life in relation to it, and only living by it, suffering from it, they sustain themselves on it, they complain of it to others, and so draw the attention of their fellows to themselves. . . . Take from them that disease, cure them, and they will be miserable, because they have lost their one resource in life—they are left empty then. . . ."*
>
> MAXIM GORKY

1

LOVE is a complex emotion. It is made up of a number of different impulses, one of the noblest of which is that of self-sacrifice. People often wonder why it is that children have been known to commit suicide at the age of twelve or thereabouts. The reason is that at that age love is awakening. Prior to that critical time the child has been dominated by the herd instinct. He wanted to be like everybody else, and it was accordingly necessary to his happiness that everybody be more or less alike, so that he could resemble them all. Hence his intolerance of all singular or unusual types of companions, cripples, specially intelligent acquaintances, or individuals with rare opinions. But at the age of puberty the child has become an idealist, a creature capable of romantic love, and therefore ready to make sacrifices. Sometimes the urge to immolate oneself becomes overpowering in its strength, and the unfortunate child may go to the extreme of sacrificing himself in deadly earnest.

It often happens that the child in whom the impulse of self-sacrifice is too strong does not actually kill himself, but comes to cherish the desire to serve in a menial sense, to be oppressed, beaten, humiliated, and dishonoured in the name of his beloved. Like everybody else he seeks happiness, but in his own perverse way. He derives pleasure from pain, and the most intense joy he can obtain in no other manner. He is the opposite of the master. He is the slave.

2

If the supernatural world is a refuge for those whose love life has been thwarted, this is especially true for that type we are speaking of as the slave. For every god, devil, or familiar spirit desires sacrifice. The immortals want men and women to be humble, submissive, and self-abasing. How can one better prove one's willingness to adore the object of one's reverence than by offering one's very life to one's lord?

This type of sacrifice once enjoyed a wide vogue. We have already mentioned the thoroughly pious, though unhappy people who are said to have thrown themselves beneath the car of Jagannath. In like manner we have the story of one Peregrinus Proteus, who was one of the early converts to Christianity. He went to an Olympian festival and there, before the eyes of the assembled crowd, burned himself to death on a wooden pyre.

In the year 1666 there was a suicide wave in Russia. According to the calculations then and there popular, Antichrist was about to appear, and it was believed to be proper to kill oneself in order to avoid meeting the Adversary. In the same country in 1897 the Government decided to take a census, which every thoroughly superstitious person knows is contrary to the will of Heaven. To avoid being counted, a number of well-intentioned persons had themselves buried alive.

3

STILL, it is not always necessary to go so far as actually to kill oneself in order to lay a supreme sacrifice on the altar. There are many religious orders whose members do not marry. They forgo the blessing of rearing families, and it must be remembered that in bygone times, in spite of the custom of exposing babies, progeny was regarded as a blessing of the highest importance.

The practice of abstaining from marriage for reasons of piety has a history. It is the product of a long process of evolution, every step of which may be traced. First comes the act of killing oneself for the glory of one's god. Next comes the practice of deliberately mutilating oneself, as in the rites undergone by the priests of the Queen of Heaven. Then comes the practice of placing marks on the devotee's body, such as the Jewish and Mohammedan signs of the covenant. Finally we have the milder customs of simply abstaining from marriage and thus renouncing the hope for offspring.

Until recent times there existed in Russia a sect called the Skoptsi, who hated their own parents because they had committed the sin of love. Their services were held at night. They danced and worked themselves into a fanatical fury, in which state they made sacrifices similar to those of the priests of Cybele. Sects of this kind, whenever they arise, are convinced that their conduct is pleasing in the sight of the supernatural world. It is probable that the Skoptsi, for example, felt that they had scriptural warrant for their idea in the twelfth verse of the nineteenth chapter of Saint Matthew.

4

SELF-ABASEMENT, of course, need not assume such indecent and horror-inspiring forms. Some of the most admired and

most saintly of souls have attained their eminence in history
because of their unquenchable desire to humble themselves,
even unto the dust, for the honour of Heaven. But the same
impulse that prompts one to abase himself in one manner,
however low, is also at the root of the habit of abasing oneself in another manner, however high.

No one will call in question the purity of motive that inspired the career of Saint Louis of Gonzaga, who is the
patron saint of young people in the Catholic Church. Says his
biography: "The inspiration came to him (at the age of ten)
to consecrate to the Mother of God his own virginity—that
being to her the most agreeable of possible presents. Without
delay, then, and with all the fervour there was in him, joyous
of heart and burning with love, he made his vow of perpetual
chastity. . . ."

Because of her deep appreciation of this vow on the part
of the child, Mary obtained for him the rare blessing of total
exemption from carnal temptation. Never at any time of his
life did he have the slightest desire for the company of the
opposite sex. On the contrary, he loathed and detested the
thought of any association between men and women. But
although he was thus blessed and might have walked with uplifted head, certain of himself and confident that temptation
could never come his way, he spent his life taking precautions
against that absent danger. He kept his eyes on the ground as
he walked in public, lest he might behold a woman. He
avoided contact, even with his own mother. He refused to
converse with a female. And at the most tender age he began
to mortify his flesh.

At the age of seventeen the saint entered the Jesuit order.
He lost contact with his family completely. He did everything
in his power to have himself falsely accused of offences and
to be punished for that which he had not done. Injustices of
that sort furnished him with opportunities for humility. He
avoided flowers or perfumed articles of any sort; but he

eagerly sought work in the hospital, where he could perform the most disgusting and most revolting services.

5

THERE is a widespread feeling on the part of people all over the world that supernatural beings are displeased if mortals appear to be happy. A human career to be acceptable on high must be a stern affair and devoid of joy.

The objection to levity and pleasure goes back to the early idea that the immortals are hostile to man, possibly jealous of him, and hence are enemies of the human race. Superstitious people are always fearful, because for them the whole scheme of reality is charged with harm. For this reason they feel that it is good policy to keep the spirits in the belief that men and women are unhappy, and we have already reviewed a number of devices to bring about that deception. From that notion it is but a step to the conclusion that there is no distinction between innocent and guilty pleasures. All pleasure is wicked.

Even among the Greeks, who were famous as seekers after joy, the idea that happiness was evil was not wholly absent. That is why in Sparta the young men used to stand of their own free will at the altar of Brimo and suffer themselves to be whipped almost to death. It explains, moreover, why the Arcadian women permitted themselves to be treated in the same manner on the advice of the Delphic oracle.

If the whip was freely used on the backs of those whose philosophic and theological opinions were regarded as erroneous, it was used just as freely for the pious purpose of self-chastisement. Possibly the most dramatic instance of this in the whole history of the supernatural is to be found in the story of the Brotherhood of Flagellants, which flourished in the fourteenth century.

That brotherhood was organized because of the circumstance that a dread plague, known as the Black Death, was sweeping over Europe. People were dying like flies as the horrible contagion spread. Obviously Heaven was displeased with the conduct of the human race and it was incumbent upon the righteous to appease the celestial wrath by undergoing penance. In order to accomplish this worthy object, bands of people organized themselves and began to walk through the highways and by-ways flogging each other as they walked. So great was the enthusiasm that all sorts of persons joined the bands. Even naked children were to be seen in the mournful and painful parades. Yet it is to be feared that this activity was misdirected, for the pilgrimages served to spread the disease wider and wider, thus defeating the very ends for which they were instituted.

Even such rigours were not sufficient to satisfy the craving for renunciation of the world and for the deliberate thwarting of all normal desires and ambitions, by way of sacrifice. In the words of no less an authority than Lecky, "To break by his ingratitude the heart of the mother who had borne him, to persuade the wife who adored him that it was her duty to separate from him for ever, to abandon his children, uncared for and beggars, to the mercies of the world, was regarded by the true hermit as the most acceptable offering he could make to his God. His business was to save his own soul. . . ."

How completely this program was carried out, a few illustrations will amply demonstrate. There is the story of Mutius, who took his child to a monastery and asked for admission. In order to discipline him the monks took the little boy and beat him, starved him, and in general mistreated him so that he languished before the eyes of his father. But the chronicler assures us that the father's piety was so great that none of this made any impression upon him. When, finally, the head of the institution ordered the parent to drown the child, he picked him up without emotion, carried him to the bank of a stream, and would have cast him into the water had not the order been countermanded at the last minute.

In like manner, the famous Saint Simeon Stylites showed utter lack of concern when his father died of a broken heart because of the conduct of his son. When, years later, his bereaved mother sought admission to his dwelling, the Saint was likewise unmoved. He refused to admit her and she died, pining away before his door. At that he went to her, prayed for her soul, and went back instanter to his devout contemplations. All of this is recorded with the keenest admiration by his biographer.

These accounts might be continued at great length. It will suffice, however, to quote the advice of Saint Jerome to Heliodorus, whom he desired to forsake the world and to become a hermit. "Though your little nephew twine his arms around your neck: though your mother, with dishevelled hair and tearing her robe asunder, point to the breast with which she suckled you; though your father fall down on the threshold before you, pass on over your father's body. . . . Your father may implore you to wait but a short time to bury those near to you, who will soon be no more; your weeping mother may recall your childish days, and may point to her shrunken breast and to her wrinkled brow. Those around you may tell you that all the household rests upon you. Such chains as these, the love of God and the fear of Hell can easily break. You say that Scripture orders you to obey your parents, but he who loves them more than Christ loses his soul. The enemy brandishes a sword to slay me. Shall I think of a mother's tears?"

6

DEEP in the hidden recesses of every man's nature there lie the impulses that incite him towards conquest and those that inspire him to sacrifice himself. The story of every life is, in part at least, the history of the conflict between those two opposing factors in his psychological make-up. Both of them are very real, and both are very powerful. Both find gratification and an outlet in the supernatural world, which is so effectively calculated to complement the cold world of which our senses tell us—that hostile environment that besets us on every hand.

CHAPTER XXV

The Inside Story of Hell

"Though love repine and reason chafe,
There came a voice without reply,—
' 'Tis man's perdition to be safe
When for the truth he ought to die.' "
RALPH WALDO EMERSON

1

THE earliest form of devotion known to students of
comparative religions is the worship of devils. Commerce with the putative world "beyond the veil" began as an
attempt to improve human luck, which meant, of course, the
averting of ill luck or evil circumstances. Even in this age of
what we are pleased to call enlightenment, a time of calamity or danger usually evokes a piteous cry for some sort
of communication with the supernatural world. This need
for supernormal assistance is felt, not only when a ship begins to sink or the Grim Reaper makes his appearance in a
family, but also when a comet shines in the sky, and the
superstitious quake for fear of the harm it must of necessity portend.

If this is so in our day, what must have been the condition in the days of prehistory? In the ages of yore, not
merely the untutored, but the greatest sages were ignorant of
the laws of nature, and they could account for the multitude
of terrors around them on no other supposition than that the
land was owned by spirits who were jealous of men and
women. The greatest and most practical art of life was that
of appeasing those spirits, or of making some arrangement
with them by which human society was afforded a measure
of security, and the besetting danger was diminished.

In the north of Europe those primitive supernatural landlords were giants, whose anger against the human usurpers resulted in all the evils that flesh is heir to. There were various methods of dealing with those powerful and vengeful creatures, as, for example, the device of cheating them in bargaining (for it is well known that devils are stupid and easily outwitted). We have the story of a giant who saw a farmer tilling his land, and demanded half of the produce as rent. The farmer readily agreed, but wanted to know in advance which half the devil desired. The spirit thought awhile and demanded the half that appeared above the ground. So the farmer planted turnips, and the fiend received merely the useless tops. The next year the giant wanted the arrangement reversed. He was to have the half beneath the soil. The planter agreed and planted wheat, and therefore the supernatural owner of the soil had to be satisfied with the stubble.

A better method of dealing with those malicious spirits was that of paying them homage and employing magic to compel them to give mankind some peace. To accomplish this, celebrations were conducted, in which the giants were represented by huge dummies, which were carried round in procession. Those great manikins are still used in Europe, but the old conceptions that called them into being in the first place have disappeared. The whole thing is now carried on in a spirit of fun, like the customs of Hallow-e'en, which were likewise superstitious in their origin.

2

IN the earliest times the inhabitants of the supernatural world were for the most part wicked and cruel. Occasionally the early peoples recognized good spirits, and even fairy-tales include accounts of "good witches." But the beneficent immortals were not worshipped. Why should they be? The purpose of worship at that time was practical in the crassest sense of the term. If the god was good anyhow, and if he was inclined by his very nature to be helpful and not harmful to mankind, why bother to induce him to do what he would certainly do without any inducement?

With devils, however, the situation was different. Those beings were ever ready to do harm to men and women. Think what they had already done, in spite of magic and in spite of worship. Had not human beings died? Were not people sick? Had not the cattle suffered calamities? Had there not been ill luck in the community? Misfortune is always present in the world, and therefore that argument was always appropriate, assuming that it was ever necessary in primitive times to justify devil-worship.

As people advanced in culture, however, and particularly after the discovery of the relation between love and life had taken place, the worship of good spirits developed. But even the beneficent gods would not serve humanity without rewards. In fact, they could not if they would, for they were as dependent upon sacrifices as men were upon supernatural blessings. The gods of life had to have living human beings (and later animals) offered to them, in order to endow them with life; and the gods of the corn had to consume the sacrifice of the first-fruits to keep full the divine reservoirs of mystic energy. Thus it happened that there came to be two distinct kinds of divinities—the good gods, and the bad devils. Yet the two were not, at first, so easily distinguishable from each other, as we shall have abundant opportunity to observe.

3

THE chief Devil of the Western World today is an individual named Satan. Like certain well-known characters in ancient mythology, he is part man and part animal in appearance. He has the leg and hoof of a goat and the horns of a bull. He also has a tail, and it resembles that of a snake.

Both the goat and the bull were symbols of the Greek god Dionysos, and both were worshipped over wide areas as divine exemplifications of love and life. Associated with Dionysos were the god Pan and his minions the satyrs, who were half man and half goat. In Rome the satyrs became the fauns, but by whatever name they were known, their chief characteristic was an excess of the flame of romance. We still use the word "satyr" in English to indicate a man who is loverlike to a fault. And, as for the serpent, was not the snake the wicked creature that tempted Adam and Eve and was therefore responsible for the downfall of mankind?

But the goat, the bull, and the serpent are by no means the only animals that are associated with evil. Among many peoples the pig is an abhorrent creature. The Jews and Mohammedans (to mention but two of the groups) do not eat the flesh of the swine. The reason why the pig is hated has nothing to do with the purely physical fact that it is dirty. The habits of the hen are just as unæsthetic, but her meat is usually a permitted delicacy. The simple truth is that, like the goat, the bull, and the snake, the pig is for many folks a devil. The list of devilish animals is fairly long, but we have mentioned enough to gain our point. If we can determine why these beings are regarded with suspicion and even hatred, we shall have gone a long way towards understanding who the Devil is and where he came from.

4

THE association of the goat with the Devil is to be found in the Bible. The holiest day in the year, according to the Jewish idea, is the Day of Atonement, which comes in the fall. In Bible times the scriptural injunctions for the observance of this festival were followed to the letter. Two goats were selected, both of which were "without blemish." Lots were cast to see which of the two should be offered to the Lord and which to Azazel. When this question had been decided by supernatural means (for the casting of lots was a universal means of letting the spirits decide a point at issue), the sins of the people were thought to be laid on the "scape-goat," which was then driven with shrieks and curses into the desert, where it became the property of Azazel. Who this Azazel was is not made plain, but the facts about devils that we shall uncover in this chapter will doubtless lead us to conclude that he was an old desert-god, transformed by a natural process into a devil.

In this classic enactment of the scapegoat drama we have two goats, equally perfect, sacrificed respectively to the god and the demon. No partiality was shown. But one was a sin-offering; the other was a mysterious sacrifice to the fell power of the abyss.

5

Now, the goat was sacrificed to other gods besides Yahweh and Azazel. It was a forbidden animal among the worshippers of the goddess Athene, and yet it was offered to her as a sacrifice once every year.

It may seem peculiar that Athene should entertain such objections to the horned creature at all times except the single occasion when she demanded it as an offering. But this sort of thing was the case in many religions, and with many different animals. The people would positively hate the animal (as the Jews hate the pig). Under no circumstances would they eat it or even touch it. But once every year the situation was reversed; the creature was sacrificed to the god and eaten by the people.

The worshippers of Attis refused to eat the meat of the pig, and among the ancient Egyptians the hatred of the creature knew no bounds. If, while walking, an Egyptian happened to touch a pig by accident, no pains were too great for him to remove the horrible contagion of that loathsome touch. He might jump into the river with all his clothes on, to wash away the spiritual uncleanness. All men in Egypt were accorded access to the temples with the single exception of the despised class of swineherds. Such people were not suffered to enter a temple, for their presence would have contaminated any holy edifice. In fact, the swineherds formed a caste by themselves. No one would give such a man a daughter to marry, so they were compelled to marry among themselves.

Since this was so, why did the Egyptians maintain swineherds at all? How did those despised people earn a living, if no one ate the meat of the pig and if the animal was detested by the gods? The answer is that, curiously enough, the pig was necessary for the worship of the very gods who loathed it. Once every year the swine was sacrificed to Osiris and the Moon. At that time the people were in duty bound to eat its flesh. To eat it at any other time would have been a grievous sin, but to consume it on the occasion of the annual sacrifice was nothing less than a sacred obligation.

The Egyptians themselves used to advance at least two reasons why they abstained from the meat of the swine. In the first place, the animal was an enemy of their Saviour, Horus. The devil Set, or Typhon, once disguised himself as a pig and in that form injured the eye of the son of Isis. In consequence the sun-god Ra issued the order that the animal was to be detested, and Horus conceived the idea of offering it as a sacrifice.

That explanation is obviously faulty, and so is the second one. It is well known that among the many crimes of Typhon was that of mutilating the body of Osiris. He happened to find the body while he was hunting a boar. Therefore the pig was hated in Egypt.

It is more than likely that the last story is a revised version of another account, according to which Osiris, like many another divinity, was actually killed by a boar. Thus, Attis was killed by a boar, and that was supposed to be the reason why his worshippers did not eat the meat of the pig.

Adonis was also connected in some way with the pig, but

just how his myth does not make clear. According to one story, he was killed by a boar, while according to another it was a boar that assisted at his birth. Adonis was the son of a damsel named Myrrh, whom Aphrodite had caused to become enamoured of her own father! Later the girl was miraculously changed into a tree in order to protect her and the unborn deity from the murderous wrath of her indignant parent. The infant grew for a period of ten months inside the tree, and then a boar cut the bark with his tusk. Thus the god was born.

The pig, then, plays the role of enemy to Osiris and Attis, while it plays a doubtful role to Adonis. But there is no doubt as to the relation of the swine to the Greek Demeter and Persephone. This is the more significant since Persephone resembled the others in that she died every year and was resurrected. The pig was sacred to Demeter and her daughter, and at the mysteries of Eleusis, which took the form of a dramatic presentation of the history of those goddesses, when the time came for the girl to descend to hell, the priests cast swine into the sacred caverns in the ground. Thus the pig was more than sacred to those deities. It actually represented Persephone. But it is now clear that originally those two goddesses were one and the same; so it is a fair conclusion that in the remotest times the pig was Demeter and her daughter.

6

IN the case of every sacred animal, the rule is to abstain from eating it; but it is the usual practice to consume it sacramentally on certain specially holy occasions, in order that the worshipper may acquire its godlike properties. But there comes a time in the development of every group when the people cease to believe that the animal is really the god. Instead the idea grows that the god is of human form, and the animal is merely "sacred to him." In time this conception also is outgrown, but the practice of abstaining from a particular kind of meat, except at certain ceremonies, remains. Gradually the duty of eating the flesh becomes obsolete, and nothing is left but the prohibition against devouring a particular animal. Since the people no longer believe that the creature is divine, they must find some other reason to explain their prohibition. So they tell stories about the forbidden creature. It killed the god and is therefore detestable. Or it injures the corn, which the god loves. Or it is a devil, the natural enemy of all the inhabitants of heaven. Sometimes the animal is hated even while it is still being sacrificed. But in general the development of this kind of practice follows the lines here laid down.

The pig god was not limited to any one part of the world. Thus the Scandinavian god Frey, who was a sun-god, was thought to have been killed by a boar. It was therefore part of the celebration of the feast of yule to sacrifice that animal to him. The people also made boars out of some kind of paste at that season and placed the images on their tables. After a while the paste boars were ground to powder. This was mixed with the food of the cattle and with the seeds that were planted. The sacred powder increased the fruitfulness of both the cattle and the crops. From what has gone before, it is plain enough that originally the god Frey was a pig. Later the animal became the enemy of the god instead of the divinity himself.

The reason why an animal is worshipped in the first place is usually that for some reason or other it suggests the idea of creation to the people. In the case of the serpent, the shape suggested the male principle of generation. The cock is not merely the herald of the dawn, but is the master of the barnyard, and soon became at least a sign of Father Sun. The fish lays thousands of eggs, and therefore it soon became a goddess of motherhood. The bull and the goat are not merely ardent lovers, but live on corn and hence appear to own it.

The shape of the pig's face seems to suggest the idea of life to primitive people. Hence the pig was one of the first gods. It was Demeter, Persephone, Attis, Adonis, Osiris, Frey, and others. But in time it was degraded. It became a devil, the hated enemy of the gods in many places and among many believers.

In like manner, the goat was Dionysos, and so was the bull. The goat was Pan, and also the satyrs and fauns. In fact, the goat was a popular god, and as late as the seventeenth century we find a sect of Tartars who used to celebrate a singular goat communion on Saint Elias's Day. First they examined the animal to be certain that it was "without blemish." Following that, they pulled its skin over its head and placed the skin on a pole. They then cooked the meat and ate it—both the men and the women. Then the men held a service in which they offered prayer to the hide.

In the ancient mysteries of Egypt the goat played a prominent part. Not much is known of the actual ceremonies, because they were kept profoundly secret. But it is known that an initiation into the goat mysteries was a prerequisite to a further initiation into the mysteries of Isis. We still have traditions concerning the use of the goat in ceremonies of initiation into lodges. As usual in such survivals, the animal, if used at all, is used for purposes that are regarded as humorous. But originally there was nothing funny about the matter. The goat initiation was the profoundest and most hallowed of rites.

7

THE gods of antiquity were all characterized by jealousy. This was due to the fact that they all had rivals. Not only did their own people tend to be fickle and to veer from the worship of one divinity to that of another, but there were many gods in the world and they were all thought to be real and powerful.

When Moses and Aaron went before Pharaoh and were asked for a sign, they demonstrated their power to work miracles. The magicians of the monarch then followed their example and showed that they, too, possessed that power. The gods of the magicians could also perform wonders.

As nations grew and as they developed in culture and the arts, they tended gradually to lessen the number of their gods, till, as with the Jews, they had but a single divinity. The prophets of Israel were convinced that there was but one God in the whole of reality; still this idea was so far ahead of the times that the prophets found few followers. The average run of people were then, as they are now, conservative, especially where the supernatural world was concerned, and they were extremely slow in appreciating the view of their seers.

But the people did look askance upon the worship of foreign gods. It became a pious duty to fight the battles of one's own god against his divine enemies. A man's own god was looked upon as a heavenly king, while the gods of other groups were his celestial enemies, powerful and even dangerous, but enemies, and to have commerce with any of them was treason against one's spiritual ruler.

At about the beginning of the Christian era the idea prevalent in Asia Minor was that the God of Israel was Yahweh, but that there were also other celestial powers, enemies of Yahweh, who were worshipped by other peoples. The rivals of Israel's God were thoroughly real and could work miracles. If a man or woman went over to the service of one of them, he could enlist supernatural help on his own behalf, but to do so was the crime of black magic, a sort of spiritual treason. For years this distinction between "white magic," or the commendable miracles of Heaven, and "black magic," or the damnable wonders of hell, persisted. One may trace it throughout the Middle Ages, till it reached its peak in the legend of Faust.

Among the Jews in ancient times, this concept of good and bad immortals was very strong. The Hebrews had come into close contact with the Persians, who had already passed through this stage of development and had come to believe that there were two great world-forces, Ahura-Mazda, the god of light, fire, life, and goodness, and Ahriman, the serpent, the god of darkness, destruction, death, and evil. According to the Persian idea, the history of the world was simply the story of the struggle for mastery waged against each other by those two great spiritual powers. The duty of every pious soul was to be allied with Ahura-Mazda, and so to order its existence as to give no aid and no comfort to the malicious Ahriman and his minions.

This Persian idea had a profound influence upon the religious development of Israel. The theory is not without a certain appeal. From the pre-scientific point of view, the world may well be interpreted as a stage upon which the forces of "good" are eternally at war with those of "evil."

There was, moreover, another reason why this idea made so powerful an appeal to the Hebrews. Yahweh was a jealous God, and His people were amazingly faithless. The prophets continually complained about the laxity of Israel, and the common people were guilty from time to time of worshipping Adonis, the Queen of Heaven, Moloch, Baal, and all the other romantic divinities whose devotions not merely afforded direct pleasure, but were warranted to provide luck and prosperity as well. Here was a ready-made explanation of the rock-bottom difference between the God of Israel and the other gods. Adonis was real enough, but he was a demon. Moloch was a devil, and *"Ge Hinnom"* (the Valley of Hinnom), where he was worshipped, became the phrase used in Hebrew to mean hell. *Ge Hinnom* (or Gehenna) is still the expression for hell in Hebrew.

The Phœnicians worshipped a fly god, much as the Egyptians adored the scarabæus or sacred beetle. The insects laid their eggs in the ground, and in another season the larvæ came forth. This was suggestive of the resurrection. (The Egyptians also credited the primitive idea that every scarab was male and that the beetle race was almost miraculously virile, since it continued to exist and increase without a female sex.) The fly divinity of Phœnicia was called "Baal Zebub," or Baal the Fly. To this day one of the names of Satan is Beelzebub.

When Christianity entered the scene, this development was still going on. In a sense the same process was taking place both among the Jews and Christians on the one hand, and among the pagans on the other. The latter were willing to admit that the Christian God could heal the sick and even raise the dead, but they attributed such acts to demoniac activity. The Christians for their part were willing to admit that the pagan deities were able to perform miracles, but the early saints insisted that those divinities were really devils and that to enlist their services was a sin.

Throughout the Middle Ages this development went on. White magic was another name for heavenly doings of a miraculous character, and there was not a village that did not boast its quota of such. Black magic was the employment of devils to bring about similar results. The two differed from each other in this particular alone. It is by no means true that while white magic concerned itself with "constructive" acts like the healing of the sick, black magic concerned itself with "destructive" acts like causing hail-storms or enchanting innocent people. Even some of the old biblical miracles were of the destructive variety, as, for instance, the killing of the children who teased the prophet. Innumerable persons have been burned at the stake for working cures by black magic. The work of God was good, and the act of His enemy was evil. That was the sole distinction.

8

SATAN is not a prominent character in the Old Testament. He appears in the Book of Job, not as a full-fledged enemy of God, but as an angel whose duty it was to walk to and fro in the world and to report human delinquencies to the Deity.

Still, in other parts of the Old Testament we find hints of the process we have been describing, in accordance with which men came to distinguish between white and black magic. We are assured, for instance, that Saul did his best to wipe sorcery and witchcraft out of the land. Yet he was by no means opposed to the use of magic as such. When his father's asses were lost, he found them by going to Samuel, paying the required money, and making inquiry. Just before his last battle he was desperate and wanted to know in advance what the outcome would be. There were of course two methods of finding out. First was the legitimate one of asking the Lord. The other was the illicit one of inquiring of the demons. Having already put himself on record in this matter by putting "those that divined by a ghost or familiar spirit out of the land," he asked the Lord. But Yahweh was angry and "answered him not, neither by dreams, nor by Urim, nor by prophets." Since Yahweh would do nothing for him, he took the next-best course and approached the Witch of En-dor, who gave him the information he sought.

9

IT is a universal phenomenon that as peoples develop and become more and more cultivated, the population of the supernatural world becomes smaller and smaller. Where once there were innumerable gods, the tendency is to combine all of the heavenly attributes in one deity, who may be served by hosts of subordinate angels. Where once there were many devils, the tendency is to reduce hell's governing class to one great Devil and his retainers.

THE INSIDE STORY OF HELL   269

The gods of love and life had a great deal in common. Their attributes were practically the same, and the methods of worshipping them were practically identical. Because of this fact, there was a noticeable tendency for all of the great male gods of fertility to be united in the person of Priapus. The attributes of the latter divinity were so unspeakably obscene that our English word "priapic" is used to connote the vilest of orgiastic characteristics.

Priapus was the son of Aphrodite, the goddess of love. Like his mother, he grew to be widely popular, and he came to be adored in many places, albeit under a variety of names. Thus in Rome he became the great Mutunus. But everywhere he was the god of fertility. In his charge was the increase of all living things. Even the fruitfulness of the bees was in his care. Gradually he became the king of life, and the situation was such that all of the gods of fertility and love became little better than manifestations of him. But in the eyes of the Yahweh-worshippers he was the basest of evils. He was real and could do marvellous deeds, but to invoke him was a sin. From the obscure station of one of the many gods of generation, he had risen to the lofty post of supreme creator. But with the triumph of the religious outlook that emanated from Palestine, he was degraded, and he became at last Satan, the King of Hell.

This does not mean that he lost caste completely, and no longer had any worshippers. Who were the obscene saints like Saint Foutin, Saint Guerlichon, Saint Guignolet, and Saints Damian and Cosmas? They were all manifestations of Priapus. The Gnostics at the beginning of the Christian era were convinced that Yahweh was a devil, for He had brought the world into being, and the world was something to flee from and renounce. They adored the serpent, the Tempter, who had induced man to eat of the tree of knowledge and thus to acquire wisdom. The Rosicrucians during the Middle Ages indulged in priapic ceremonies, and there were other such sects, including an organization known as the "Witches' Sabbath." That group of fanatical women used to worship Satan in deadly earnest. In their services the Devil was conventionally represented as a goat or a serpent or a brass ox. Obviously the women were continuing the old tradition of paganism, though they knew it not. Occasionally, in the meetings of the Witches' Sabbath, Satan was represented as an oak-tree. But the oak was originally the king of the gods, Jupiter—no less. Apparently even Zeus, when he fell from Olympus, became Satan of hell. How have the mighty fallen!

It was necessary, of course, for such worship as that to be carried on under the rose. Still, the tradition kept developing and growing, so that the Witches' Sabbath reached its flower as late as the fourteenth century. The women actually thought that they had entered into a mystic union with the kingdom of hell. The great witchcraft trials and persecutions were based upon something more than the human imagination. The Inquisitors did have something to go on. There was a witchcraft tradition. It was a developed (or should we not say "decadent"?) form of the old worship of Priapus.

10

IN addition to Satan, mediæval Europe knew a number of subordinate demons, and knew them by name. Like the Prince of Darkness himself, these demons had histories of their own and were not created out of nothing by the imaginative and credulous people who feared them. They were the primitive gods of those groups that were converted to Christianity. The old gods did not die. They simply fell into hell and became devils.

Among the evil spirits who inhabit the supernatural world are the goblins. Most of them were originally Teutonic gods of the wood, comparable to the satyrs of the Greeks and the fauns of the Romans. They continued to inhabit the

forests, though they occasionally invaded the haunts of
men, in order to gratify their depraved desires. One of the
most famous of the goblins is Robin Goodfellow, an English
spirit, the early pictures of whom show the creature in the
indecent pose and with the obscene attribute of Priapus.
Time was when Robin Goodfellow was a god. But he fell
upon evil times, and he became first a goblin and then a
caricature.

The goblins are sometimes useful to ignorant parents who
wish to frighten their children in order to render them obedient. Equally useful, if not more so, is the bogy man, or the
bugaboo, who usually lives in dark rooms, where he deliberately lies in wait to frighten the young. Apparently he is
afraid of adults or else he is powerless against them, for he
directs his malice against children alone.

The word "bogy" is derived from a Slavonic word "bog,"
which means god. The Hindus know a Bhaga, who is a
divinity of life. In the ancient cuneiform inscriptions Baga
was one of the names of the supreme god.

The bogy man, or the bugaboo, or the buggey, as he is
occasionally called, is the greatest tragedy of the supernatural
world. Originally he was the supreme god of the universe.
Not only has he fallen from his high estate, but he has become the basest of knaves. All he is capable of doing now is
hiding in dark rooms in order to frighten children. The great
ruler of heaven has become the vilest rascal in hell.

11

WHEN two rival groups of believers come in contact with
each other, the tendency is for each to regard as devils the
spirits whom the other reveres. Thus the Spiritists (or
Spiritualists) of our own day feel that they are able to converse with their deceased relatives and friends. But a number
of sects which do not share this view (notably the Roman
Catholics and the Seventh Day Adventists) feel that the

minions of Satan are in the habit of attending seances, in order to impersonate the souls of the departed, and in such disguise to lure trusting men and women to hell, through their deception. Thus the spirits to whom the Spiritists talk are real enough, but they are devils—nothing more.

Now, the eerie beings with whom the Spiritists hold conversations are not regarded by them as gods. They are merely the souls of human beings who have "passed over." If they are degraded into hell by other sects and are accounted as devils, this is not because they are the deities of rival groups of believers, but because they appear to be dangerous to the institutions that their detractors hold dear.

Among the modern tales that treat of the supernatural world, there is none more outstanding than the legend of Faust. Like the immortals of whom Spiritism treats, Faust was not a god. In fact, he was not a spirit at all, but a mere man of flesh and blood. He was a chemist, and he lived in an age when laboratory science was looked upon as dangerous to those institutions that were founded upon faith rather than upon experiment.

Dr. Johann Faustus lived in the sixteenth century, at the time of that great spiritual controversy known as the Reformation. Of his actual life little is known. It is certain, however, that he was a student of chemistry. Shortly after his death a legend grew up concerning his career.

According to the story, Faust had discovered, through his research, a method of summoning a demon from hell. The demon's name was Mephistopheles ("not loving the light"). Since it happened that Faust was growing old, he determined to make a pact with hell; he would turn over his soul to the Devil in return for the spry feeling of youth. The contract was drawn up and signed with blood.

At once Faust became young. Moreover, Mephistopheles attended him at all times and carried him through the air to enable him to witness marvellous sights. According to the

Protestant version, he entered the Vatican in invisible form, but the Pope was unable to exorcize either the man or his demoniac attendant. According to the Catholic version, Faust studied in the very city where Luther nailed his theses to the church door.

Faust even attended a meeting of the notables of hell. There he beheld the beautiful Lilith, but was warned against her charms.

At last the time came for Faust to die. He retired to his room and was blown to bits, just as if he had been victimized by an explosion in his laboratory.

At bottom the legend of Faust is a modern example of the tendency of believers to degrade the objects of the other man's admiration. The story is a folk-protest against modern science in general and chemistry in particular. The moral of the tale is that the marvels of laboratory science are in essence the sinful wonders of black magic.

12

THE great devil of Buddhism is a being named Mara. He resembles the devils of other faiths in many ways. It is his function, not merely to serve as adversary to mankind, but also to oppose the heavenly hosts themselves.

When it appeared that Siddhartha Gautama was likely to achieve the Buddahood, Mara did everything in his power to prevent this consummation. First he offered the prophet a number of inducements to abandon the project; for example, he promised to make him "sovereign over the four continents and the two thousand adjacent isles." Gautama began to fail in health, due to his mortification of the flesh. Mara used this as an argument. Was not the man ill? Was he not likely to be the cause of his own premature death? Could he not be of greater service and be able to do more "good works" living than dead? This is a modern argument. But it did not avail with Buddha.

At last the holy man went to sit beneath the Bo tree, where fortunately he managed to attain the grace of Buddahood. But no sooner had he taken his seat than Mara advanced with his whole army to dislodge him. This frightened the gods and they did their best to beat the devil off. But they were not able.

Thereupon Mara tried his diabolical magic. First he brought on a hurricane. Then he caused a rain-storm. Buddha did not even become wet. Then came a hail of rocks, but they turned into flowers before they struck the prophet. Following these attempts there came storms of weapons, hot coals, ashes, sand, and mud. All of them were transformed into objects of value and beauty. The last of the plagues was darkness, but the darkness turned to light about the sacred person.

Unsuccessful in his violent attempts, Mara started to argue the point. He demanded that Buddha vacate the seat, as it rightly belonged to him (Mara). But Gautama called upon the earth to witness that he of right owned it because he and he alone had attained to the "perfections." In a loud and terrible voice Mother Earth did attest this. Then the hosts of the devil fled in alarm. The gods were happy and shouted for joy.

13

WHILE there have usually been demons who inhabited the forests, and there still are ghosts who for one reason or another haunt particular houses or other geographic spots, the powers of evil for the most part live in a place called hell. The exact location of this place is a matter under dispute; some have held that it was in the sun, but as a rule it is located in the underworld. The word "hell" is derived from an old northern source. Hel was the goddess of the dead. The Teutonic hell was under the earth. It was not a warm place, but a frigid one—a gargantuan refrigerator.

The abode of the dead was usually conceived as a cheerless place. Among ancient peoples it was always a shadowy country, and at best the dead were worse off than the living. But at its worst hell was a frightful place of supernatural torment. In later times people made a distinction between the realm of the blessed and that of the damned. The former was as pleasant as man could conceive. The American Indians looked forward to their happy hunting-ground. The Norsemen expected to go to a place where there was war all day long, but in the evening all wounds were miraculously healed. The fighters rested and enjoyed themselves all night. In the morning the fight began again. The Mohammedans look forward to a place of sensuous delight featuring wine, woman, and song. The Christians anticipate a heaven of golden streets and the music of harps. The Jews hope for an academy on high, where God joins with the faithful in ceaseless study.

In passing, it will not be out of place to mention that there is a song of the American Marine Corps which speaks of the abode of the blessed, albeit the reference is humorous. The ballad ends with the words:

If the Army and the Navy ever look on heaven's scenes,
They will find the streets are guarded by United States Marines.

14

BUT hell is a place of infinite horror. People are cast into that pit for a variety of reasons, and frequently they are denied hope of eventual deliverance. Usually the reasons why people are consigned to that place are ecclesiastical rather than ethical, in the secular sense of that word.

For instance, Buddha taught that men should do good without hope of reward or fear of punishment. But after the death of the teacher the priests constructed a most elaborate place of torment. The Buddhist hell is divided into eight sections, one more terrible than the other.

The first seven of the Buddhist hells are for persons who have been guilty of committing different sins and are destined to be purged of iniquity by punishment. But the eighth and worst hell is reserved for those who have been remiss in the giving of alms to Buddhist priests or who do not believe in the "gospel of evidences." From any of the first seven hells one might expect relief when guilt has been expiated. But those in the eighth hell have no hope. From that place of torment there is no escape. The souls of misbelievers rot there, for ever.

The nature of hellish tortures has differed from age to age and from land to land. Thus, in Greece there were a number of ingenious devices for punishing the wicked. One man was compelled to roll a rock up a hill, but he never could get it to the top, for it kept rolling backwards. Another stood in a pool of clear water that reached to his chin; but whenever he stooped to drink, the water receded, and he was destined to be thirsty for eternity.

The northern hell was a place of refrigeration. Dante embodied that tradition in his inferno. The lowest hell, for Dante, was an icy place. The King of Hell lived in a palace of ice, and the worst of the damned stood partly frozen in the element.

When missionaries approached the Eskimos and told them of the heat of hell, the poor natives were impressed. They were so cold and so afraid of frigidity that they asked how to get to hell. Anything suggestive of warmth appealed to them. A lake of perpetual fire they regarded as paradise.

CHAPTER XXVI

The Legend of Lilith

> "[*The people*] *that say: 'Stand by thy-*
> *self, come not near to me; for I am*
> *holier than thou.' These are a smoke*
> *in my nose, a fire that burneth all the*
> *time.*"
>
> ISAIAH LXV. 5

1

SATAN has ever been an ardent lover. Did he not go so far as to impersonate Saint Sylvanus in order to seduce a girl by making her believe that not the fiend but the good man had come to her? Frequently he was compelled to resort to such tricks in order to break down the natural resistance of good maidens. But occasionally he found a woman who would freely give herself to him. Such a female was Angele, Lady of Labarthe, if we may credit the court record of the Inquisition. She was burned alive at Toulouse in 1275 for the crime, not merely of giving herself to Satan, but of bearing him a son. The child was a horrible creature with the head of a wolf and the tail of a serpent. He had, moreover, an unspeakable appetite for babies; in fact he subsisted on such a diet. Angele was sixty-five years old when she was burned for this crime.

Then there is the famous story of Robert the Devil. His mother was a Duchess of Normandy. She was grieved because it had not pleased Heaven to vouchsafe to her a son. At last, weary of presenting her fruitless petitions to the throne of God, she addressed the Prince of Hell. Immediately he answered her, and Robert was born. He became a wicked man, by profession a robber chief. At length, however, he discovered the truth about his birth and was so pained by the knowledge that he repented. According to one account, he married the Emperor's daughter and lived happily ever after. According to another version, he declined the offer of imperial marriage and ended his days as a hermit.

Still, Satan was not satisfied with such love and allegiance as that which came to him unsolicited. He was a master of intrigue and he resorted to strategy in his love-affairs. Take, for example, the well-known case of Merlin.

Merlin was the son of Satan and a good and pious maiden. The girl's family had been ruined by the magic of the Devil. One by one the members of that family fell by the way-side, till at last there was but one maid who was steadfast in her faith and piety in spite of all that Satan could do. What rendered her so completely unapproachable as far as the Devil was concerned was her habit of continually crossing herself.

One night, however, the girl forgot to make the sign. In consequence of that omission, a child was born to her, and she gave her son the name. Merlin. The whole incident was pleasing rather than the reverse in the sight of Heaven, for would it not be a splendid consummation to win to the side of God the very child of the Devil? So God gave the boy a knowledge of the future, while Satan gave him a knowledge of the past. With so much wisdom, he naturally turned to heaven instead of hell, and he is said to have gone straight to the region of the blessed after he finished a glorious earthly career.

2

BUT although devils have always been given to the hideous practice of carrying on intrigues with mortals, there is a love life in hell itself. Thus, according to the early mystics of Europe (especially the Jewish mystics), there was a story of the union of the devil Samael with Lilith, who became the Queen of the Succubi and the First Lady of Hell.

3

LILITH is an old demon known to Semitic peoples, and her name occurs once in the Bible (Isaiah xxxiv. 14). The Hebrew is clear, but in the English translation Lilith is rendered "screech-owl," while in the Vulgate it is rendered "Lamia." Literally the passage means: "The wild beasts of the desert shall also meet with the wild beasts of the island, and the satyr shall cry to his fellow; Lilith shall also rest there, and find for herself a place of rest."

The connexion of Lilith with the satyr is of course significant. The goat was everywhere a god of fertility, till in later years he became discredited and one of his legs was appropriated by Satan. Lilith has a similar history. Upon analysis, it will be found that she is a fallen goddess.

The ancient rabbins were confronted with the problem of explaining who Lilith was and where she had come from. They were willing to assume that she was real enough, but the question was, how did she happen to be born? Or, if God had created her, how did He happen to do so, and when? They explained the matter as follows:

It seems that in the first chapter of Genesis it is expressly stated that God created a human pair. "Male and female created He them." But in the second chapter it is said that God put man in the garden and then decided that it was not good for him to live alone. Accordingly, after trying the animals and finding that they were not fitted for the duty, He put Adam into a sound sleep and made Eve out of one of his ribs.

The rabbins felt that if God had created man and woman by the same act (as in the first chapter), it could not be that He had made first Adam and then Eve (as in the second chapter). So they harmonized the passages by introducing Lilith into their calculations and explaining that she was the first wife of Adam. Eve was the second.

4

THE rabbins explained that the two stories referred to two separate and distinct events. In the first place, God created man and woman together, joined back to back like Siamese twins, for the text says: "Male and female He created them, and called their name Adam." But this did not prove to be a satisfactory arrangement, for the two quarrelled continually; so the Lord decided to separate their bodies and see if they could agree and be happy.

But they were miserable from the very start. Since the two had been created at exactly the same time, there was no reason why the woman should consider herself the servant (or helpmate) of her husband, and there was likewise no reason why the husband should take orders from his wife. Both Adam and Lilith were of an aggressive spirit, and each was determined to rule. Lilith was the first to tire of the wrangling, which was turning Eden into a veritable hell. So in her distress she pronounced the ineffable name, which has always been a cabbalistic charm, and thus she acquired wings. With them she flew out of the garden.

No sooner had she gone than Adam become lonesome, and he cried aloud to the Lord. So God took pity on him and sent three angels to find her and to persuade her to return to her husband. They found her flying over the Red Sea, and they transmitted to her the divine message. But she utterly refused to go back and endure the domineering attitude of Adam.

Sorely disappointed, the angels returned to God and told Him of their failure. He thereupon sent them once more and allowed them to threaten the woman with the curse that if she refused to go back to the garden, she would give birth to many children, but they would all die in infancy. The alternative presented no acceptable possibility to the harassed beauty. In despair she was about to cast herself into the sea, when the angels took pity on her plight and offered her some compensation for the curse they had just inflicted. That is, they promised that she should have power over all children till they were eight days of age. In turn she promised that she would never molest any youngsters who had been specially committed to the care of those three angels. Orthodox Jews still use a charm called the *camea*. They hang it upon the necks of babies at birth. The *camea* contains the names of the angels.

While Lilith sat brooding over her wrongs, she met the demon Samael. Being by this time divorced from Adam, she married the devil. According to the Christian idea in the Middle Ages, she was not married, for marriage is a sacrament and cannot take place outside of the Church. Still, she was the Queen of the Succubi and, like her subjects, a most romantic lover.

There were three proofs of the existence and power of Lilith. In the first place there were the facts of infant mortality, which have always been difficult to reconcile with the mercy of the omnipotent supernatural Ruler. To this day, infant mortality is variously explained in mystic lore. One of the old explanations was that Lilith was responsible for the evil.

A second proof of the existence of Lilith was found in the fact that infants were known to smile in their sleep. What had they to smile about? Obviously Lilith was playing with them. It was customary, on noticing that phenomenon, to strike the child on the nose three times and to say: "Away, cursed Lilith." It has been suggested by certain scholars that our word "lullaby" comes from an ancient expression that meant: "Avaunt thee, Lilith."

The third proof is derived from the fact that even married men were known to have dreams in which they felt that they were in love with some strange beauty. Among African Negroes, Legba in female form causes these dreams to this very day. Lilith used to cause them in Europe. Perhaps in some spots she still does!

5

LILITH and Samael had much in common. It happened that the devils were created at about the time when the woman left the garden of Eden. Samael had originally been a leader of the seraphim, but he had fallen by virtue of his ungovernable jealousy. He then saw Adam, who by that time was married to the humble Eve and was enjoying his sojourn in paradise. The devil was consumed with envy, and it was while he was filled with hatred of Adam that he encountered Lilith. No wonder he courted her and married her.

Since that time Lilith has held the highest rank among the succubi. Borrowed from her Semitic creators by the superstitious folks of the North, she changed her appearance a bit in order to conform to northern standards of beauty. She acquired golden hair, which became her most attractive glory. She has been known to kill a human lover; but fortunately there is a method of knowing in every such case that it is she who is the guilty party. Superstition is (or was) clear on this point—when Lilith kills a human being, she strangles her victim by winding one of her golden hairs round his heart.

Hair is also the crowning glory of the daughters of Eve. As men have been known to be attracted by the hair of Lilith, so devils have been attracted by the hair of women. Jewish women scrupulously cover their hair after marriage (that is to say, Orthodox Jewish women do), and they never appear afterwards without a wig. This is supposed to be a measure of modesty, but it clearly had its origin in superstition. Saint Paul warned the maidens to cover their hair because of "angels."

The hair plays a prominent part in the lore of the supernatural. One remembers the snaky locks of the gorgon

Medusa, and such long-haired heroes as Samson. According to the legend of Faust, when that misguided scientist attended the witches' sabbath, his guide, Mephistopheles, warned him to beware of the golden hair on the head of the gorgeous demoness Lilith.

6

Poor, beautiful Lilith has always been unhappy. If there are folks today who still are convinced of her reality, they know that she is unhappy. What are the sighing sounds one sometimes hears in the country during the stillness of the night? Lilith is sighing because of the sadness of her lot.

Eve, doubtless, is happier. Lilith was charming enough, but she was unable to be the servant of man. She was a feminist. Eve knew her place. Be it understood at this point that myths have grown up among other peoples which illustrate the primitive struggle for mastery between the sexes. The story we are considering points a moral. "The function of a wife," it seems to say, "is to serve."

But the usefulness of the story does not explain the origin of the character we know as Lilith. Who was she in the first place? What is the true inwardness of her secret?

According to an ancient Sumerian tablet, the goddess Ishtar, the mother and lover of the divine Tammuz, sent a gorgeous and attractive demon to seduce men and to urge them to indulge in that form of embrace with which she, as a goddess of fertility, was most pleased. The name of this demoness who represented Isthar was Lilitu, which has been changed to Lilith in Hebrew. There is no reason why Ishtar should have sent a special messenger to do this work of seduction except that, as her people developed in culture and refinement, the goddess began to outgrow her primitive habits. For Ishtar was Venus, and she required no representative in this work of romance. She herself was capable of performing that function.

Originally, of course, this romantic activity was no disgrace for a goddess. The very name "Ishtar" basically means either a goddess or a lewd woman, and the connexion was once plain. Divinity and easy virtue went hand in hand in the old days. Certainly the combined mother and lover of Adonis was the patroness of motherhood, love, and licence. In her earliest days she was a serpent goddess, and in some of her representations she holds in her hand the mystic caduceus. But in later years, when this form of activity began to be regarded as slightly beneath the divine dignity, she sent a messenger to do her work of seduction. Originally Ishtar and Lilitu were one and the same.

Thus we have in our female devil but another instance of the tragedy that runs through the whole history of hell. Ishtar was the goddess of love and creation. She was adored for her gifts to mankind. She was at once the mother, lover, and rescuer of Adonis, the victory over death, destruction, and winter. But as the years wore on, her worship was outgrown, and slowly she passed from the centre of the supernatural scene. The divine Venus became the accursed Lilith. The All-Mother became the beautiful fiend, whose children died in infancy and who hovered over the babies of her rival, Eve. The lover of Tammuz the Good, she deteriorated till she became the bride of Samael the Vengeful and the Wicked. The shining princess of the heavens, who once presided over beauty and romance, has become the Queen of Hell.

CHAPTER XXVII

The Spirits Perish

*"No indeed, man is neither the begin-
ning nor the end of terrestrial life. . . .
A future race, born perhaps of our
own, but having perchance no bond of
origin with us, will succeed us in the
empire of the planet. These new spirits
of the earth will ignore or despise
us. The monuments of our arts, should
they discover vestiges of them, will
have no meaning for them. Rulers of
the future, whose mind we can no
more divine than the Palæopithekos of
the Siwalik Mountains was able to forecast the trains of thought of Aristotle,
Newton, and Poincaré."*

(From a dialogue in *The White Stone*)

ANATOLE FRANCE

1

THE history of human thought is the story of errors,
some of them painful and ugly, but many of them beautiful and ennobling. Cast upon the world without the guid-
ance that only knowledge could afford, primitive men
endeavoured to survive. They were confronted with the alternative of adapting themselves to a hostile environment
and thus continuing to live, or else of becoming extinct like
the brontosaurus and the pterodactyl. Earlier species have
managed to adapt themselves by effecting physical changes in
their structures, which enabled them to find food and to
protect themselves against ever present enemies. Man has
not only survived, but has well nigh conquered the earth, not
by the power of his body, but by the force of his mind.

There is no living creature that fits in so perfectly with the background that the world affords that it is not subject to disease or accident. Some animals have evolved traits so inimical to their own preservation that if they did not have compensating features, their species would surely die out. The moth lives on, not because it flies into the flame, but in spite of that unfortunate tendency.

Men, too, have their points of imperfect adaptation, in spite of which, rather than because of which, they survive. Thus the arch of the foot is better adapted for tree-climbers than for riders and walkers. The intestines of a man are attached by mesenteries to his back, as in a four-footed creature. This is a splendid arrangement in the bull or the lion, but in man it makes for enlarged abdomens and other strange conditions and is indirectly responsible for the painful lot of woman. The list of penalties humanity pays for the privilege of walking on two legs instead of four is by no means a short one.

Among the many disabilities of the human race, though we share it with the brutes, is the phenomenon of death. It is the great error, the skeleton at the feast, the negation of life itself. For ages it has been the supreme mystery, a mystery which has been explained by a number of myths, and for the solution of which the unseen forces of the supernatural world have been called into play.

In our own times, with the assistance of scientific technique, this mystery has at last yielded a portion of its secret. Death is the price that organisms pay for advancing in the scale of evolution. The lowest forms of life, the amœba for example, do not die; they are potentially immortal. As living beings become more and more complex, parts of them are sloughed off by nature. At first the portion which is discarded is very small, but when we reach such large creatures as the elephant, the part which is sloughed off is gigantic, while the immortal part, that which transmits life from generation to generation, remains microscopic. Simple cells, which form the physical basis of life, can be kept alive indefinitely; and such a group of cells, detached from the organism of which it once formed part, is being kept alive today at the Rockefeller Foundation in New York City. It is unlikely that scientists (in spite of the work they are doing to determine the nature of life on the one hand and of death on the other) will ever achieve actual physical immortality for humanity. And yet it would be rash to become dogmatic and assert with any degree of assurance that such a consummation will never be attained.

The scientific method itself is the result of ages and ages of experience, and ages and ages of error. Men have always sought life; but the methods of search have been conditioned by their lights. Sometimes those have been dim.

2

PRIMARILY the world of the supernatural is the world of love. This is so for two reasons. In the first place, love is life, the enemy of death. Even devils were once gods or angels of light, till they were forced to abandon the field to rival divinities and were cast into the pit.

But over and above this fact, which is the golden key to unlock the mysteries of the supernatural, there is the further fact that love is primary among human instincts, and, alas, it is often thwarted. But the disappointed man did not pine away and die. He put his faith above and lived. If credulity was responsible for much bloodshed, if it is to blame for much cruelty on the part of those who refused to heed the prophet's warning concerning the "holier than thou," it has been at the same time essential to the continued life of humanity. Without the faith and confidence it afforded, men would have become dispirited and despondent. With no knowledge of natural law, man groped in the dark, and found —faith. Out of what we now call "superstition" has devel-

oped man's present regard for truth, man's faith in the salvation that comes out of the laboratory. Every tree is a
revelation of the truth that lies at the bottom of things, and
every microscope is an oracle. The heavens above refused to
reveal the truth to Saul "either by dreams or by Urim or by
prophets," but they have begun to yield their secret through
the instrumentality of the telescope.

The first great spiritual revolution was brought about
when men discovered the relation between love and life. The
present spiritual awakening is related to another discovery
to the effect that life and death are products of and con-
tributors to a chain of evolution. Through the application of
this knowledge, and of the knowledge of related facts, men
are able to command the powers that underlie reality. Science is the magic of modern times.

Still, like all modern products of the human mind, science
is an outgrowth of speculation concerning the supernatural.
Who does not know that chemistry has developed out of
alchemy, the superstitious attempt to transmute base metals
into gold, and that astronomy has grown out of astrology, the
effort to read human destiny in the motions of the stars?
Even the arts have been bequeathed to us by those who
sought communication with the world beyond the veil. Painting, sculpture, music, and the dance all arose in the first place
as channels of communion between the worlds. Even ethics
developed out of the eerie fears of men long ago. The very
idea that murder is wrong may be traced to a primitive dread
of ghosts.

Truly, our debt to the supernatural world is tremendous.

3

THOSE who have followed us this far may pause at this
point to inquire whether or not there is a measure of truth
in the basic idea of the supernatural. Does such a world exist,
over and above our own?

To attempt to answer this question would carry us far beyond the realm of demonstrable fact into the trackless domain of theory. Therefore, interesting as it would be to inquire whether or not there is truth in the conception of the supernatural, it would be beyond the scope of our modest effort.

Still, this much is fact and not theory: the scientific method, with its emphasis on impartial research and ruthless testing of all items of experience has tended to push the supernatural world farther and farther from the consciousness of men. Earthquakes are no longer caused by the struggling of gigantic devils under the ground. The thunder has long since ceased to be caused by Jove and his bolts. Even Lilith has been exorcized at last, and dreams no longer issue from her romantic attentions.

As that shining authority, Sir James G. Frazer, has aptly observed: "The spirits are gone even from their last stronghold in the sky, whose blue arch no longer passes, except with children, for the screen that hides from mortal eyes the glories of the celestial world. Only in poets' dreams or impassioned flights of oratory is it given to catch a glimpse of the last flutter of the standards of the retreating host, to hear the beat of their invisible wings, the sound of their mocking laughter, or the swell of angel music dying away in the distance. . . ."

BIBLIOGRAPHY

The author is aware of no one work that treats between its covers all of the items that have been discussed in this volume. There is, however, no single phase of our subject which has not been carefully investigated by scholars and which has not been adequately dealt with in one book or another. Should the reader desire to pursue the matter further, the writer begs leave to recommend the following selected and authoritative works:

BLAKE, WILLSON W.: *The Cross Ancient and Modern*. New York, 1889.

BRAND, JOHN: *Observations on the Popular Antiquities of Great Britain*. London, 1902.

BRIFFAULT, ROBERT: *The Mothers*. New York, 1927.

BROWN, SANGER: *The Sex Worship and Symbolism of Primitive Races*. Boston, 1916.

CARUS, PAUL: *The History of the Devil and the Idea of Evil*. Chicago, 1900.

CATHOLIC ENCYCLOPEDIA.

CONWAY, MONCURE DANIEL: *Demonology and Devil Lore*. New York, 1879.

CRAWLEY, ERNEST: *The Mystic Rose*. London, 1902.

EICHLER, LILLIAN: *The Customs of Mankind*. New York, 1925.

ELWORTHY, FREDERICK THOMAS: *The Evil Eye*. London, 1895.

FORLONG, J. G. R.: *Rivers of Life*. London, 1883.

FRAZER, SIR JAMES G.: *The Golden Bough*. New York, 1924.

— *The Belief in Immortality and the Worship of the Dead*. London, 1913.

HARTLAND, EDWIN SIDNEY: *Primitive Society*. New York.

HASTINGS, JAMES, editor: *Encyclopædia of Religion and Ethics*. New York, 1908 et seq.

HECKETHORN, CHARLES WILLIAM: *The Secret Societies of All Ages and Countries*. London, 1897.

HOWARD, CLIFFORD: *Sex Worship*. Chicago, 1917.

INMAN, THOMAS: *Ancient Pagan and Modern Christian Symbolism*. New York, 1922.

JAMES, WILLIAM: *The Varieties of Religious Experience*. London, 1916.

JEWISH ENCYCLOPEDIA.

LA CROIX, PAUL: *History of Prostitution*, translated by Samuel Putnam. Chicago, 1926.

LANGDON, S.: *Tammuz and Ishtar*. Oxford, 1914.

LEA, HENRY CHARLES: *History of the Inquisition of the Middle Ages*. New York, 1888.

— *A History of the Inquisition of Spain*. New York and London, 1906.

LECKY, W. E. H.: *History of the Rise and Influence of the Spirit of Rationalism in Europe*. New York, 1878.

— *History of European Morals*. New York and London, 1919.

LEUBA, JAMES H.: *The Belief in God and Immortality*. Boston, 1916.

NEWTON, JOHN: *Assyrian Grove Worship*. New York, 1922.

PRATT, JAMES BISSETT: *India and its Faiths*. New York, 1915.

PRESCOTT, WILLIAM H.: *History of the Conquest of Mexico*. New York.

— *History of the Conquest of Peru*. Philadelphia, 1902.

STORY, WILLIAM W.: *Castle St. Angelo and the Evil Eye*. London and Philadelphia, 1877.

TYLOR, EDWARD B.: *Primitive Culture*. London, 1873.

WESTERMARCK, EDWARD: *The Origin and Development of the Moral Ideas*. London, 1906.

— *The History of Human Marriage*. London, 1921.

INDEX

Aaron, and legend of Micah, 10-11; rod of, 74-6, 84, 128, 265

Abbot of Unreason, 176, 197

Abiram, and building of Jericho, 8

Abraham, as host to angels, 36-7, 79; oåk of, 79; and method of taking oath, 130; footprint of, 134; sign of covenant of, 180; subjection of Sarah to, 201

Adam, as first possessor of Aaron's rod, 74; forbidden to molest magic trees in Eden, 80; tempted with apple, 102; and Eve, 199, 279, 282; foredoomed to sin, 234; and Lilith, 279-80

Adonis, 64, 195, 205, 261-2, 264, 266, 284

Africa, temples to Venus in, 55; snake-worship in, 89, 167, 216-17; blood on gateways in, 107; Arab method of averting evil eye in, 142; Livingstone in, 150-1

African superstitions: shadow believed to be soul, 11; sneezing as source of happiness, 33; belief in Legba, 42-3, 281-2; veneration for trees, 79

Agni, 189

Ahriman, 188, 266

Ahura-Mazda, 188, 266

Albigenses, charms of, against sickness, 97

Alexander the Great, 88

Alpha, as symbol, 159

Altar, origin of, 128

Amber, as amulet, 145

America, belief in horseshoe as lucky in, 13; sceptres among Indians in, 73; preaching to fish among Indians in, 154, 155

Amiel, quoted, 212

Ammon, as divine lover, 39

Amon-Ra, 211

Amulets, 144-9

Anaitis, 54

Angele, Lady of Labarthe, 277

Anjou, 70

Anne of Austria, Empress, 104

Antæus, 187

Antichrist, 249

Anu, 208, 216

Aphrodite, 96, 103, 262, 269; *and see* Venus

Apocalypse, 159

Apollo, 78, 91

Apple of Love, and baptism, in Bengal, 97; and bridal bouquet, 101; awarded by Paris, 102-3; as symbol of sex, 104

Arab: rite on opening door, 108; use of salt, 123; method of taking oath, 130; method of averting evil eye, 142; comment on magic knots, 212

Arches, magical use of, 109

Aristotle, on sneezing, 33

Ark of the Testimony, 128-9

Armenian goddess Anaitis, 54

Arrow, of Cupid, 121, 132; leaden, destructive of love, 121

Artemis, 142, 203, 205, 216, 217; *and see* Diana, Astarte

Arunta, the, primitive beliefs among, 20-1

Asher, 129

Ash-tree, as Scandinavian tree of life, 80-4; and ancient English method of curing rickets, 106

Asmodeus, 231

Ass, Feast of the, 197-8

Assassins, sect of, 238, 240-1

Asshur, 216

Shinto custom of ceremonial whipping, 245-6
Siberian legend of "eye of God," 120
Sibyls, 45
Silver, magic potency of, 121-2
Sigismund, King, of Poland, 207
Simeli Mountain, tale of, 152
Simeon Stylites, Saint, 166, 254
Simon Maccabeus, 132
Sin, calamities as punishment for, 221, 228; origin of idea of, 219-29
Sirens, 152
Siva, as divine lover, 42; sacred symbol of, 56, 161; festivals of, 69; temples of, 89; father of Sani, 138, 139; and trinity, 216; husband of Kali, 238, 239
Skoptsi, 250
Sleeping Beauty, the, folk-tale, 138
Snake, believed to bear jewel in head, 24; as demon lover, 24-5; as object of worship, 76, 86-7, 88-9, 91, 208, 216-17, 269; and magic wand, 74, 76, 84-6; as ancestor of famous men, 87-8; forbidden as food, 90; as symbolic of generation, 90, 91, 92, 202, 208, 263; in ark of Osiris, 91, 130; as symbol of heaven, 91; as banner of Roman *Draconarii*, 91; snake-stone effective against bite of, 126; as possessor of evil eye, 140; phylacteries as relic of worship of, 146; associated with pillar, 166-7; Hea as, 211
Sneezing, beliefs about, 33, 107
Sodom, 221
Soldiers, magic charms used by, 91, 141
Solomon, Temple of, 104, 165, 185
Song of Songs, quoted, 103
Soul, shadow as, 11; disembodied during lifetime, 32
Sparta, 68, 252
Spiritists, 271-2
Spring, festival of, 56, 60, 66, 67, 69
Sri Iantra, Hindu emblem, 161-2
Star, as Jewish symbol, 157

Star and crescent, 73
Stonehenge, 125
Stones, as abode of discarnate spirits, 21; as objects of worship, 124-5, 126, 128; as charms, 125-6; as male symbol, 125, 126, 127, 202; to mark graves, 132
Strassburg Cathedral, and human sacrifice, 9
Strassburg Synagogue, 168
Succubi, 28-9; Queen of, 278, 281, 282
Sun, as divinity, 47, 68, 82, 83-4, 120, 181, 182, 186-7, 191, 217; palm sacred to, 82; worshipped at Stonehenge, 125; and rock, 125; worshipped in Mexico, 126-7; cock as emblem of, 160, 263; nativity of, 179; ghosts exorcized by, 188
Supernatural world, hostility of, 12, 15, 18, 26-7, 31, 137, 226, 252, 257-8; foundation of belief in, 14, 18; as composed of warring factions, 15-16, 17-18, 165, 266; as sanctuary, 231, 249; human desire for communication with, 256
Swastika, 162-3
Swine, sacrificed at the Thesmophoria, 63; sacrificed to Osiris, 107, 261; Ulysses' men changed to, 151-2; abhorrence for, 63, 259-62; associated with Adonis, 261-2; as divinity, 263, 264
Switzerland, practice at time of death in, 112
Sylphs, cabbalistic belief in, 29
Sylvanus, Saint, impersonated by Satan, 277

Tabernacles, Feast of, 83, 104
Tablets of stone, 128, 129
Talmud, cited, 86, 92, 131
Tamar, 219
Tammuz, cross in sign of, 164-5; as Adonis, 205; and Ishtar, 283, 284
Tartars, celebration of goat communion by, 264
Thebes, temple at, 44; Amon-Ra of, 211
Thesmophoria, festival of the, 60, 63

Wine, Bacchus as god of, 60; at
Jewish Passover, 60; at Roman
Bacchanalia, 69; used in revering
St. Foutin, 69-70; at Christian
festivals in Italy, 70; in revering
sex symbols, 127
Wings, symbolic of love, 132
Witches, and demon lovers, 28; body-
fluids as protection against, 97;
immune to lead bullets, 121;
mediæval beliefs about, 139, 149,
243-4; on Hallow-e'en, 183; and
broomsticks, 183; whips effective
against, 184-5; method of detecting, 244; driven out by Saul,
268
Witches' Sabbath, 270
Winter, Greek myth of origin of,
60-2; solstice feast of, 181, 188
Woden, 68
Wreath, as precaution against spirits,
108

Xenophon, view of, on sneezing, 33

Yahweh, oak sacred to, 78; and the
healing serpent, 86; name of, con-
cealed, 153; as one God among
many, 265; as jealous God, 266;
and Saul, 268
Yucatan, method of averting evil eye
in, 142; "shield of David" in, 161;
serpent goddess of, 167
Yule, 177-8, 182, 189, 263
Yuste, monastery at, 242

Zeus, as divine lover, 37, 40, 121,
231; father of Persephone, 60;
Sabazios, 73; oracle of, at Dodona, 78, 86; father of Heracles,
101; and golden apples of the Hesperides, 102; and Trojan War,
102-3; and Danaë, 121; as oak-
tree, 211, 270; as Satan, 270;
and see Jupiter
Zipporah, daughter of Jethro, 75